This book is dedicated to the wond
all profits from its sale w

Mission Morogoro focus on develc
rural upland villages of Berega,
Tanzania.

MW00480054

It is also devoted to the rural women's movement called 'Tushikamane', which Mission Morogoro has supported in the hamlets surrounding Tunguli and Msamvu.

'Tushikamane' means 'We are sticking together' (to be empowered), and its mission is to set up and work through women's groups – mainly young, rural, poorly educated women – so as to try to reduce the enormous burden of child and maternal mortality in this beautiful and peaceful country.

The entire set of exercises from this book is available as two audio files with the Swahili spoken by a first-language Swahili speaker.

Buy Section 1 at: https://sellfy.com/p/sgql/
Buy Section 2 at: https://sellfy.com/p/69Tr/

This two-hour auditory experience provides the vital component in the learning of any language: auditory learning.
By listening to these exercises repeatedly, the language will sink in without effort - just as a child learns its native tongue.

This process is fast-tracked when you understand WHY the translation is as it is, and the text book provides this information, in exactly the same sequence.

In case of problems buying the audio CD / mp3, please email:
email.lozza@gmail.com

Table of Contents

Introduction – how the course works 10

Learn Swahili quickly and easily – Section One: Some simple rules 11

Learn Swahili quickly and easily – Section Two: The Theory 11

Learn Swahili quickly and easily – Listening 11

Learn Swahili quickly and easily – Pronunciation 12

Section 1: Understand the way the language works 13

1.   'Na'= Currently happening 13

Exercise 1: (Answers at the end of this part of the book) 14

2.   M-MI words 19

Exercise 2: 20

3.   Ki-Vi and Ch-Vy words 21

Exercise 3: 22

4.   Na = is currently; and; with; & to have 23

Exercise 4: 25

5.   Ni = am /are. Si = am not /are not. Descriptions – e.g. 'is good' 26

Exercise 5: 27

6.   Not doing things – the negative of action words 28

Exercise 6: 30

7.   That is so! That is not so! 31

Exercise 7: 31

8.   Where is it? 32

Exercise 8: 33

9.   In; on; nearby = -ni. 34

Exercise 9 35

10.   Here = Hapa or Huku. There = Pale or Kule. 36

Exercise 10 37

11.   (In that place) there is; there are 38

Exercise 11 39

12.   A: This; these 40

12 B. That; those 40

Exercise 12 41

13.   Where? In front of, on top of, behind of, etc. (Yes, behind of) 42

Exercise 13: 43

14. Other directions 44
  Exercise 14: 45
15. More on possession 46
  Exercise 15: 48
16. Descriptions 49
  Exercise 16: 52
17. Greetings 53
  Exercise 17: 54
18. I have gone, I went. I have spoken, I spoke – the past 55
  Exercise 18: 56
19. I have not gone. I did not go – the negative in the past 57
  Exercise 19: 58
20. I will go, I will not go – the future 59
  Exercise 20: 60
21. Giving orders and making requests 61
22. If … 67
  Exercise 22: 69
23. Me, you, him/her, us, them 70
  Exercise 23: 72
24. Nicely, badly, fairly – descriptions of actions 73
  Exercise 24: 74
25. When? 76
  Exercise 25: 78
26. Numbers and telling the time 79
  Exercise 26: 82
27. How many? Quantity 83
  Exercise 27: 84
28. All and any: '-ote' and '-o -ote' 85
  Exercise 28: 86
29. Actions to, at, or for someone or something 87
  Exercise 29: 88
30. Making an action reciprocal – another use of '-na' 89
  Exercise 30: 90

31. Doing things to oneself – '-ji-' 91

Exercise 31: 91

32. Connecting words 92

Exercise 32: 93

33. Which, whom, whose, and other questions 94

Exercise 33: 95

34. Who, which and whom as explanations – 'amba'. When as explanation. 96

Exercise 34: 97

35. 'With it' – Na + it 98

Exercise 35: 98

36. The way things are done – jinsi; kama; kadiri 99

Exercise 36: 99

37. N class words 100

37C: Still more on N-class: The family, and N-class words dealing with living things 105

38. Ji-Ma Class of words 107

Exercise 38: 110

39. U class words 112

Exercise 39: 115

40. Pa Class, plus more on location 116

Exercise 40: 118

41. W: Being done to you, rather than doing it 119

Exercise 41 121

42. K: more on the passive 122

Exercise 42: 124

43. Causing things to happen – '-isha'; '-esha'; and '-za' 125

Exercise 43: 126

Section 1: Exercises and answers 128

Exercise 1A: 'Na'= Currently happening 128

Exercise 1B M-Wa 128

Exercise 1C More on M-Wa 128

Exercise 2 M-Mi 128

Exercise 3 Ki-Vi and Ch-Vy 129

Exercise 4 Na & possession 129

Exercise 5 Ni = am /are. Si = am not /are not 129

Exercise 6 Si & Ha: Negatives 130

Exercise 7 Ndiyo & Siyo 130

Exercise 8 PKM: location 130

Exercise 9 Ni: in or near to 131

Exercise 10 Here = Hapa or Huku. There = Pale or Kule. 131

Exercise 11: There is /There are = Pana, kuna, mna 131

Exercise 12: h-: this/these; -le: that/those 132

Exercise 13: More on location 132

Exercise 14: Other directions 132

Exercise 15: More on possession 133

Exercise 16: Agreement of descriptions 133

Exercise 17: Greetings 134

Exercise 18: -li- : The completed past;   -me- : 'have' + the past 134

Exercise 19: -ku- & -ja- : The negatives of the past 135

Exercise 20: -ta- : The future 135

Exercise 21A: Commands and requests 135

Exercise 21B: Hopes and aspirations 136

Exercise 22: -ki- : If 137

Exercise 23: To me, to you, to it, to them 137

Exercise 24: Vi- Ki- and kwa: Describing an action 138

Exercise 25: Expressions of time 138

Exercise 26: Numbers and clocks 138

Exercise 27: Quantities 139

Exercise 28: -ote and -o –ote: All and any 139

Exercise 29: -i- -li- etc: Actions to, at or for 140

Exercise 30: -na : Reciprocal actions 140

Exercise 31: -ji- : Action to one's self 140

Exercise 32: Connecting words 140

Exercise 33: Questions 141

Exercise 34: -amba- : Who and which as explanations 141

Exercise 35: Nayo etc: With it/them 141

Exercise 36: Jinsi Kama Kadiri: The way things are done 142

Exercise 37A: N-class words 142

Exercise 37B: More on N-class words 143

Exercise 37C: The family 143

Exercise: 38 Ji-Ma class... 143

Exercise 39: U-class 144

Exercise 40: Mahali; Pa class; Location 144

Exercise 41: -w- : It being done to you 144

Exercise 42: -k- : The state things are in 145

Exercise 43: –isha –esha –za : Causing things to happen....................... 145

Section 2: Practise and assimilate the way the language works 147

1. '-na-' Present continuous. M-Wa nouns 148

2. M-Mi nouns 149

3. Ki-Vi and Ch-Vy nouns.. 149

4. Na = To have 150

5. The verb 'To be' 151

6. Expressing the negative of verbs 152

7. Agreement & disagreement with statements 153

8. Location – the PKM system 154

9. Location – In; on; nearby = -ni. 155

10. Location – Here = Hapa or Huku. There = Pale or Kule. 155

11. Location – (In that place) there is; there are: Pana, Kuna & Mna 156

12. Location – Nearby: this; these: H- Further away: that; those: -le 156

13. Location – In front of, on top of, behind of, etc. 157

    Location – Directions... 158

14. Location versus Possession and the possessive 158

15. Adjectives 160

16. Greetings 162

17. The past – to have done something = '-me-'; did something = '-li-' 163

18. Negative of the past – '-ja-' and '-ku-' 164

19. The future – '-ta-' 165

20. The imperative and the subjunctive: Giving orders and making
requests 166

21. The conditional: If: '-ki-'. If not: 'kama' or 'sipo' 168

22. Object pronouns: Me, you, him/her, us, them 171

23. Adverbs: Descriptions of actions. Prepositions and conjunctions ... 172

24. Expressions of relationships in time 173

25. Numbers and telling the time 175

26. Quantity 176

27. All and any: '-ote' and '-o -ote' 177

28. Indirect object pronouns: Actions to, at, or for someone or something 178

29. Making an action reciprocal – another use of '-na' 179

30. Doing things to oneself – '-ji-' 179

31. Conjunctions and adverbial connecting words 180

32. Questions 180

33. Relatives: Who, which and whom – 'amba'; 'must'; and the letter 'o' 181

34. Preposition + object: 'With it' – Na +it 185

35. Relatives of manner – jinsi; kama; kadiri 186

36. N class words 188

37. Ji-Ma Class of words 190

38. U class words 191

39. Pa Class, plus more on location 193

40. Passive – insertion of '-w-' 194

41. The stative – insertion of '-k-' 194

42. Causing things to happen – '-isha'; '-esha'; '-ka' and '-za' 195

43. The present indefinite tense: -a- 197

44. The 'Hu-' tense – 'usually' 198

45. The '-ka-' narrative tense: 'and so I...'; 'he went and...'; 'go and...', etc 199

46. The infinitive, the gerund, and the uses of 'ku' 200

47. Swahili translation of the word 'it' and 'they / them' – summary 201

48. Summary of verb modifications to produce related meanings 203

Section 2: Translation Exercises - sehemu 2: Zoezi la kutafsiri 205

1. '-na-' Present continuous. M-Wa nouns 205

2. M-Mi nouns 205

3. Ki-Vi and Ch-Vy words 206

4. Na = To have 206

5. The verb 'To be' 207

7. That is so! That is not so! 207

8. Location – the PKM system 208

9. Location – In; on; nearby = -ni. 208

10. Location – Here = Hapa or Huku. There = Pale or Kule. 208

11. Location – (In that place) there is; there are: Pana, Kuna & Mna 209

12. Location – Nearby: this; these: H- Further away: that; those: -le 209

13. Location – In front of, on top of, behind of, etc. 210

Location – Directions 210

14. Possession and the possessive 210

15. Adjectives 211

16. Greetings 212

17. The past – to have done something = '-me-'; did something = '-li-' 213

18. Negative of the past – '-ja-', '-kwe-', '-ae-', '-hu-', '-ha-' and '-ku-' 213

19. The future – '-ta-' 213

20. The imperative and the subjunctive: Giving orders and making requests 214

21. The conditional: If: '-ki-'. If not: 'kama' or 'sipo' 214

22. Object pronouns: Me, you, him/her, us, them 215

23. Adverbs: Descriptions of actions 216

24. Expressions of relationships in time 216

25. Numbers and telling the time 217

26. Quantity 218

27. All and any: '-ote' and '-o -ote' 219

28. Indirect object pronouns: Actions to, at, or for someone/ something 219

29. Making an action reciprocal – another use of '-na' 219

30. Doing things to oneself – '-ji-' u 220

31. Conjunctions and adverbial connecting words 220

32. Questions 220

33. Relatives: Who, which and whom – 'amba' 221

34. Preposition + object: 'With it' – Na +it 222

35. Relatives of manner – jinsi; kama; kadiri 222

36. N class words 223

37. Ji-Ma Class of words 224

38.	U class words	225
39.	Pa Class, plus more on location	225
40.	Passive – insertion of '-w-'	226
41.	The stative – insertion of '-k-'	226
42.	Causing things to happen – '-isha'; '-esha'; and '-za'	226
43.	The present indefinite	227
44.	The 'hu' tense – usually	227
45.	The '-ka-' narrative tense: 'and so I...'; 'he went and...'; etc	227
46.	Gerunds, and the uses of Ku.	228
	Annexe 1: Vocabulary Summary	229
	Annexe 2: (Ki)Swahili Metaphorical Expressions	23939
	Annexe 3: (Ki)Swahili Proverbs	241
	Annexe 4: Street Phrases & Slang	2455
	Annexe 5: (Ki)Swahili Taboo Words	2500
	Annexe 6: (Ki)Swahili links	2511
	Annexe 7: (Ki)Swahili-speaking countries	2533

Learn Swahili quickly and easily

Introduction – how the course works

The first section of this book does not use any grammatical terms whatsoever, but still gets the ideas across. It is a rebellion against all those 'teach yourself' language books that seem to think that grammar is the very first thing to take in. That is not how you learnt your native language – you learnt it by making sense of it and by gentle immersion. That is what this book will do.

Swahili is quite an easy language to learn, once you get past two tricky aspects. Firstly, in English, we change the <u>end</u> of a word according to the context, (eg when speaking about the past, load becomes loaded; or when changing from single to many, 'thing' becomes 'things'). In Swahili, however, the changes are often at the <u>front</u>, and sometimes at both ends of the word.

The second awkward thing is that there are a number of different sets of rules for changing the beginnings and ends of words, depending on what type of thing you are talking about – for instance the rules for people are different from the rules for plants.

Putting these two things together, it gets confusing at the start of learning Swahili to see that the plural of mtu (person), is watu. The beginning of the word has changed from 'm' to 'wa', whereas in English we just put 's' on the end. But the change is not always from 'M' to 'Wa'. Sometimes, the change might be from 'M' to 'Mi' – for instance, the word for tree is 'mti', but the plural is 'miti'. So, some word-beginnings change from m- to wa-; (typically those that deal with people); and others change from m- to mi-, (typically those that deal with certain types of things). There are five other types of change. However, once you know how it works for one, it is exactly the same for all words of that type, with few exceptions. You quickly get to know which type is which – the beginning of the word being an important clue.

So, don't worry – in a few weeks these types of words will be second nature to you, and you can get on with learning the language. Once you get past this unfamiliarity, the rest of the rules of Swahili are much easier than English, with far fewer irregularities. For instance, if you know the way to say something that is happening now, you will also be able very easily to work out how to say the same thing in the past or the future. Furthermore, Swahili words are often short and simple, and the connecting words are short and multi-purpose. Swahili speakers realise that the person you are speaking to has mainly cottoned on to what you are saying whilst you are still saying it, so you do not need elaborate grammar and long words to say something simple!

Learn Swahili quickly and easily – Section One: Some simple rules

The first section of this book, then, is designed for painless understanding of the way in which the language works. It uses only a very limited vocabulary, and absolutely no technical terms, but nevertheless explains, in gentle steps, the way the language functions. By doing this with only a limited number of new words to learn, you will only have to concentrate on learning the new concepts, which are really not that difficult.

At the end of the section, and at the end of each short chapter within it, are straightforward tests to drive home the understanding.

Learn Swahili quickly and easily – Section Two: The Theory

Thereafter, once the concepts are clear, the second section summarises the first, and uses simple sentences to illustrate all the key points. In making a limited number of carefully crafted sentences, the second section translates the learning of the first section everyday language into the grammatical concepts. The idea is that once you can translate these sentences, and understand why, you will have a very good working grasp of the way the language works. Once again, at the end of the section, and at the end of each short chapter within it, are straightforward tests to enhance further the understanding. If you are very grammar-minded, by all means move to the second section quickly.

Learn Swahili quickly and easily – Listening

All the exercises should also be listened to as well as read. Listening is a very powerful tool for driving home learning – especially repetitive listening combined with making sense of what you are hearing. (Which is the way that children learn a language). Listen to the recordings repeatedly. One day, you will find that the entire vocabulary has entered into your deep learning.

If you study only from books, this simply does not happen. How often do you pick up your book, and think, "I did this yesterday, but have already forgotten!" By contrast, the process of learning by listening, and using the book to check understanding, will make the language sink into your deep and long-term memory, without effort. By virtue of your earlier work, you will also understand why the translation is as it is – and if you do not, you can go back and check that section. This 'active listening' is the secret to all deep language learning.

Listen to Swahili for just 20 minutes every day – in a queue in a shop, walking along the street, driving to work – and back this up by checking understanding and making sense of it where there is any confusion. Within six months, you will be able to have fairly detailed and fluent conversations.

Learn Swahili quickly and easily – Pronunciation

The pronunciation of Swahili is very little different from English, and is just about always the same in all Swahili words, no matter what the grammatical context.

If you want to be perfect, then concentrate on getting the vowels (a, e, i, o, u), to sound more African. This is much easier than in English, where the same vowel can be pronounced in many different ways. (Look at that last sentence, for example: look at the letter 'e' and see how often we pronounce it differently in different words!). In Swahili, the vowels are always pronounced the same way:

The letter A is pronounced like in the word 'car', but shorter. The letter E is pronounced as in the word 'bed'. The letter 'i' is pronounced like 'ee'. The letter O is like 'off'. The letter U is like 'oo'.

However, please note that in Swahili, the vowel sounds are shorter than English – e.g., 'O' is never long like in 'Oh!' It is always short like in 'off'. If you were saying the word 'bingo' in English, the end would sound long and weird in African ears. To get it more African, you would have to pretend that you were saying "bingot", then not pronounce the T.

With longer words, the stress is always on the next-to-last syllable, e.g., wanawake is pronounced "wana**wa**ke". Swahili words almost exclusively end in a vowel, such that when Swahili speakers talk in English, they often add a vowel sound 'ee' at the end of English words. Be sure then, to pronounce final vowels, though without giving them special emphasis.

By the way, you may at times see the name of the language written as 'Kiswahili'. That is the Swahili word for the language, but in English we call it 'Swahili'. In the same way, for example, the Spanish word for Spanish is 'español', but we call it 'Spanish'. You would not say, "I'm learning español", and technically speaking, neither should you say, "I am learning Kiswahili"!

This section is all about painless explanation. There are no grammatical terms, but simply readily understandable explanations of how Swahili is constructed. Just start reading. At the end of each part, test yourself on the easy short sentences <u>until you get it right each time!</u>

Note: To begin with, until you are used to the compound words made up of different elements, they will be written with hyphens, so that you can see how they are put together.

1. 'Na'= Currently happening

1A: People doing things – first part

Child	is	*M-toto*
To visit	is	*Ku-zuru*
Town	is	*M-ji*
s/he is (currently)	is	*a-na-*
they are (currently)	is	*wa-na-*

The child is currently visiting the town	is	*M-toto a-na-zuru m-ji*
The children are visiting the town	is	*Wa-toto wa-na-zuru m-ji*
The children are visiting the towns	is	*Wa-toto wa-na-zuru mi-ji*

Points to note:
When you change 'child' to 'children', you change the front of the word from M to Wa. This class of word is therefore called 'M-Wa'. However, when you change from town to towns, the front of the word changes from M to Mi. This class of word is 'M-Mi'.

'To visit' is 'Kuzuru': ku- means 'to' and -zuru means 'visit'. This is important. The 'ku' part means 'to' and is at the front of all general action words, eg kuficha – to hide; kupika – to cook.

When making words about (e.g.) visiting, you drop the 'ku' in the same way that in English we drop the 'to' – we don't say 'He <u>to</u> is visiting', we say 'He is visiting'. In the same way in Swahili, when using an action word, you drop the 'ku' at the start. (Unless it leaves the word too short – see below).

So: '-na-' means 'it is happening right now, at this time, currently'.
Therefore '…-na-zuru' means 'visiting currently'.

However, in Swahili, you don't just say "the child is visiting the town, (Mtoto na-zuru mji), you say "the child, <u>he</u> is-currently visiting the town', (Mtoto <u>a</u>nazuru mji). 'a' means he or she.

He-is-currrently-visiting is 'a-na-zuru'. They-are currently-visiting is 'wa-na-zuru'. 'wa' means 'they'.

Exercise 1: (Answers at the end of this part of the book)
Translate:
The child is visiting the town.
The children are visiting the town.
The children are visiting the towns.

Do not progress unless you got all three right!

1B: People doing things – second part

Teacher	is	M-walimu (M-Wa class)
Pupil	is	M-wanafunzi (M-Wa class)
To bake	is	Ku-oka
To hide	is	Ku-ficha
Bread	is	M-kate (M-Mi class)
Bag	is	M-fuko (M-Mi class)

The teacher is cooking food	is	M-walimu a-na-pika m-kate
The teachers are baking bread	is	Wa-limu wa-na-oka m-kate
The pupil is hiding the bag	is	M-wanafunzi a-na-ficha m-fuko
The pupils are hiding the bag	is	Wa-nafunzi wa-na-ficha m-fuko
The pupils are hiding the bags	is	Wa-nafunzi wa-na-ficha mi-fuko

Points to note:

The M-Wa class of nouns tends to refer to people. The basic stem of the word for teacher is '-walimu'. When changing teacher to 'teachers', being an M-Wa class of word, it should change from M-walimu to Wa-walimu. But the main part of the word already starts with 'wa', so putting another 'wa' in front is not done. Similarly, the word for pupils is 'wa-nafunzi', not 'wa-wanafunzi'.

The words for 'to bake' and 'to hide' both end in 'a' in Swahili. This is a common ending for Swahili action words, (ie words that tell what something or someone is doing). Indeed, it is only really action words of foreign origin that do not end in 'a' – typically ending in 'i' and 'u'. So, you can get a feel for what type of word each word might be, from its ending. If a word ends in 'o', for example, it is not an action, and is probably a 'thing' of some sort.

'They are hiding' is wa (they) na (are currently) ficha (hiding). So 'they are hiding' is 'wa-na-ficha'.

A word starting with 'wana…' that is describing an action, is saying 'they are currently…'

A word starting with 'wa-…' if it is a person, means more than one of them:

SUMMARY:

'wana...' means 'they are currently...'
'wanafunzi' means 'pupils'
'wanafunzi wanaficha' means 'the pupils, they are currently hiding'

Exercise 1B:

Translate:
"The pupils are cooking /baking bread".
"The teachers are hiding the bag".
Do not progress unless you get both right!

1C: People doing things – third part

'To come'	is	'Ku-ja'
'To eat'	is	'Ku-la'
'To go'	is	'Ku-enda' (also written 'kwenda')
'To arrive'	is	'Ku-fika' or 'kuwasili'
'To beat'	is	'Ku-piga'
`The man'	is	'M-wanaume (M-Wa class)
`The men'	is	'Wa-naume (M-Wa class)
`The woman'	is	'M-wanamke (M-Wa class)
`The women'	is	'Wa-nawake' (M-Wa class)
'The man is arriving'	is	'M-wanaume a-na-fika' / a-na-wasili
'The women are arriving''	is	'Wa-nawake wa-na-fika' / wa-na-wasili
'I am at this moment coming'	is	'Ni-na-kuja'
'We are beating'	is	'Tu-na-piga'
'You are at this moment going'	is	'U-na-enda' (if just one person)

(NB: Also, you can say, 'U-na-<u>kw</u>enda' – see below)

'You are at this moment going'	is	'Mnaenda' (if more than one)

Points to note

'You are currently going' is 'u-na-enda', but this sounds a bit weird, so often people say "unakwenda" – in other words they do not bother dropping the 'kw' sound at the beginning of the word. Similarly, on short words like kula and kuja, you do not drop the 'ku' when using the word. So, for instance, 'I-am-eating' is 'ni-na-kula', not 'ni-na-la'.

In Swahili, the letter M is often a syllable by itself, pronounced 'mmm'. You can spot this, because it will be when m is before another consonant – e.g. <u>m</u>wanaume. Pronounce it "mmm-wana-oomi".

SUMMARY:

When dealing with M-Wa words (ie people):
ni=I;   u=you;   a=s/he
(the word for he and she is the same)
tu=we;   m=you;   wa=they

kukuja = to come
'ninakuja...' means 'I am currently coming'
'unakuja...' means 'you are currently coming' (just one)
'anakuja...' means 's/he is currently coming'
'tunakuja...' means 'we are currently coming'
'mnakuja...' means 'you are currently coming' (more than one)
'wanakuja...' means 'they are currently coming'

'Kupiga' means 'to beat', but is used as a simple way of saying many different actions, as long as they involve doing something to an object – e.g. to beat the piano (play it), to beat the clothes, (iron them), to beat the hands, (clap them), to beat the phone, (make a call), to beat the picture, (take a photo), etc. So, if you need an action word and can't remember it, it is often OK to use 'kupiga'!

Some Swahili words were originally two words, but have been compressed into one. So, the word for man is 'mwanamume', but this was originally 'mwana' ('someone's offspring'), and 'mume' or 'mme', (male or husband). Similarly, the word for woman was originally two words: 'mwana' - 'mke' (mwanamke) = 'someone's female offspring'. When making the plural, then, both bits of the word change. So, in the word for 'men', 'mwana' becomes 'wana'. (It is an M-Wa word, and so should change to wawana, but that is too much of a mouthful, so 'wana' is enough). The second part of the word also takes a short-cut, and simply drops the 'm'. So 'mwanamume or mwanaume' (man), becomes 'wanaume' (men).

Exercise 1C:
Translate:
You (plural) are beating the men.
We are currently arriving.
The women are currently cooking.
Do not progress unless you get all correct!

2. M-MI words

'To smell not nice'	is	'Ku-nuka'
'To be sufficient'	is	'Ku-tosha'
'To touch'	is	'Ku-gusa'
'To burn' (i.e. to be flaming)	is	'Ku-waka'
'Plant' or 'crop'	is	'M-mea' (M-Mi class)
'Plants' or 'crops'	is	'Mi-mea' (M-Mi)
'Smoke'	is	'M-oshi' (M-Mi)
'Tree' (also wood from tree)	is	'M-ti' (M-Mi)
'Mango tree'	is	'M-wembe' (M-Mi)
'Hand'	is	'M-kono' (M-Mi)
'The smoke is smelling'	is	'M-oshi u-na-nuka'
'The bread is burning'	is	'M-kate u-na-waka'
'The bag is sufficient'	is	'M-foko u-na-tosha'
'The hands are touching'	is	'Mi-kono i-na-gusa'
'The crops are arriving'	is	'Mi-mea i-na-fika'
'To be aflame'	is	'Kuwaka'
'To burn' e.g. food	is	'Kuungua' / 'Kuunguza'
'To burn up'	is	'Kuunguza'
'To set fire to'	is	'Kuwasha' / 'Kuchoma'
'The trees are aflame'	is	'Mi-ti i-na-waka'
'The mango trees are aflame'	is	'Mi-embe i-na-waka'

Points to note:

M-Mi words form their plurals, (obviously!), by changing the M to Mi. There are some straightforward exceptions to this rule – for instance when the word starts with Mw, you drop the w as well as the m, before substituting Mi. (e.g. 'Mwili' – body; 'Miili' – bodies.)

Once more, the action being done by the M-Mi word needs also to change its front letters.

Remember that in Swahili, they do not say "The crops are arriving", they say "the crops, they are arriving". With M-Wa words, 'they' was 'Wa'. (e.g. they are arriving = wanafika). With M-Mi words, however, 'they' is 'i'. So 'kufika' (to arrive), becomes 'i-na-fika' – they are currently arriving. 'The trees (they) are arriving is therefore 'Miti inafika'.

Please note something which confuses slightly at first, but which quickly you will not even notice: 'unakuja' when applying to an M-Wa word means 'you are coming'. When applied to an M-Mi word, it means 'it is coming'. The interpretation is usually obvious from the context.

Exercise 2:
Translate:
The bread is arriving
The smoke is sufficient
The mango trees are smelling
The hands are touching
Do not progress unless you get them all right!

(From now on, compound words will mainly not be broken down with hyphens. Hopefully, you now have the gist of how it works!)

3. Ki-Vi and Ch-Vy words

'Thing'	is	'Kitu' (Ki-Vi class)
'Things'	is	'Vitu' (Ki-Vi)
'Book/books'	is	'Kitabu/vitabu' (Ki-Vi)
'Bed/beds'	is	'Kitanda/vitanda' (Ki-Vi)
'Village/villages	is	'Kijiji/vijiji' (Ki-Vi)
'Food/foods'	is	'Chakula/vyakula' (Ch-Vy class)
'Toilet/toilets	is	'Choo/vyoo' (Ch-Vy class)
'To grow'	is	'Kukua'
'To look at'	is	'Kutazama' (or kutizama)
'To bring'	is	'Kuleta'
'To find'	is	'kutafuta' or 'kupata'
'The things are touching'	is	'Vitu vinagusa'
'The food is growing'	is	'Chakula kinakua'
'The man is bringing beds'	is	'Mwanaume analeta vitanda'
'The toilet is smelling'	is	'Choo kinanuka'
'The toilets are smelling'	is	'Vyoo vinanuka'
'The villages are burning' (fire)	is	'Vijiji vinawaka' (moto)
'The village is burning'	is	'Kijiji kinawaka'
'The beds are arriving'	is	'Vitanda vinafika'

Points to note:
It is important to get past this section, after which things get easier. When first coming across all different classes of word, the temptation is to say, "I'll never get this".

But you will! Just read it over until you do.

Once you get familiar with the way the whole language depends on just a few different classes of word, which allow a very thrifty way of expressing yourself, your understanding will suddenly open up.

Like the M-Mi class of words, the Ki-Vi class comprises only names of things, never of types of people.

Remember that in Swahili, you have to say, "the thing, it is doing something", (not "the thing is doing something"). So, as we have already noted, when something is doing something currently, you take the action word, (e.g. kupika, to cook), knock off the 'ku', and add 'na'. Do you remember that 'the man is cooking' is 'mwanamume anapika.' 'A-na... means 'he-is-currently'. So 'mwanamume anapika' is 'the man, he-is-currently-cooking'.

So, the word for 'he' in M-Wa words, (which deal with people), is 'a'. You remember that in this class, there is a word for I, you, s/he, we, etc. In all other classes of words, however, which only deal with things and not people, you only ever need to talk about 'it' and 'they': ('the tree, it burns'; 'the toilets, they smell', etc). You never need to say, "The tree, I burn", or "the toilets, we smell".

The words for 'it' and 'they' with M-Mi words were 'u' and 'i'. For Ki-Vi words, they are 'ki' (it) and 'vi', (they). So 'it-is-currently-burning' is ki-na-waka'. They-are-currently-burning is 'vi-na-waka', (when talking of the burning of Ki-Vi things). The book, it is burning is therefore: 'Kitabu kinawaka'. The books are burning is 'vitabu vinawaka'. In Swahili, then, it is very common to have a sequence of two or three words starting with the same letter/s, all derived from the starting letters of whatever thing or things is doing the action.

The Ch-Vy class of words are really just a sub-group of the Ki-Vi words, and so exactly the same words are used for 'it' and 'they' – ki and vi. So 'the toilet-is-currently-smelling' is 'choo ki-na-nuka'. The toilets are smelling is 'Vyoo vinanuka'.

SUMMARY:
When dealing with Ki-Vi (and Ch-Vy) words
ki=it;   vi=they

'kinakuja…' means 'it is currently coming'
'vinakuja…' means 'they are currently coming'

Exercise 3:
Translate:
The toilet is coming
The mango trees are growing
The things are arriving
The book is burning

4. Na = is currently; and; with; & to have

'Is-currently'	*is*	*'Na'*
'And'	*is*	*'Na'*
'With'	*is*	*'Na'*
'Have'	*is*	*'Na'*

Points to note:

'Na' means 'is-currently' when talking about an action – e.g. kupika = to cook. Anapika = s/he is currently cooking. However, 'na' also means 'and', and it also means 'with', and it is used to mean 'have'!!! There are even other nuances of the word, which we will come to, but in each case, you can work out what is going on from the place of 'na' within the word or sentence.

When used to mean 'is-currently', it is within a word, soon after the beginning – e.g. a<u>na</u>pika. When used to mean 'and', it is a separate word: 'beds and books' – 'vitabu <u>na</u> vitanda'.

When it is used as 'with', it is at the end of a short word: 'She is cooking <u>with</u> a thing' = 'anapika a<u>na</u> kitu'. (Notice that you still have to say, "she is cooking, <u>she</u> with thing". So, the 'with' word needs a letter or two before it to say who it is with. 'Anapika <u>a</u>na kitu' = 'she is cooking, <u>she</u>-with thing'.

Finally, there is no special word for 'to have'. You just say (for instance') 'he-with book', instead of 'he has a book': ana kitabu.

SUMMARY:
When dealing with M-Wa words (ie people):
ni=I; u=you; a=s/he
tu=we; m=you; wa=they
To these, add '-na' to make 'I have', 'you have' etc.

'nina kitabu' means 'I have a book' (= 'I-with book')
'una kitabu' means 'You have a book' (Just one of you)
'ana kitabu' means 's/he has a book'
'tuna kitabu' means 'we have a book'
'mna kitabu' means 'you have a book (more than one of you)
'wana kitabu' means 'they have a book'

M-Mi class:
una = it has   ina = they have

Ki-Vi class
kina = it has   vina = they have

'The villages have food'	is	'Vijiji vina chakula'
'The village is growing and has beds'	is	'Kijiji kinakua na kina vitanda'
'I have a bed and a book'	is	'Nina kitanda na kitabu'
'The books and beds are burning'	is	'Vitabu na vitanda vinawaka'
'The toilets and things are burning and smelling'		

is 'Vyoo na vitu vinawaka na vinanuka'

'I have food and books. They are sufficient'

is 'Nina chakula na vitabu. Vinatosha'

The opposite of 'na' is 'bila', which simply means 'without; not having (something)'. It does not change in any situation:

'Villages without food'	is	'Vijiji bila chakula'
'The village without beds'	is	'Kijiji bila vitanda'
'The child without bed and without book'		

is 'Mtoto bila kitanda na bila kitabu'

('Vijiji bila chakula' can mean 'The villages have no food', but this is more correctly expressed as 'vijiji **ha**vina chakula' – the 'ha-' prefix meaning 'not' – see Chapter 6.)

In the examples above, 'anapika ana kitu', means 'she is cooking with a thing', and 'ana kitu' by itself means she has/possesses a thing. In this example, where 'na' is used to signify possession, there is another way to express it, using the word '-enye', meaning 'possessing' or 'having'.

It is a somewhat cumbersome way of doing it, because not only does the front end of '-enye' have to agree with the thing being possessed, but also, that agreement is not straightforward to work out, because '-enye' starts with an 'e'. So, for instance, 'A man with a book', (ie 'A man possessing/having a book'), should be 'Mwanaume kienye kitabu', and 'A man with a child', should be 'Mwanaume menye mtoto'. However, because of the vowel clash in the first case, and the loss of importance of the 'm' in the second case, 'kienye' and 'menye' are not allowed, so we have the following changes:

M-Wa class:	M + -enye = mwenye
	Wa + -enye = wenye
M-Mi class:	U + -enye = wenye
	I + -enye = yenye
Ki-Vi class:	Ki + -enye = chenye
	Vi + -enye = vyenye

(These same changes are the usual ones for combining two vowels, and will be met often when the agreement letters meet an 'e' at the front a describing word).

'The villages with food'	*is*	*'Vijiji vyenye chakula'*
'The village with beds'	*is*	*'Kijiji chenye vitanda'*
'The child with a bed'	*is*	*'Mtoto mwenye kitanda'*
'The child with a tree'	*is*	*'Mtoto mwenye mti'*
'The child with trees'	*is*	*'Mtoto mwenye miti'*

Thus, the use of '-na' to signify possession is easier: 'He has a book' = 'Ana kitabu'!

Exercise 4:

Translate:
The village has mango trees and crops
Men and women have hands and are beating
The teacher and pupils have food and are hiding.

Please note how far you have come! And, once again, please make sure you have taken these things on board before moving on. If you do, from now on, the next stages of the journey are much easier than in European languages, because in many cases, the Swahili way to get the meaning across just means the addition of a few small letters, plus agreement between the words, and there are few exceptions to the rules.

5. Ni = am /are. Si = am not /are not. Descriptions – e.g. 'is good'

'I am'		*is*	*'Ni'*
'You are, he is, we are, they are'		*is also*	*'Ni'*
'I am not'		*is*	*'Si'*
'You are not, he is not, we are not, etc.'		*is also*	*'Si'*
'The tree is ...'		*is*	*'Mti ni ...'*
'The book is ...'		*is*	*'Kitabu ni ...'*
'Nice / good'		*is*	*'-zuri'*
'The book is good'		*is*	*'Kitabu ni kizuri'*
'The tree is good'		*is*	*'Mti ni mzuri'*
'The villages are good'		*is*	*'Vijiji ni vizuri'*
'The man is good'	*is*		*'Mwanaume ni mzuri/mwema'*
'You are good'		*is*	*'Wewe ni mzuri/mwema'*
'You are not good'		*is*	*'Wewe si mzuri/mwema'*
			Wewe ni mbaya
'I am good'		*is*	*'Mimi ni mzuri/mwema'*
'I am not good'		*is*	*'Mimi si mzuri/mwema'*
			Mimi ni mbaya

Points to note:

Yes, it is true, you can use the word 'ni' to mean 'I am', 'you are', 'it is'; and 'si' to mean the opposite, for all cases! Probably originally this was not perfect grammar, but it works. However, if you are not using the normal starting letters to tell you who is doing the action, (ni-, u-, a-, tu-, etc), then something needs to be done to show who you are talking about. Sometimes it is obvious – e.g. 'the book is…' ('Kitabu ni …)

When it is not otherwise clear, Swahili has a special set of words for clarifying or emphasising the words for 'I', 'You', 'He', etc:

When needing to emphasise or clarify:
mimi=I;   wewe=you, (one only);   yeye=s/he
sisi=we;   ninyi=you, (more than one);   wao=they

' mimi ninakuja' means 'I am currently coming'
'wewe unakuja' means 'you are currently coming' (just one)
'yeye anakuja' means 's/he is currently coming'
'sisi tunakuja' means 'we are currently coming'
'ninyi mnakuja' means 'you are currently coming' (more than one)
'wao wanakuja' means 'they are currently coming'

Normally, when no emphasis is required, the first word is omitted, (mimi, wewe, etc). Without these words, the meaning is still clear.

Note that the word for good, (-zuri), because it is a description of something or someone, has to have its front end modified by the normal starting letters of that class of word. So, when describing M-Wa words, 'good' can be either mzuri or wazuri; for M-Mi words, 'good' can be mzuri or mizuri; for Ki-Vi words, 'good' can be kizuri or vizuri; etc. The same need for front-end changes is true for many Swahili words.

Examples:

'The book is good'	*is*	*'Kitabu ni kizuri'*
'The book is not good'	*is*	*'Kitabu si kizuri'*
'The food and the beds are good'	*is*	*'Chakula na vitanda ni vizuri'*
'The food and the beds are not good'	*is*	*'Chakula na vitanda si vizuri'*
'The children are growing. They are good'		
	is	*'Watoto wanakua. Ni wazuri'*

One more point on the use of 'na': when saying 'with me', it should be 'na mimi'. However, this is contracted to 'nami'. Similarly, 'with you' is 'nawe', not 'na wewe'. The full list of these contractions is:

SUMMARY

with me	=	nami
With you (one)	=	nawe
With him/her	=	naye
With us	=	nasi
With you (>one)	=	nanyi
With them	=	nao

Exercise 5:
Translate:
The books and beds are good.
The toilets and villages are good.
We are good.
You are good.
The book is not good
The book is with me
The trees are with them
The trees are not with them

6. Not doing things – the negative of action words

We have seen just above that one way of expressing the negative is to use 'si'. This particularly applies to descriptions – e.g. when saying that I, you, he, etc., are not good, or not big, or not dirty. 'I am not good' is 'mimi si mzuri/mwema' (Mimi ni mbaya); 'they are not good' is 'wao si wazuri/wema' (wao ni wabaya); etc. The use of 'ni' and 'si' is therefore particularly for descriptions.

However, when dealing with action words as opposed to descriptions – something or someone not doing something – there is a different way to express the negative. It involves adding some short starting letters to the action word stem. These letters signify I-not; you-not; we-not; etc.

You remember that the words for I, you, etc, were: ni-, u-, a-, tu-, m-, wa-; and for it & they were u-, i-, ki-, vi-, etc. The negative forms of these mainly just adds ha- (or h-). For instance, to form (e.g.) the word 'they not', you just add 'ha' in front of the word for 'they', (wa), making 'hawa'. I-not is the principle exception to the addition of 'ha-' or 'h' to make the negative: it changes from 'ni' to 'si', instead of from 'ni' to 'hani'. So:

'I-not'	*'You-not'*	*'S/he-not'*	*is*	*'si-'*	*'hu'*	*'ha'*
'We-not'	*'You-not'*	*'They-not'*	*is*	*'ha-tu'*	*'ha-m'*	*'ha-wa'*
'It-not'	*'They-not'*	*(M-Mi class)*	*is*	*'ha-u'*	*'ha-i'*	
'It-not'	*'They-not'*	*(Ki-Vi class)*	*is*	*'ha-ki'*	*'ha-vi'*	

For example: 'things' is 'vitu'; and 'the things are burning is 'vitu vinawaka/vinaungua'. 'The things are <u>not</u> burning is 'vitu <u>ha</u>viwaki/<u>ha</u>viungui'. When you see 'ha' at the beginning of an action word, it means 'not'.

'The tree, it is burning'	*is*	*'Mti unawaka/unaungua'*
'The tree, it is not burning'	*is*	*'Mti hauwaki/hauungui'*
'Water'	*is*	*'Maji'*
'To shut'	*is*	*'Kufunga'*
'To feed'	*is*	*'Kulisha'*
'To eat'	*is*	*'Kula'*
'To wash'	*is*	*'Kuosha'*
'To come'	*is*	*'Kuja'*
'To succeed'	*is*	*'Kufaulu/kufanikiwa'*

Note: the 'u' ending which some action words have.

'To know'	*is*	*'Kujua'*
'I do not know'	*is*	*'Sijui'*
'You do not know'	*is*	*'Hujui'*
'We do not know'	*is*	*'Hatujui'*
'The plant does not feed'	*is*	*'Mmea haulishi/hauli'*
'The plants do not feed'	*is*	*'Mimea hailishi'*

'The teachers do not succeed'	is	'Walimu hawafanikiwi'
'The toilet does not shut'	is	'Choo hakifungi'
'The pupils do not come'	is	'Wanafunzi hawaji'
'I do not come – I am feeding'	is	'Siji – ninalisha'
'He does not feed and does not wash'	is	'Halishi na haoshi'
'<u>He</u> does not feed and does not wash'	is	'<u>Yeye</u> halishi na haoshi' (emphasising 'he')
'We do not eat'	is	'Hatuli'
'No!'	is	'La!' / 'hapana' / 'acha'

Points to note:

As mentioned above, most Swahili action words end in the letter 'a', when talking about things in the positive, but changes to an 'i' when talking of the negative. Thus 'they are cooking' is 'wanapika'; but 'they are not cooking' is 'hawapiki'. Note that you also lose the 'na', (which means 'is/are currently'). So, 'wa-na-pika' is literally 'they-are currently-cooking', whereas 'ha-wa-piki' is 'not-they-cooking.'

Changing the last letter to an 'i' lets the hearer know clearly that you are saying 'not'. (In Swahili, the various words in a sentence often reinforce each other – e.g. <u>wa</u>toto <u>wa</u>napika; <u>vi</u>tabu <u>vi</u>nawaka/vinaungua; etc).

Some action words of Arabic origin, however, end in 'u', and they lose meaning if you change this to an 'i', so the u remains. Some other few actions words already end in 'i'.

A final point on expressing the negative is when saying that you do not have something:

'I do not have water'	is	'Sina maji'
'We do not have trees'	is	'Hatuna miti'
'The teachers do not eat...	is	'Walimu hawali'
... they have no mango trees'	is	'... hawana miembe'
'The men do not wash	is	'Wanaume hawaoshi
... they have no water'	is	... hawana maji'

You remember that there is no separate word for 'to have' in Swahili. We saw before that when you say, 'I have', you say 'ni-na', meaning 'I-with'. 'He has' is 'ana', etc. When saying 'I have not' got something, then instead you use the 'I-not' or 'You-not' or 'she-not' etc words, (si, hu, ha, etc – see the list just above), and then add 'na'. So 'sina' is 'I-not-with' = I have not got. 'Hawana' = they have not got, etc. In other words, to make 'not' into 'have not', just add 'na'.

I-not'	'You-not'	'S/he-not'	is	'si-'	'hu-'	'ha-'

'We-not'	'You-not'	'They-not'	is	'hatu-'	'ham-'	'hawa-'

'It-not'	'They-not'	(M-Mi class)	is	'hau-'	'hai-'
'It-not'	'They-not'	(Ki-Vi class)	is	'haki-'	'havi-'

'I have not'		'You have not'	S/he has not'		is
'sina'		'huna'	'hana'		

'We have not'	'You have not'	'They have not'	is
'hatuna-'	'hamna-'	'hawana-'	

It has not'	'They have not'	(M-Mi class) is	'hauna'	'haina'
'It has not'	'They have not'	(Ki-Vi class) is	'hakina'	'havina'

It can be seen that Swahili can often get the message across in far fewer words. If writing English literature, then having plenty of words and constructions to choose from is our way of painting a picture with words. But having so many words and uses and rules makes the language much tougher to learn. Swahili, by contrast, is thrifty in the number of words you need to know, but equally can paint vivid pictures because each part of each word conveys meaning.

Exercise 6:

Translate:
The pupils are not eating the plants
The villages are not feeding the teachers
The teachers and the pupils have no books
The villages have no toilets and no mango trees.

SUMMARY of "do, be and have":

I am cooking:	Ninapika
I am nice:	Mimi ni mzuri
I have bread:	Nina mkate
I am not cooking:	Sipiki
I am not nice:	Mimi si mzuri
I have no bread:	Sina mkate

They are cooking:	Wanapika
They are nice:	(Wao) ni wazuri
They have bread:	Wana mkate
They are not cooking:	Hawapiki
They are not nice:	(Wao) si wazuri
They have no bread:	Hawana mkate

7. That is so! That is not so!

'That is so!'	is	'Ndiyo!' (or ndivyo)
'That is not so!'	is	'Siyo! (or si-vyo)

'Are the villages growing?' – 'Yes!'
        is   'Vijiji vinakua?'– 'Ndiyo!'
'Are the villages growing?' – 'No!'
        is   'Vijiji vinakua?' – 'Siyo!' (or 'La!' or 'hapana')
'Are the teachers eating?' – 'Yes!'
        is   'Walimu wanakula?' – 'Ndiyo!'
'Are the teachers not eating?' –'They are not!'
        is   'Walimu hawa(ku)li?' – 'Ndiyo!'
'Are the teachers not eating?' –'They are!'
        is   'Walimu hawali?' – 'Siyo!' or 'hapana, wanakula'.

Points to note:

These two expressions do not exactly mean 'Yes' and 'No'. They mean 'That is so' or 'That is not so'. They therefore are expressing either agreement or disagreement with what was just said.

This makes even more sense when you consider that in Swahili, the order of the words is not changed when you make a question. In English, we say, "The teachers are eating", and to turn it to a question, we say, "Are the teachers eating?" By contrast, in Swahili they just say the statement with a questioning tone: "The teachers are eating?" The response is then that you either agree or disagree with the statement made. "That is so", or "that is not so".

SUMMARY:

'That is so!'	is	'Ndiyo/ndivyo!'
'That is not so!'	is	'Siyo/sivyo/hapana!'

Exercise 7:

Translate:
Are the pupils growing? – Yes!
Are the pupils growing? – No!
Are the teachers eating? – Yes!
Are the teachers not eating? –They are not!
Is the tree burning? Yes, that is so.
Is the tree not burning? Yes, that is so.

8. Where is it?

'Is located kind-of ...'	*is*	*'-ko'*
'Is located precisely..'	*is*	*'-po'*
'Is located within..'	*is*	*'-mo'*

These three letters – k, p and m – crop up in various ways when you are saying where something is. 'K' signifies an approximate location. (Think of 'K' for Kind-of!). So when asking questions about location, ('Where is..'), the 'is' word will be formed using a 'k', because by definition you do not know the precise location. You use 'P' when you are talking about Precise location, and 'M' when something is within something, (think of 'Middle'):

'The children are located hereabouts ...'	*is*	*'Watoto wako ...'*
'The children are located precisely...'	*is*	*'Watoto wapo ...'*
'The children are located within..'	*is*	*'Watoto wamo...'*
'The children are not located precisely...'	*is*	*'Watoto hawapo ...'*
'The book is located precisely .. .'	*is*	*'Kitabu kipo ...'*
'The books are located precisely ...'	*is*	*'Vitabu vipo ...'*
'The books are within ...'	*is*	*'Vitabu vimo ...'*
'Where?'	*is*	*'Wapi?'*

'Where are the children?' (approximately)

    is   *'Watoto wako wapi?'* (i.e. 'the children are-located where?)

'Where are the children?' (precisely)

    is   *'Watoto wapo wapi?'*

'Where are the books?'	*is*	*'Vitabu viko wapi?'*
'The books? They are not located ...'	*is*	*'Vitabu? Havipo ...*
'The books? They are not within ...'	*is*	*'Vitabu? Havimo ...*
'The children are not located within..'	*is*	*'Watoto hawamo...'*

Points to note:

The front of the location word is formed by the normal front-end word changes: ki-, vi-, wa-, etc. So, you get kiko, (it is approximately located); wapo, (they are precisely located), etc.

Swahili has far fewer irregularities than English, but one of them crops up here: 'They are located...' is 'wapo...', and so you would expect 'he is located...' to be 'apo...' (Remember that 'he is cooking' is 'anapika'.) However, for some reason lost in time, 's/he is located...' is 'yupo'. 'Yu' also crops up in one or two other settings for 's/he' or 's/he is'. (By the way, there is no difference between the words for 'he' and 'she').

To form the negative, ha- is put in front: hakiko, hawapo, etc. (Ha- is an all-purpose negative beginning: You remember that to make the negative of having something, you also add 'ha-', e.g.: 'they have' is 'wana'; 'they have not' is 'hawana'.)

SUMMARY:
Regarding being precisely located somewhere:

M-Wa:	'I am ...'	is	'Nipo...'
	'We are...'	is	'Tupo...'
M-Wa:	'You are...'	is	'Upo...'
	'You are...'	is	'Wapo...'
M-Wa:	'S/he is...'	is	'Yupo...'
	'They are...'	is	'Wapo...'
M-Mi class	'It is...'	is	'Upo...'
	'They are...'	is	'Ipo...'
Ki-Vi class	'It is...'	is	'Kipo...'
	'They are...'	is	'Vipo...'

Regarding _NOT_ being precisely located somewhere:

M-Wa:	'S/he is not...'	is	'Hayupo...'
	'They are not...'	is	'Hawapo...'
M-Mi class	'It is not...'	is	'Hakipo...'
	'They are not...'	is	'Havipo...'
Ki-Vi class	'It is not...'	is	'Hakipo...'
	'They are not...'	is	'Havipo...'

Exercise 8:

Translate:
He is located somewhere …
They are located somewhere …
He is (precisely) located …
I am (precisely) located …
The books are not approximately located …
The books are not within…
Where are the children?
The children are within…

9. In; on; nearby = -ni.

'Table'	is	'Meza'
'On the table'	is	'Mezani'
'Bag'	is	'Mfuko' (M-Mi)
'In the bag'	is	'Mfukoni'
'Bed'	is	'Kitanda' (Ki-Vi)
'By the bed'	is	'Kitandani'
'River'	is	'Mto' (M-Mi)
'Where is the bread? It's on the table'	is	'Mkate uko wapi? Upo mezani'

'Where are the children? They're in the village' is 'Watoto wako wapi? Wapo kijijini'

'By the river'	is	'Mtoni'
'By the good river'	is	'Katika mto mzuri'
'By the rivers'	is	'Mitoni'
'By the good rivers'	is	'Katika mito mizuri'
'On the good bed'	is	'Katika kitanda kizuri'
'On the beds'	is	'Katika vitanda/vitandani'

Points to note:

At the beginning, it was said that Swahili is in many ways easier than English, and 'ni' is one of those all-purpose words that proves the point. Just add it to the end of any phrase and it signifies that you are describing where that thing is.

The other words in the sentence then tell you all you need to know: the location, (eg village, table, river); and whether it is thereabouts, (-ko), precisely there, (-po), or within, (-mo). The -ko/-po/-mo are preceded by the word for it, (eg u- or ki-); or they, (eg i- or vi- or wa-); or s/he, (yu-); or we, (tu-); or you, (u-, m-).

Another way of saying '-ni', meaning 'in, on, by', is 'katika'. This is the only way to say it, if the thing you are talking about has a describing word attached. Thus 'by the river' can be: 'Mtoni'; or 'Katika mto'. But 'by the good river' can only be 'katika mto mzuri'. When it means 'outside', "by" can also be translated as "kando ya…" 'At the edge of would be: "pembeni mwa/ya…"

'In the bag'	is	'Katika mfuko/mfukoni'
'By the town'	is	'Katika mji/mjini'
'Outside the town'	is	'Kando ya mji/mjini'
'At the edge of the town'	is	'Pembeni ya mji/mjini'

'Where is the bread? It's on the table'

is   *'Mkate uko wapi? Upo katika meza'*
'Where are the children? They're in the village'
        is   *'Watoto wako wapi? Wapo katika kijiji/wako kijijini'*

Nearby can also be translated as 'karibu' – which otherwise means 'Welcome!'

Where is the book? It is near the table
        is   *'Kitabu kiko wapi? Kiko karibu na meza'*

SUMMARY:		
'Where?'	is	'Wapi?'
'Is located kind-of ...'	is	'-ko'
'Is located precisely...'	is	'-po'
'Is located within...'	is	'-mo'
'In, on, by'	is	'-ni'
'Where is the bread?'	is	'Mkate uko wapi?'
'The bread is on the table'	is	'Mkate upo mezani'
	or	'Mkate upo katika meza'

Exercise 9

Translate:
Where is the book? It is on the table
Where are the children? They are at the town
Where are the teachers? They are in the river

10.   Here = Hapa or Huku. There = Pale or Kule.

'Hereabouts'	*is*	*'Huku'*
'Thereabouts'	*is*	*'Kule'*
'Right here'	*is*	*'Hapa'*
'Right there'	*is*	*'Pale'*
'The children are (located) right here'	*is*	*'Watoto wapo/wako hapa'*
'The children are right there'	*is*	*'Watoto wapo/wako pale'*
'The books are somewhere round here'		*is* *'Vitabu viko huku'*
'The rivers are somewhere there'		*is* *'Mito iko kule'*

Points to note:

Note that the words for not-very-sure location, (hereabouts and thereabouts – huku & kule), have got the characteristic letter 'k' in them. The words for precise location, (right here, right there – hapa & pale), have got a 'p'. Note that Kiswahili gets the message across in fewer words.

To help you remember: the two words dealing with 'here' both begin with 'H'. The two words dealing with 'there' both end in -le. Later, we will deal with the words 'this' and 'that', and will see that in Swahili, the word for 'this', (the nearby thing), also begins with an H-; and the word for 'that', (the far thing), also ends in -le.

Note that for perfect agreement, one should say 'Watoto wapo hapa', but that it is entirely normal instead to say 'Watoto wako hapa'.

'Doctor'	*is*	*'Mganga' (M-Wa)*
'Where is the doctor?'	*is*	*'Mganga yuko wapi?'*
'The doctor is here somewhere'	*is*	*'Mganga yuko huku'*
'Is the doctor right here?'	*is*	*'Mganga yupo hapa?'*

'The doctor is not here. He is in the village'
     is   *'Mganga hayupo hapa. Yuko kijijini'*
'The doctor is not there. He is in the town somewhere'
     is   *'Mganga hayuko kule/huko. Yuko mjini'*

'Where are the children?'	*is*	*'Watoto wako wapi?'*
'Kitchen'	*is*	*'Jiko'*

'The children are in the kitchen'	*is*	*'Watoto wapo jikoni'*
'The books are in the kitchen somewhere'	*is*	*'Vitabu viko jikoni'*
'The books? They are not here'	*is*	*'Vitabu? Havipo hapa'*
'The children? They are not here'	*is*	*'Watoto? Hawapo hapa'*

Exercise 10

Translate:

The teachers do not have bread here.

The bread is there in the house (somewhere).

Where are the books? They are right here.

The river there has no water.

The books are over there in the river.

The students are not here.

11. (In that place) there is; there are

'There is/are' (precise location)	is	'Pana'
'There is/are' (rough location)	is	'Kuna'
'There is/are' (within)	is	'Mna' (said 'mmm-na')
'There are books right here'	is	'Pana vitabu hapa'
'There are books right there'	is	'Pana vitabu pale'
'There are books hereabouts'	is	'Kuna vitabu huku'
'There are some books thereabouts'	is	'Kuna vitabu kule'
'There are children thereabouts'	is	'Kuna watoto kule'
'There are books somewhere in the kitchen'	is	'Kuna vitabu jikoni'
'The books are somewhere in the kitchen'	is	'Vitabu viko jikoni'
'There are books in the river'	is	'Mna vitabu mtoni'
'There are children in the river'	is	'Mna watoto mtoni'
'There are children in the river'	is	'Mna watoto mtoni'
'There is not/are not' (precise location)	is	'Hapana'
'There is/are not' (rough location)	is	'Hakuna'
'There is/are not' (within)	is	'Hamna'
'There is no book hereabouts	is	'Hakuna kitabu huku'
'There are no books hereabouts	is	'Hakuna vitabu huku'

Points to note:

You may remember that '-na' means 'with' – eg ni-na kitabu: I-with book – in other words, nina kitabu means 'I have a book'. The three words that say that in a certain location 'there is or there are', all end in -na. This is because they are in fact saying: precise-place-with, (pana); approximate-place-with, (kuna); or within-with, (mna). The P, K, M code once again applies.

Note that when you say, 'there is…here', (pana … hapa); or 'there is … over there somewhere', (kuna … kule); that the P or the K is specified both in the 'there is' word, and in the 'here/there' word. Neither of these words needs to change to accommodate the thing being talked about – irrespective of whether it is a M-Wa word, and M-Mi word, a singular, a plural, etc.

In saying a sentence like "The book is in the river", Swahili makes no distinction between 'a' book and 'the' book, ('kitabu'). In saying "The books are in the river", it makes no distinction between 'the' books and 'some' books, ('vitabu').

To convert 'there is/are' (pana) into 'there is not/are not', simply add 'ha' to the front of the word: 'hapana'

SUMMARY		
'There is/are' (precise location)	is	'Pana'
There is/are' (rough location)	is	'Kuna'
'There is/are' (within)	is	'Mna'
'There is not/are not	is	'Hapana'

Exercise 11

Translate:

There are mango trees right here in the village

There are teachers over there in the river somewhere

There are some books on the table.

Some books are somewhere in the kitchen

There is water over there somewhere.

12.   A: This; these

'This man'	*is*	*'Mwanaume huyu'* (M-Wa)
'These men'	*is*	*'Wanaume hawa' (M-Wa)*
'This tree'	*is*	*'Mti huu' (M-Mi)*
'These trees'	*is*	*'Miti hii' (M-Mi)*
'This book'	*is*	*'Kitabu hiki'* (Ki-Vi)
'These books'	*is*	*'Vitabu hivi' (Ki-Vi)*

Points to note:

When talking of things nearby, (this and these), the word in Swahili starts with an H. (You remember that the word for here is 'hapa' and for hereabouts is 'huku', both beginning with an H).

You can almost work out the words for 'this' and 'these' by putting an H in front of the word for (eg) 'it' and 'they'. For instance, in M-Wa words, the word for 'they' is 'wa-', so the word for 'these' is 'hawa', (H + wa). In M-Mi words, the word for 'it' is 'u', so the word for 'this' is 'huu'. The end of the word thus changes with the class of word being talked about. For instance, the words for this and these when talking about books are hiki and hivi – for Kitabu it ends in -ki; for Vitabu it ends in -vi. You may recall that the words for 'it' and 'them' in M-MI words are 'u' and 'i', and so the words for 'this' and 'these' when talking of M-Mi words, end in 'u' and 'i'.

The only irregularity is the M-Wa word for 'this'. 'He' is 'a' (e.g. he is cooking – 'anapika'), However, 'this' in 'this man' is not (H+a) Ha, but huyu, so 'this man' is mwanamume huyu'. We saw this same irregularity when saying, 'He is precisely located': 'Yupo'; 'He is approximately located': 'Yuko'; etc.

12 B. That; those

'That man'	*is*	*'Mwanaume yule'*
'Those men'	*is*	*'Wanaume wale'*
'That tree'	*is*	*'Mti ule'*
'Those trees'	*is*	*'Miti ile'*
'That book'	*is*	*'Kitabu kile'*
'Those books'	*is*	*'Vitabu vile'*

Points to note:

When talking of things further away, (that and those), the word in Swahili ends with -le. You remember that the word for 'there' is 'pale', and for thereabouts is 'kule': both deal with things further away, and both ending with -le. In these short Swahili words, the ending -le means far, and the beginning h- means here.

For 'that' and 'those', the letters of agreement go <u>in front of</u> the '-le'. This contrasts with 'this' and 'these', where the agreeing letters came <u>after</u> the 'h-'. Therefore, the words for 'that' and 'those' are yule; wale; ule; ile; kile; & vile. The words for 'this' and 'these' are huyu; hawa; huu; hii; hiki; & hivi.

When you know how a class of words changes its beginning, you can apply this to all the other words which have to agree with it – eg this nice book is burning – kitabu kizuri hiki kinawaka, (book nice this it-is-currently-burning): in each word, the 'ki' change occurred. 'That nice book is burning' also contains the 'ki' change in every word: 'kitabu kizuri kile kinawaka'.

SUMMARY:

'This man'	*is*	*'Mwanaume huyu'*
'These men'	*is*	*'Wanaume hawa'*
'That man'	*is*	*'Mwanaume yule'*
'Those men'	*is*	*'Wanaume wale'*

Exercise 12

Translate:
Where is that child?
Where are those children?
Those books are in the river.
These books are right there on the table in the kitchen.
That is not so! They are in the bag.

13. Where? In front of, on top of, behind of, etc. (Yes, behind of)

'Where?'	is	'Wapi?'
'On top of ...'	is	'Juu ya...'
'Inside of ...'	is	'Ndani ya...'
'Outside of ...'	is	'Nje ya...'
'In front of ...'	is	'Mbele ya...'
'Among, between ...'	is	'Kati ya.../katikati ya..'
'Behind ...'	is	'Nyuma ya...'
'Below ...'	is	'Chini ya...'
'Beside...'	is	'Kando ya...'
'Beyond ...'	is	'Ng'ambo ya...'
'Where is the book?'	is	'Kitabu kiko wapi?'
'The book is on top of the tree'	is	'Kitabu kipo juu ya mti'
'The book is in front of the tree'	is	'Kitabu kipo mbele ya mti'
'The book is among 'of' the trees'	is	'Kitabu kiko kati ya miti'
'Under the bed'	is	'Chini ya kitanda'
'Beside me'	is	'Kando yangu'
'Beside you' (One person)	is	'Kando yako'
'Beside him'	is	'Kando yake'
'Beside us'	is	'Kando yetu'
'Beside you' (>One person)	is	'Kando yako/yenu'
'Beside them'	is	'Kando yao'
'Close to...'	is	'Karibu na...'
'Far from...'	is	'Mbali na...'

Points to note:

When used with the words above, 'ya' means 'of', in the sense of 'on top of'; 'outside of', etc.

As you can see from the list, you still use 'ya', for instance in saying 'Nyuma ya...', which means 'behind'. In English, we don't say 'behind of', we say 'behind the'. In Swahili however, they always say 'of' – eg 'behind of'; 'inside of'; 'among of'; etc.; Therefore, the connecting word is always 'ya'.

It is not exactly true to say that 'ya' always means 'of' – 'Ya' implies belonging to something or someone. 'Beside the tree' is translated in Swahili as 'beside of tree', ('Kando ya mti'), and to the Swahili speaker, it sort-of implies that the thing somehow belongs to the tree, however temporarily.

This idea of 'ya' meaning belonging is carried through when talking about people – when something is beside or beyond or behind a person. For this reason, there is a special set of words to express 'of me', of you' etc. You will notice in the list above, that when saying 'beside me', it is not 'kando ya mimi', but rather 'kando yangu'. 'Yangu' means not 'me', but 'of me' (or 'my'). 'Kando yangu' means 'Beside of-me'. Similarly, 'yako' is 'of-your'; 'yetu' is 'of-us'; etc.

Notice that these words all begin with 'ya' (or at least with 'y'), which often signifies possession, but in this context, means location. We will see later that a similar set of words is formed by the combination of 'kwa', (to, by, with, towards or for), plus the endings below, to make: 'to me' (kwangu); 'to you', ('kwako'), etc.

SUMMARY:		
'On top ...	is	'Juu ...
... of me'	is	yangu'
... of you' (one person)	is	yako'
... of him'	is	yake'
... of us'	is	yetu'
... of you' (two+ people)	is	yenu'
... of them'	is	yao'
... of the tree'	is	ya mti'
... of the trees'	is	ya miti'
i.e. when dealing with location, 'of'	is	'ya'

Some explanations of location use 'na' instead of 'ya', for instance 'mbali na vijiji' – 'far from the village'. When standing alone as a word, 'na' usually means 'and'; but can mean 'by' or 'from', in a phrase like 'mbali na vijiji'. A Swahili speaker will not be worried by you selecting the wrong one, as it will be precisely clear what you are saying. It is only convention in English that sometimes makes us use 'from', sometimes 'to' and sometimes no connecting word at all, (e.g. 'near **to** the village' = 'near the village')

'Ya' has other 'connecting' uses, where again the explicit meaning of 'ya' is not that important:

'Concerning...'	is	'Kuhusiana na/kuhusu.../juu ya'
'Instead of...'	is	'Badala ya...'
'After that time...'	is	'Baada ya...'
'Before that time...'	is	'Kabla ya...'
'More than...'	is	'Zaidi ya...'

Exercise 13:
Translate:
Where is that man? He is in front of the river.
Where are the women? They are among the trees.
That book is beside the bed.
Those toilets are hereabouts. They are within the village.
That is so! They are behind us.
The bread is hereabouts. That is so! It is under the bed.

14.   Other directions

'Towards'	*is*	*'Kwa'*

('Kwa' is a general connector, and can sometimes mean to, by, with or for!)

'To the right'	*is*	*'Kulia'*
'To the left'	*is*	*'Kushoto'*
'Straight on'	*is*	*'Nyosha/nyoosha'*
'Until, up to, as far as'	*is*	*'Mpaka'*
'Far'	*is*	*'Mbali'*
'Far from'	*is*	*'Mbali na'*
'Near'	*is*	*'Karibu'*
'Near to'	*is*	*'Karibu na'*
'Before'	*is*	*'Kabla'*
'Before …'	*is*	*'Kabla ya'*
'More'	*is*	*'Zaidi'*
'More than'	*is*	*'Zaidi ya'*
'In here'	*is*	*'Humu'*
'In there'	*is*	*'Mle'*

Points to note:

There is not much to say about these words, as none alters in the various situations in which they are used, and they occur in the same place in the sentence as in English.

'Towards', when talking about direction, is 'kwa'. You will find this word recurring in several contexts, each time with the sense of something being towards something else. One example is in the formation of words which describe actions or behaviours: 'truth' is 'kweli'; but 'truthfully' is 'kwa kweli'.

As with English, these words can be used to signify things beyond their literal meaning. So, for instance, in English, 'straight' means 'not bent', but it can also mean 'honest', ('he is a straight-up person'); or it can mean 'directly', ('I went straight there'). Similarly, in Swahili, the meaning of these words can depend on context, and 'kwa nyosha' can mean 'safely', or 'in a hurry'. To signify 'straight on', by contrast, it is common to say, 'moja kwa moja', which technically means 'one by one'!

Note that in giving directions, the words for left and right are as shown, and can be preceded by 'kwa'. However, when these words are used as descriptions, the beginning of the word 'kwa' might not be 'kw-' in front of the '-a', but might be an agreement with the thing being described. So 'right hand' is 'mkono <u>mwa</u> kulia', not '<u>kwa</u> kulia'. This is explained below in the section on descriptions.

You may have spotted that 'in here' and 'in there' have the already familiar 'hu-' and '-le', plus an 'm' sound.

'Towards'	*is*	*'Kwa' (or 'kuelekea')*
'He went to the right'	*is*	*'Alikwenda kulia'*
'Travel'	*is*	*'Kusafiri/safiri'*
'Travel straight on...'	*is*	*'Safiri kwa kunyosha'* (or 'nenda moja kwa moja...')
'... as far as the town'	*is*	*'... mpaka mjini'*
'Morogoro is far from Arusha'	*is*	*'Morogoro ni mbali na Arusha'*

Exercise 14:

Translate:
I am cooking near the river
We are travelling to the left as far as the town
We are going far from the river
They are travelling straight on by the river
He is going in there
He is travelling to the right towards the village

15. More on possession

'The pupil of the teacher'	is	'Mwanafunzi wa mwalimu'
'The pupil of the teachers'	is	'Mwanafunzi wa walimu'
'The pupils of the teacher'	is	'Wanafunzi wa mwalimu'
'The tree of the village'	is	'Mti wa kijiji'
'The trees of the village'	is	'Miti ya kijiji'
'The thing of the teacher'	is	'Kitu cha mwalimu'
'The things of the teacher'	is	'Vitu vya mwalimu'
'The things of the teachers'	is	'Vitu vya walimu'
'Beside me' (location)	is	'Kando yangu'
'Beside you' (location)	is	'Kando yako'
'My pupil' (possession)	is	'Mwanafunzi wangu' (M-Wa)
'Your pupil' (just one of you) (possession)	is	'Mwanafunzi wako' (M-Wa)
'His pupil'	is	'Mwanafunzi wake' (M-Wa)
'Our pupil'	is	'Mwanafunzi wetu' (M-Wa)
'Your pupil' (>one of you)	is	'Mwanafunzi wako/wenu' (M-Wa)
'Their pupil'	is	'Mwanafunzi wao' (M-Wa)
'My pupils'	is	'Wanafunzi wangu' (M-Wa)
'My tree'	is	'Mti wangu' (M-Mi)
'My trees'	is	'Miti yangu' (M-Mi)
'My book'	is	'Kitabu changu' (K-Vi)
'My books'	is	'Vitabu vyangu' (K-Vi)

Points to note:

When we were talking about location, (e.g. on top of, etc), we noted that in Swahili you need to say 'ya' for 'of'. 'Juu ya mwalimu' therefore means 'on top of the teacher'. So, 'ya' means 'of' when dealing with where something is – belonging to a place.

When talking about possession /ownership rather than location, however, the most common word for 'of' is 'wa' – e.g. 'Mti wa kijiji': 'the tree of the village'. (By the way, please note that in Swahili you cannot say 'The teacher's pupils'. You have to say, 'The pupils of the teacher'. Whenever there is possession in Swahili, where one thing or person has or owns another, you cannot say 'Jim's book', or 'the dog's bone'. You have to say, 'the book of Jim'; or 'the bone of the dog'. The 'of' word must always be there.)

This particular use of 'of' therefore deals with possession or belonging. For the M-Wa group of words, you use 'wa' for 'of' when dealing with possession – eg 'mwanafunzi wa mwalimu' – 'the pupils of the teacher'. The 'wa' word is the same for one person being possessed as it is for more than one, for M-Wa words.

'Wa-' is also the word used to mean possession when a single M-Mi thing is being possessed. For instance, to say 'the tree of the village' is: 'Mti wa kijiji'.

However, as with many other Swahili words, the front end of this word for 'of' changes according to context. Therefore 'the tre<u>es</u> of the village' is 'Miti <u>ya</u> kijiji'. 'Wa' has changed to 'ya' because the number of trees possessed has changed from one to more than one, and because 'trees' is an M-Mi word. It is the thing being possessed which determines this change, not the possessor. Therefore, for instance, 'The trees of the teacher' is 'Miti ya walimu'. You still use 'ya', because the thing being possessed is trees, and 'ya' is the word for possessing M-Mi things, when there is more than one of them. (It is annoying that 'ya' meaning possessing more than one M-Mi thing is the same word as 'ya' referring to location. Nevertheless, in Swahili it is common to have these short words serving more than one purpose, the meaning is almost always obvious from the context. In fact, when you get used to it, you see that not only is there a pattern, but the words flow naturally).

As you might expect, there are other versions of wa, depending on the class of thing being possessed: So whereas for M-Mi words, when more than one is possessed, the word for 'of' is 'ya', for Ki-Vi words it is 'cha' (just one thing possessed); or 'vya', (more than one).

These words, (wa, ya, cha, vya), are used when you are naming the owner – the pupil of the teacher, the tree of the village, etc. However, when you just say 'mine' or 'yours', (ie 'of me' or 'of you'), there is again a specific set of words. You remember that in the previous chapter we noted that when talking about location of people, there was a special set of words based on 'ya': yangu, yako, yake, etc. So 'on top <u>of</u> the tree' was 'juu <u>ya</u> mti', but 'on top <u>of</u> me' was 'juu <u>yangu</u>'. 'Ya' became 'yangu'. The changes for 'wa' and 'wangu' are precisely the same as the changes for 'ya' and 'yangu'. Therefore, for instance, 'On top <u>of me</u>' was 'Juu <u>yangu</u>', and 'on top <u>of us</u>' was 'Juu <u>yetu</u>'. In the same way, 'my pupil' (the pupil <u>of me</u>) is 'mwanafunzi <u>wangu</u>', and 'our pupil' (the pupil <u>of us</u>) is 'mwanafunzi <u>wetu</u>'.

When talking about possession instead of location of people, then, the initial letter 'y' is changed to 'w'. So 'my /mine' is typically 'wangu'; 'yours' is typically 'wako'; 'his/hers/its' is 'wake'; 'ours' is 'wetu'; 'yours' (more than one owner is 'wenu'; and 'theirs' is 'wao'.

SUMMARY:

Of (possession):	wa,	ya,	cha, vya, etc
My /mine:	wangu,	yangu,	changu, vyangu, etc
Your/s (just one of you):	wako,	yako,	chako, vyako, etc
His/ hers/ its:	wake,	yake,	chake, vyake, etc
Our/s:	wetu,	yetu,	chetu, vyetu, etc
Your/s (more than 1 owner):	wenu,	yenu,	chenu, vyenu, etc
Their/s:	wao,	yao,	chao, vyao

Just to clarify, then, as this is a confusing area until you get used to it: 'Wa', 'ya', 'cha', and 'vya' mean 'of' in sentences like 'the teacher's book', (i.e. 'the book of the teacher' – 'Kitabu cha mwalimu'); or 'the village's tree', (i.e. 'the tree of the village' – 'mti wa mjiji').

However, when you say, 'His book', or 'its tree', instead of using 'wa', 'ya', 'cha', etc, you use 'wangu', 'yangu' 'changu', etc. So '-angu' means 'my' or 'mine', and the beginning you put in front of -angu is determined according to what is being possessed. Who or what possesses them does not affect things. (In English, is a female possesses something, it is 'hers'. For a male, it is 'his'. Not so in Swahili. In Swahili, the thing being possessed determines the change.)

Therefore, possessing a person will for instance use the words 'wake' for 'his', and 'wao' for 'theirs', etc. When possessing an M-Mi thing, then 'wake' is still the word 'his' or 'her' for possessing one thing. However, this becomes 'yake' when possessing more than one M-MI thing. It becomes 'chake' when possessing one Ki-Vi thing. Similarly, 'yao' means 'theirs' for possession of more than one M-Mi thing. For Ki-Vi things, the respective words for 'theirs' are 'chao' and 'vyao'.

The thing being possessed determines the word for 'my', 'his', 'her', etc. ... _Not_ the possessor.

A final point to make when talking about possession, is the use of the insert 'enye', which signifies possession in certain circumstances, and will be dealt with later.

Exercise 15:
Translate:
Where are my books? They are beside you.
The student's bread is under the bed
Where is your village? Mine is over there somewhere.
Those trees just there are theirs.
I am cooking my food
The teacher's plants are beside the river.
Your pupils are here somewhere

16.   Descriptions

'Nice'	*is*	*'-zuri' (-jema)*
'Bad'	*is*	*'-baya*
'Big'	*is*	*'-kubwa'*
'Little'	*is*	*'-dogo'*
'Tall/Long'	*is*	*'-fupi/ndefu'*
'Dirty'	*is*	*'-chafu'*
'New'	*is*	*'-pya'*
'Old' (person)	*is*	*'-zee'*
'Old' (thing)	*is*	*'-kuukuu'*
'Important'	*is*	*'-kuu' (muhimu)*
'Good' (person)	*is*	*'-ema'*
'Black'	*is*	*'-eusi'*
'White'	*is*	*'-eupe'*
'Red'	*is*	*'-ekundu'*
'Blue'	*is*	*'bluu'*
'Green'	*is*	*'Kijani'*
'Very'	*is*	*'Sana' (mno)*
'Best'	*is*	*'Bora'*
'Clean'	*is*	*'Safi'*
'Ready'	*is*	*'Tayari'*
'Equal'	*is*	*'Sawa'*
'Easy/Cheap'	*is*	*'Rahisi'*
'Open'	*is*	*'Wazi'*
'Normal'	*is*	*'-a kawaida'*
'Male'	*is*	*'-a kiume'*
'Female'	*is*	*'-a kike'*
'Hot'	*is*	*'-a moto'/-a joto*
'Cold'	*is*	*'-a baridi'*
'Big child'	*is*	*'Mtoto mkubwa'*
'Big trees'	*is*	*'Miti mikubwa'*
'Big book'	*is*	*'Kitabu kikubwa'*
'Big books'	*is*	*'Vitabu vikubwa'*
'A good book'	*is*	*'Kitabu kizuri'*
'A big man'	*is*	*'Mwanaume mkubwa'*

Points to note:

Note that, unlike English, the describing word always comes <u>after</u> the thing it is describing – e.g. '<u>Big</u> trees' is 'Miti <u>mikubwa</u>'.

We have already noted that the word for good, (-zuri), because it is a description of something or someone, has to have its front end modified by the normal agreement letters. So, when describing M-Wa words, 'good' can be either mzuri or wazuri; for M-Mi words, 'good' can be mzuri or mizuri; for Ki-Vi words, 'good' can be kizuri or vizuri; etc.

The same need for front-end changes is true for many, but not all describing words.

'Sana', for instance, is an all-purpose word for saying 'very' and comes at the end of the description – eg 'very big trees' is 'miti mikubwa sana'. 'Sana' never changes its letters. There are other describing words which never change, (e.g. bluu, kijani, safi, bora). These tend to be words that originated in Arabic.

Some describing words are saying that the thing is 'as…' or 'like…' something, eg 'as normal' – '-a kawaida'; 'as a man' (ie male) – '-a kiume'; etc. These words are preceded by the single-letter word
'-a', which is then modified to make it agree with what is being described – see below.

Further points to note about decriptions and their agreement with the thing being described

As just said, some describing words do not change at all. For the others, the agreements are straightforward for those words whose stem begins with a consonant, such as -zuri, -kubwa, etc. However, when the stem of the describing word starts with a vowel, it gets more complicated, even though it is not difficult once you know what is going on. Look at the table below first, and then the explanation.

SUMMARY:
Rules for agreement of describing words
Some descriptions never change – eg sana, bora, safi

The remainder change in the normal way, as long as the stem starts with a consonant – eg -zuri, -baya, -kubya.

**If the stem begins with a vowel,
then the agreement and the stem get squashed together,
sometimes with a 'w' or a 'y' in between:**

More rules for agreement of describing words

m- plus -a…	becomes mwa…
wa- plus -a…	becomes wa…
wa- plus -e… or -i…	becomes we…
m- plus -e…	becomes mwe…
m- plus -i…	becomes mwi…
mi- plus -e…	becomes mye…

mi- plus -i...	*becomes mi...*
ki- plus -e...	*becomes che...*
ki- plus -i...	*becomes ki...*
vi- plus -e...	*becomes vye...*
vi- plus -i...	*becomes vi...*

Explanation of agreement of describing words starting with a vowel

When the describing word begins with a vowel, and the agreement letters need to be added to the front, there is often a merging – e.g. one of the vowels might disappear. So, for instance, 'Big children' is 'watoto wakubwa'. 'Wa-' has been added to '-kubwa' to make it agree with 'watoto'. However, when you add 'wa' in front of a describing word starting with a vowel, you lose the 'a'. So, 'dark children' is 'wototo weusi', not 'watoto waeusi'.

Any time the stem of the describing word starts with an 'a' or an 'e', if you want to make it agree with 'wa', you only add 'w' instead of 'wa'. Similar losses of vowels occur with other combinations of agreement + stem. For instance, when the agreement is vi-, and the stem starts with an 'i', then one of the 'i's is dropped. 'Many books' is 'vitabu vingi', not 'vitabu vi-ingi'.

There are other rules to note when the stem starts with a vowel, and they all relate to making the word simpler to say and spell, and yet easy to distinguish from similar meanings. For instance, whenever the agreement is m-, and it is followed by a vowel, a 'w' is inserted. 'A red tree' should be 'mti mekundu', because the agreement is m- (for a singular M-Mi word), and the word for 'red' is '-ekundu'. Thus m-ekundu' should become 'mekundu'. However, this does not sound right in Swahili, because the 'm' sound should be long, like 'mmm'. A 'w' is therefore inserted to make it 'mwekundu'. Similarly, 'A good man' should be 'Mwanamume mema', because the agreement is m- (for a singular M-Wa word), and the word for 'good' is '-ema'. However, a 'w' is again added: 'Mwanaume mwema'.

In most cases, however, the change is a sort of squashing together of the agreement and the vowel stem. So, for instance, two letters 'a's will become just one. The same is usually true of two letters 'i's. A mixture of vowels often is just replaced by 'e' or 'ye'.

An oddity is that in the case that the describing word starts with an 'i', the combination of eg 'a' & 'i' can change to an 'e'. For example, 'many' is '-ingi', but 'many children' is 'watoto wengi', not 'watoto wa-ingi'. You still lose the 'a' of 'wa', but the 'i' changes to 'e'.

One final strange change that needs specific mention is that ki- plus a stem starting with -e... changes to che-. (i.e. ki + e = che-, not ke- or kye-.)

'A black child'	is	'Mtoto mweusi'
'Some black teachers'	is	'Baadhi ya walimu weusi'
'A black tree'	is	'Mti mweusi'
'Some black trees'	is	'Miti myeusi'
'A black book'	is	'Kitabu cheusi'
'Black books'	is	'Vitabu vyeusi'

Further points about two-word descriptions starting with -a, (e.g. -a kawaida – 'normal')

We have noted that the describing words that are preceded by '-a' are saying 'as' or 'like'. In fact, you can turn just about anything into a description this way – e.g. 'like John' could be '-a John'. It is not only people and things that can be used in this way, but also actions and states-of-being, (e.g. '-a kutosha', meaning 'as to-be-satisfied' – ie 'sufficient').

The -a must agree with the thing being described, and so might turn out to be for example 'w-a' (e.g. 'wanafunzi wa kweli' – 'true pupils'); or 'ch-a' (e.g. 'chakula cha bure' – free food); etc. The agreements are as mentioned above: 'wa' for M-Mwa words and single M-Mi words; 'ya' for plural M-Mi words; and 'cha' and 'vya' for Ki-Vi words. Some more of these descriptions are given below.

'True'	is	'-a kweli' (= 'like truth')
'False'	is	'-a uongo' (-a + uongo, a lie)
'Last'	is	'-a mwisho' (= 'like the end')
'Free'	is	'-a bure' (= 'like useless')
'Right'	is	'-a kulia' (sawa)
'Left'	is	'-a kushoto' (-ondoka)
'Cold'	is	'-a baridi'
'Dangerous men'	is	'Wanaume hatari'
'Dangerous food'	is	'Chakula hatari'
'Dangerous trees'	is	'Miti hatari'

Exercise 16:

Translate:
Some dangerous black foods are under the bed
I am cooking some very black bread
The very big child is in the kitchen
The bad old toilet is in the village
The best child has my book
My clean child is ready
The big woman is cold but the child is hot. ('But' is 'lakini')

17. Greetings

'Hi!'	is	'Jambo!' or mambo?
response:		'Jambo! /poa'
'Hi!' (to man)	is	'Jambo bwana!'
'Hi! (to woman)	is	'Jambo mama!'
'Hi!' (to child)	is	'Jambo mtoto!'
'(polite greeting from child)	is	'Shikamoo'
response:		'Marahaba!'
'How's it going?	is also	'Vipi?'
response:		e.g. 'Nimesha poa, asante!'
		(I am fine, thanks!)
'How's it going?	is	'Vipi?'
response:		eg 'Poa!' (Cool!)
'How's it going?' (to 1)	is	'Hujambo?'
response:		'Sijambo!' ('no problem!')
'How's it going?' (to 2+)	is	'Hamjambo?'
response:		'Hatujambo!' ('no problem!')
'Are you well?'	is	'Mzima?'
response:		'Mzima!'
'What news?'	is	'Habari gani?'
response:		'Nzuri!' (fine!)
'What news of the morning?'	is	'Habari ya asubuhi?'
response:		'Nzuri!' (fine!)
'What news of the daylight?'	is	'Habari ya mchana?'
response:		'Nzuri!' (fine!)
'What news in home?'	is	'Habari ya nyumbani?'
response:		'Nzuri!' (fine!)
'Good day, ladies and gentlemen!'	is	'Habari ya mchana mabibi na mabwana!'
'Very'	is	'Sana' or 'mno'
'Until'	is	'Mpaka'
'Again'	is	'Tena'
'God'	is	'Mungu'

'God be with you until we meet again!'
        is   'Mungu awe nanyi mpaka tutakapoonana tena!'

'It's very good to be here!'	is	'Ni vizuri sana kuwa hapa!'
'Praise the Lord!'	is	'Bwana asifiwe!'
'Goodbye!' (end of day)	is	'Kwaheri!'
response:		'Kwaheri!'
'Goodbye!' (to 2+)	is	'Kwaherini!'
response (to 2+):		'Kwaherini!'
'Safe /Safely!'	is	'Salama!'
response		'Salama!'
'Safe journey!'	is	'Safiri salama!'
'Good journey!	is	'Safari Njema!'

'Journey safely!'	*is*	*'Safiri salama'*
'Thanks' (very much)	*is*	*'Asante' (sana)*

Points to note:

Greetings are massively important in Swahili-speaking countries. Even in the most urgent of settings, even between sworn enemies, the greetings need to be first. Sometimes they can be elaborate and might consist of a sequence of mutual enquiries about all sorts of things.

Similarly, on parting, it is important to exchange good wishes. For this reason, there are far too many greetings to learn, and it is best to get used to a few in the first instance. E.g. 'Hujambo bwana/mama?' … 'Sijambo!' would be a reasonable opener and response to and from one person. Note that 'habari' is followed by 'ya' when asking about one thing, (e.g. today); or 'za' when asking about many things, (e.g. the children).

Exercise 17:

Translate:
From a child to an adult polite greeting:
Response from the adult to a child
Greet the child's parent as he arrives
Ask if he is well
Ask about his family and home
Say 'Thanks. Safe journey. Goodbye'

18.   I have gone, I went. I have spoken, I spoke – the past

'To go'	*is*	*'Kwenda'*
'To speak'	*is*	*'Kusema'*
'To converse'	*is*	*'Kuongea'*
'To open'	*is*	*'Kufungua'*
'To shut'	*is*	*'Kufunga'*
'To start'	*is*	*'Kuanza'*
'To use'	*is*	*'Kutumia'*
'Door'	*is*	*'Mlango'*
'I have gone'	*is*	*'Nimekwenda'*
'I went'	*is*	*'Nilikwenda'*
'I have spoken'	*is*	*'Nimesema'*
'I spoke'	*is*	*'Nilisema'*
'We have gone'	*is*	*'Tumekwenda'*
'We went'	*is*	*'Tulikwenda'*
'We have spoken'	*is*	*'Tumesema'*
'We spoke'	*is*	*'Tulisema'*
'The bag has (been) opened'	*is*	*'Mfuko umefungua'*
'The doors have (been) shut'	*is*	*'Milango imefunga'*
'The doors (were) shut'	*is*	*'Milango ilifunga'*
'The teachers have started'	*is*	*'Walimu wameanza'*
'The teachers started'	*is*	*'Walimu walianza'*

Points to note:

To express the past in Swahili is extraordinarily easy. You remember that i-na-waka means, 'they are currently burning', (when applied to M-Mi words such as 'miti'), and ni-na-kwenda means 'I am currently going'. The -na- part of the word means 'is/are currently'. To express the past, you simply replace this with either '-me-' or '-li-'.

There are two options, because these are two different ways to describe the past: One way uses 'have/has' done something. This is often used to convey something where, instead of just telling what happened, the issue is whether you have or have not done something. For this option in English, you use 'has' or 'have'. In Swahili, you substitute -me- for -na-.

The other way of talking about the past is when something is clearly over, or happened some time ago – the way of speaking you use in telling what happened. For this type of expression of the past, you substitute -li- for -na-.

Thus: Ninakula = I am eating. Nimekula = I have eaten. Nilikula = I ate.
(Notice by the way that once again with the very short action words like 'kula', (to eat), you do not lose the 'ku' when making phrases. Compare that with, eg kuanza = to start. Ninaanza = I am starting. Nimeanza = I have started. Nilianza = I started).

There is another way of expressing the past: 'I was eating'. In this case, the action was happening continuously in the past. One way to express this in Swahili is to use a separate word to convey this sense of continuous action. In this case, we use the word '-kuwa', (which means 'be'), and add the 'li' to make it in the past: -likuwa = 'was'. Therefore 'I was eating' becomes 'nilikuwa nilikula'. (Literally 'I was, I ate'.)

SUMMARY:

Ninakula	= I am eating
Nimekula	= I have eaten
Nilikula	= I ate
Nilikuwa nilikula	= I was eating

Exercise 18:

Translate:
I have eaten the black bread
I ate the black bread
That very big man went
This very clean book succeeded
That big tree has started
Those crops did grow over there somewhere
Hi! How are you? Have you already succeeded?

19.   I have not gone. I did not go – the negative in the past

'I have not gone'	*is*	*'Sijakwenda'*
'I did not go'	*is*	*'Sikwenda'*
'You have not gone'	*is*	*'Hujakwenda'*
'You did not go'	*is*	*'Hukwenda'*
'I have not spoken'	*is*	*'Sijasema'*
'I did not speak'	*is*	*'Sikusema'*
'We have not gone'	*is*	*'Hatujakwenda'*
'We did not go'	*is*	*'Hatukwenda'*
'We have not spoken'	*is*	*'Hatujasema'*
'We did not speak'	*is*	*'Hatukusema'*
'The bag has not opened'	*is*	*'Mfuko haujafunguka'*
'The doors have not shut'	*is*	*'Milango haijafunga/ haijafunwa'*
'The doors did not shut'	*is*	*'Milango haikufunga/haikufungwa'*
'The teachers have not started'	*is*	*'Walimu hawajaanza'*
'The teachers did not start'	*is*	*'Walimu hawakuanza'*

Points to note:

To make -me- into the negative, you change it to -ja-. To make -li- into the negative, you change it to -ku-. In addition, in most cases, you have to add ha- to the front of the word, to indicate 'Not'. So, eg, 'We have spoken' is 'tu-me-sema', but 'we have <u>not</u> spoken' is 'hatu-ja-sema'. In other words:

- 'tu-' means 'we'
- 'hatu-' means 'not-we'.
- '-me-' means 'have/has'. and
- '-ja-' means 'have/has not'.

So 'we have not spoken' is 'hatujasema': 'Not-we have-not spoken'. As we will see in other situations, Swahili likes to cram as much meaning into each word, and into each bit of the word, so do not be surprised that <u>both</u> the 'tu-' is changed to 'hatu', and the '-me-' is changed into the negative form '-ja-'. Therefore, the idea of negativity is expressed twice. In English, by contrast, one small negative word, ('not'), infects the whole sentence.

In relation to the thing doing the deed, adding the sense of 'not' means adding 'ha-'. (We have just seen that 'tu-' became 'hatu-'.) The exceptions are the words for I and you. (Exactly as we saw when talking about the present). 'I' is 'ni-', but 'I-not' is not hani, but 'si'. 'You' is 'u-', but 'you-not' is not 'hau', but 'hu'.

You may remember at the very start, when talking about the present, that when referring to the negative, you dropped the '-na-'. Additionally, you needed to change the last letter of the word from 'a' to 'i', to convey extra negativity. (eg 'to look at' is 'kutazama'. I am looking at: ninatazama. I am not looking at – Sitazami.) When talking about the past, this final letter change from 'a' to 'i' is not needed – eg 'nimetazama' is 'I have looked at', and 'sijatazama' is 'I have not looked at'. The double negative is already achieved by changing 'ni' to 'si', and by changing 'me' to 'ja'.

By the way, the negative form -ja- also implies 'not yet'. So 'I have eaten' is 'nimekula', and 'I have not eaten' is 'sijala'. 'I have not <u>yet</u> eaten' is translated identically to 'I have not eaten' – 'sijala'.

Note that the 'ku' is dropped from the word to eat, ('kula'), whereas when expressing the positive with these very short action words, the 'ku' is retained. This seems more reasonable when you consider that 'I ate' is 'Nilikula', but if you did not drop the 'ku' in the negative, 'I did not eat' would be 'sikukula' – ie 'ku' would be in there twice. 'Ku' is also dropped before 'kw', eg sikwenda, hukwenda, hatukwenda.

> **SUMMARY:**
> **Negative in the past**
> ...has...   = -me-
> ...has not (yet)... = -ja-
> ...did...   = -li-
> ...did not...   = -ku-

I not;	you not;	s/he not	= si-;	hu-;	ha-
We not;	you not;	they not	= hatu-;	ham-;	hawa-

Exercise 19:

Translate:
Those plants did not arrive
He has not come yet – he is somewhere in the village
He did not talk and they failed
The big child has not yet eaten
The very clean toilets over there somewhere did not shut
The men did not eat in the village
The trees have not yet succeeded in the town

20.   I will go, I will not go – the future

'I will go'	*is*	*'Nitakwenda'*
'I will not go'	*is*	*'Sitakwenda'*
'To come'	*is*	*'Kuja'*
'I will not come'	*is*	*'Sitakuja'*
'You will go' (one person)	*is*	*'Utakwenda'*
'You will not go' (one person)	*is*	*'Hautakwenda'*
'You will go' (>one person)	*is*	*'Mtakwenda'*
'You will not go' (>one person)	*is*	*'Hamtakwenda'*
'We will speak'	*is*	*'Tutasema'*
'We will not speak'	*is*	*'Hatutasema'*
'The bag will open'	*is*	*'Mfuko utafunguka'*
'The bag will not open'	*is*	*'Mfuko hautafunguka'*
'The doors will shut'	*is*	*'Milango itafunga'*
'The doors will not shut'	*is*	*'Milango haitafunga'*
'The teachers will start'	*is*	*'Walimu wataanza'*
'The teachers will not start'	*is*	*'Walimu hawataanza'*

Points to note:

Speaking about the future is even easier. The -na- changes to -ta-. Note that with very short action words such as kuja, the 'ku' is retained. It is often even retained in kuenda, because 'utakwenda' is easier to say than 'utaenda'.

When speaking of the negative, you do not even bother to change the -ta-. 'Ha-' once again is the all-purpose negative beginning of an action word. To express the negative of the future, you simply change the front of the word – from 'wa-' to 'hawa-', from 'u-' to 'hau-'; etc. So 'We will eat' is 'Watakula'. 'We will not eat' is 'Hawatakula'. Once again, 'I' is the exception, and changes from 'ni' to 'si-', not from 'ni-' to 'hani-'; eg 'I will eat' is 'nitakula', and 'I will not eat' is 'sitakula'.

There is one other way to talk about the future: In English, when talking about what is going to happen, we sometimes say, for example, I am going to do it', rather than 'I will do it'. Swahili has an equivalent – 'kutaka' – which means 'to be going to…':

'To be going to…'	*is*	*'Kutaka'*
'I am going to fall'	*is*	*'Ninataka kuanguka'*
'They are going to go'	*is*	*'Wanataka kwenda'*
'To rain'	*is*	*'Kunyesha'*
'It is going to rain'	*is*	*'Inataka kunyesha'*

SUMMARY:
The future

I will...	=	*nita-*
I will not...	=	*sita-*
They will...	=	*wata-*
They will not...	=	*hawata-*
It will...	=	*uta- (M-Mi)*
It will not...	=	*hauta- (M-Mi)*

'To be going to...'	*is*	*'Kutaka'*
'I am going to fall'	*is*	*'Ninataka kuanguka'*
'It is going to rain'	*is*	*'Inataka kunyesha'*

Exercise 20:

Translate:

The very big children will not eat in the town

The big black tree just there will not burn

These teachers will eat these plants

Those pupils are in the town somewhere. They will come.

My big clean bag will open in the kitchen.

Good morning! I will come to the town early ('early' = 'mapema')

The men? They will not speak. They have already spoken

21. Giving orders and making requests

'To do'	is	'Kufanya'
'To put or to place'	is	'Kuweka'
'To cook'	is	'Kupika'
'To eat'	is	'Kula'

'Would you do...? (to one person)
     is   'Ufanye...?' or 'Ungefanya...?' or 'Utafanya...?'
'Would you put...? (to one person)
     is   'Uweke...?' or 'Ungeweka...?' or 'Utaweka...?'
'Would you cook...? (to one person)
     is   'Upike...?' or 'Ungepika...?' or 'Utapika...?'
'Would you eat...? (to one person)
     is   'Ule...?' or 'Ungekula...?' or 'Utakula...?'

'Would you do...? (to 2+ people)
     is   'Mfanye...?' or 'Mngefanya...?' or 'Mtafanya...?'
'Would you put...? (to 2+ people)
     is   'Mweke...?' or 'Mngeweka...?' or 'Mtaweka...?'
'Would you cook...? (to 2+ people)
     is   'Mpike...?' or 'Mngepika...?' or 'Mtapika...?'
'Would you eat...? (to 2+ people)
     is   'Mle...?' or 'Mngekula...?' or 'Mtakula...?'

'Please'	is	'Tafadhali'
'Please would you cook ...?'	is	'Ungepika...?'
(It is already polite)		
'<u>Please</u> would you cook ...?'	is	'Tafadhali ungepika'
(extra polite!)		

Points to note:

When asking someone to do something in English, we might say "Please would you...", or "please can you..." In Swahili, the whole of that idea can be conveyed by two very simple changes to the action word: drop the 'ku-' at the front, and replace it with u- (for speaking to one person), or m- (for speaking to more than one); and change the last 'a' to an 'e'.

Therefore 'ufanya' means 'you do', and 'ufanye' means the more poilte version, 'might you do?' Just as in English, however, much of the politeness comes from the tone of the voice, and there are two other ways of expressing the same thing: 'Would you do...?', ('ungefanya?'), and 'will you do ...?', ('utafanya?').

The word 'ungefanya' (ie 'would you do', or 'if you were to do') comes from the insertion of -nge-. This addition of -nge- turns a statement into a polite request.

You only add the word for 'please' at the beginning of the phrase if you want to be extra-polite. The reason for this is that changing 'kupika' into 'upike…?' or 'ungepika…?' already implies politeness. The change from 'a' to 'e' at the end of the word, or the addition of -nge-, implies having said 'please'.

To turn this request into the negative, simply add '-si-':

'Would you not do…? (to one person)	*is*	*'Usingefanya…?'*
'Would you not put…? (to one person)	*is*	*'Usingeweka…?'*
'Would you not cook…? (to one person)	*is*	*'Usingepika…?'*
'Would you not eat…? (to one person)	*is*	*'Usingekula…?'*
'Would you not do…? (to 2+ people)	*is*	*'Msingefanya…?'*
'Would you not put…? (to 2+ people)	*is*	*'Msingeweka…?'*
'Would you not cook…? (to 2+ people)	*is*	*'Msingepika…?'*
'Would you not eat…? (to 2+ people)	*is*	*'Msingekula…?'*

Once again, this is automatically polite. If you wanted to be bossier, there is another form of telling someone what to do:

'Do… (to one person)	*is*	*'Fanya…'*
'Put… (to one person)	*is*	*'Weka…'*
'Cook… (to one person)	*is*	*'Pika…'*
'Eat… (to one person)	*is*	*'Kula…'*
'Do… (to 2+ people)	*is*	*'Fanyeni…'*
'Put… (to 2+ people)	*is*	*'Wekeni…'*
'Cook… (to 2+ people)	*is*	*'Pikeni…'*
'Eat… (to 2+ people)	*is*	*'Kuleni…'*

This is a more formal way of expressing an order, typically used when a boss is talking to an employee. It still drops the 'ku-' at the front of the action word, but does not add in 'u-' or 'm-'. (In the very short words, such as kula, it does not drop the 'ku', or else there would not be much left!).

Furthermore, this bossy version of giving an order does not change the end letter to 'e'. This part is particularly important, as it will be seen later that changing the end letter to 'e' makes the action seem less definite – less of a command and more of a suggestion.

When speaking to more than one person, however, the final 'a' is replaced with '-eni'.

SUMMARY:

To cook	**= kupika**
Would you cook? (to one person)	**= Ungepika/Upike?**
Would you cook? (to > one person)	**= Mngepika/Mpike?**
Would you not cook? (to one person)	**= Usingepika/usipike?**
Cook! (to one person)	**= Pika!**
Cook! (to >one person)	**= Pikeni!**

Exercise 21A:

Translate (to one person and to two):

Do not burn the plant! Cook it! (to burn = kuungua)

Come! We are going to the village over there.

Speak! We will listen. ('listen' is 'kusikiliza')

Might you go with me and my child?

Would you cook this plant?

Please can you come to the village?

Would you kindly burn that plant?

Would you not go to the village?

21B: Actions that might or might not happen – eg desires, hopes, polite requests

'To want'	is	'Kutaka'
'To cook'	is	'Kupika'
'To eat'	is	'Kula'
'Would you cook...? (to one person)	is	'Ungepika/Upike...?'
'Would you eat...? (to one person)	is	'Ungekula/ule...?'
'I want...' ('I currently am wanting')	is	'Ninataka...'
'I want you to cook' ('I want that you might cook')	is	
		'Ninataka upike'

'Best'	is	'Bora'
'Now'	is	'Sasa'
'It's best that you eat now'	is	'Bora ule sasa'
'It's best that you cook now'	is	'Bora upike sasa'
'To succeed'	is	'Kufaulu/kufanikiwa'
'It's best that you succeed now'	is	'Bora ufaulu/ufanikiwe sasa'
'I am cooking'	is	'Ninapika'
'In order that'	is	'Ili'
'I am cooking in order that you might eat'	is	'Ninapika ili ule'
'I am cooking in order that he might eat'	is	'Ninapika ili ale'

'Let him eat' (i.e. 'might he eat?')	is	'Acha/ngoja ale'
'Let him cook' (ie 'might he cook?')	is	'Acha/ngoja apike'
'Let's cook' (ie 'might we cook?')	is	'Ngoja tupike'
'Let's not cook' (ie 'might we not cook?')	is	'Ngoja tusipike'

'I might cook'	is	'Lazima nipike'
'I might not cook'	is	'Nisipike'
'Am I not to cook?'	is	'Nisipike?' or 'Si mimi wa kupika'
'Let me not cook'	is	'Ngoja nisipike'
'Let them not cook'	is	'Waache wasipike'
'They might not cook'	is	'Ngoja/acha Wasipike'

'To refuse'	is	'Kukataa'
'We refused'	is	'Tulikataa'
'We refused them'	is	'Tuliwakataza'
'We refused to let them cook'	is	'Tuliwakataza wasipike'

Points to note:

We have already noted that when making a polite request to one person, you change the ku- to u-, and change the -a to an -e. For example, 'to cook' is 'kupika', and 'please might you cook?' is 'upike?'

This final letter change to an 'e' signifies that the action has changed from one which definitely has happened or will happen, to one which only might happen. Indeed, you could associate this change with anything where we in English use the word 'might'. If you ask someone a request politely, it is not very polite to say it in a way that makes it certain it will happen. When we are being really polite, we should say 'Please might you …'

In formal English, there are quite a few situations in which strictly speaking we should use the word 'might': When you are saying 'would you cook?', a more formal way of saying it is 'might you cook?'. In Swahili, as in formal English, you have to say: 'I hope that we might win', instead of 'I hope we win'; I am cooking so that you might eat', instead of 'I am cooking so you can eat'; etc. In each of these situations in Swahili, you use the polite/uncertain form of the action word, and change the final letter from 'a' to 'e'. In this way, you will be conveying that you are not taking it for granted that it will happen.

Therefore, for instance, when saying "it's best that…", ("Bora…"), it is followed by the action word with the final 'a' changed to an 'e'. Additionally, when saying "in order that…", ("ili…"), you use the polite form of the action word, eg 'ili upike', ('in order that you might cook' – or we normally say, "so that you can cook").

This change of the last letter only applies to action words normally ending in -a. For those ending in -u (eg kujaulu, to succeed); or -i, (eg kufikiri, to think); there is no final letter change in the polite version. However, you can still tell that this is a polite version, as the '-na-' has been omitted. ('-na-' means 'is currently', and is omitted in this type of statement or request – eg 'I am thinking' is 'ninafikiri', but 'I might think' is 'nifikiri'.

The negative form of the polite version is created simply by inserting -si-. Please note that when talking about refusing that someone might do something, a double-negative is used: 'We refused to let them cook' is 'Tuliwakataza wasipike' – ie 'we refused … that they might <u>not</u> cook'. You would have thought it should be 'tuliwakataza wapike', but -si- has been added to convey 'not'. Putting in a double negative in English is a bit coarse, eg "I ain't never done it". In Swahili, as already discussed, it is actually often correct. This minor detail, however, is not something to get too worried about – you would be understood if you got it a bit wrong.

By the way, just look again at the phrase 'tuliwakataza wasipike': **first word:** tu = we; li = in the past; wa = them; kataza = refused; **second word:** wa = they; si = not; pike = might cook. So much meaning in just two words! We have already dealt with the use of -wa- to mean 'they', as in 'wasipike'. We will deal later with the idea of inserting -wa- to mean 'them', as in tuli-wa-kataza. This illustrates an important difference between English and Swahili. English tends to clarify meaning by adding more words. Swahili does it by putting small bits into the word until the meaning is clear, but will often do the same change to several words in the sentence. In this way, Swahili uses fewer words, but each word is more stand-alone in its meaning.

Translate

I am going so that he might succeed

Might you eat this bread so that I won't cook?

It's best that you eat this food now ('Now' is 'sasa')

They will be succeeding in order that you (more than one) might eat

They succeeded in order that you (one person) might eat

We have not yet gone so that we can cook

The trees over there will not burn now – it is best that they do not burn

22.   If …

'If I cook…'	*is*	*'nikipika'*
'If you cook'	*is*	*'ukipika'*
'To agree'	*is*	*'kukubali'*
(one of the action words ending in 'i')		
'If I agree…'	*is*	*'nikikubali'*
'If I go…'	*is*	*'nikienda'*
'If they go…'	*is*	*'wakienda'*
'To be, to become'	*is*	*'kuwa'*
'If they are/if they become'	*is*	*'wakiwa'*
'If they have'	*is*	*'wakiwa na' ('if they are with')*
'To come'	*is*	*'kuja'*
'If we come'	*is*	*'tukija'*

Points to note:

Once again, Swahili makes the use of action words very simple – to convey the sense of 'if', you insert -ki- instead of eg -na- or -ta-. For instance, 'I am cooking' is 'ninapika'; 'I will cook' is 'nitapika'; if I cook' is 'nikipika'.

Note that even in the very short words such as kuwa and kuja, you still drop the 'ku'. This did not happen with eg the present and the past, (eg 'I am coming' – 'ninakuja'; 'I came' – 'nilikuja'). However, when dealing with 'if', you drop the 'ku' at the start of kuja, so 'if I come' is 'nikija', not 'nikikuja'. (We have already seen that this same loss of 'ku-' on short action words also happened with expressing 'might'. For instance, 'I might come' is 'nije', not 'nikuje'.)

The opposite of 'if I cook' is 'if I do not cook'. To say this in Swahili, the word 'kama', (which means 'if … not'), is inserted at the front of the sentence: 'Kama nitapika'. Note that the '-ta-' form of the action is used, signifying that the doubt about me cooking is to do with the future.

There is another way to say, 'if not'. In this case, you can simply use '-sipo-' instead of '-ki-': 'Ni**ki**pika' means '**If** I cook'; and 'Ni**sipo**pika' means '**If** I do **not** cook'. This can also mean 'Unless I cook', and the meaning is derived from the context.

In all types of sentence and classes of word, '-sipo-' can be used as the opposite of '-ki-', when talking about 'if …not' (or 'unless'). The only point to clarify is that when saying 'if I come', the 'ku' of 'kuja' is dropped. This does not happen with '-sipo-' plus very short action words, and so 'unless I come' is 'nisipokuja'. (Or 'kama nitakuja'.)

When a sentence begins with 'If I…', there is usually a second part: 'I would…' As we have already noted, this concept of 'would' is expressed by substituting '-nge-' for '-ki-'(future tense).

'If I go, I would return soon'   is   'Nikienda, ningerudi mapema'

However, this sentence would normally be translated without using this format, by saying:

'I will go, but I will be back soon'   is 'Nitaenda lakini nitarudia mapema'.

There is, (as discussed in Chapter 21), a common situation in which -nge- is used, and that is to say what you want in a shop, more politely that just saying 'I want' (Ninataka):

'I would like…'   *is*   *'Ningependa'*

The substitution of -ki- for -nge- would change the meaning to 'if' – eg 'nikipenda' means 'if I want'.

In addition to its meaning as 'if', there is another use of -ki-:

'To see'   *is*   *'Kuona'*
'We saw them cooking'   *is*   *'Tuliwaona wakipika'*

We saw them cooking: **Tu** (we) **li** (in the past) **wa** (them – M-Wa word) **ona** (saw), **wa** (they) **kipika** (cooking).

'The trees? We saw them burning' is   'Miti? Tuliiona ikiwaka/ikiungua'
'The books? They saw them burning'
                 is 'Vitabu? Waliviona vikiwaka/vikiungua'

In other words, putting -ki- before the final stem of the action word turns it into what we would translate as '-ing'. E.g. 'nimepika' = 'I have cooked', but 'nimekipika' = 'I was cooking'.

As already noted, this is one of the prices we pay for the compactness of Swahili – that two-letter combinations can have different functions in different settings. But don't worry – they are indeed different settings and it does not take long to get used to how each word part is used.

Just to revise, then, '-ki-' as the <u>second</u> part of the word means 'if' – eg nikipika', 'if I cooked'. However, '-ki- as the <u>third</u> part of the word means '-ing' – 'nilikipika', 'I was cooking'.

Exercise 22:

Translate

Those big black trees? We saw them burning

If I come to the village, I might cook the food

Those little children will come to the town if we give them food (To give to = kupatia)

Come here! If you come, I will give you some books

The toilets over there by the river are opening

Those big dirty toilets in the town are closing

If the tree burns, I will go over there

If I cook the food, will the teachers eat it?

If I cook the foods, will the teachers eat them?

23.   Me, you, him/her, us, them

'To give to'	*is*	*'Ku-pa' or 'ku-patia' or 'ku-toa'*
'They are giving me the tree'	*is*	*'Wa-na-ni-pa mti'*

(wa = they; na = currently; ni = to me; pa = give; mti = the tree)

'They are giving you the tree' (to 1 person)	*is*	*'Wana-ku-pa mti'*
'They are giving him/her the tree'	*is*	*'Wana-m-pa mti'*
'They are giving us the tree'	*is*	*'Wana-tu-pa mti'*
'They are giving you the tree' (>1 person)	*is*	*'Wana-wa-pa mti'*
'They are giving them the tree'	*is*	*'Wana-wa-pa mti'*

'The village? They are giving it the tree'
                    is   *'Kijiji? Wa-na-ki-pa mti'*
'The village? They are giving it some toilets'
                    is   *'kijiji? Wa-na-ki-pa vyoo'*

Points to note:

When talking about things to which an action is done, (eg gave **me;** hit **him;** cooked **them),** a two-letter insertion goes into the word to signify who is the object of the action – eg '-ni-' for 'me'. However, some of these two-letter inserts do not quite follow the normal pattern.

For M-Mi and Ki-Vi words, there is no problem – the words for 'it' and 'them' are the same as normal, respectively '-u-', '-i-', '-ki-' and '-vi-'. For example, if you throw a book and it hits a tree, then 'the book hit the tree' is 'Kitabu **kilipiga** mti'. (**ki** = because Ki-Vi word; **li =** in the past; **piga** = hit). However, if you want to say: 'The book hit **it**', you say: 'Kitabu kiliu̱piga', where the 'u' means 'it', (the tree). 'The book hit them', (if it hit more than one tree!), is: 'Kitabu kili̱ipiga'. (You leave both 'i's in place – 'ki-li-i-piga' – otherwise you lose some meaning.)

If you just say, 'It hit it', this is therefore **ki** (it, the book) **li** (in the past) **u** (it, the tree), **piga** (hit) = kiliupiga. So, 'Kitabu kiliupiga' means 'the book, it hit it', but 'kiliupiga' alone means 'it hit it'.

The words for me, us and them are also as expected: '-ni-', '-tu-' and '-wa'. So

'The book? It hit <u>me</u>'	*is*	*'Kitabu? Kili̱nipiga'*
'The book? It hit <u>us</u>'	*is*	*'Kitabu? Kili̱tupiga'*
'The book? It hit <u>them</u>'	*is*	*'Kitabu? Kili̱wapiga'*

The word for 'you' (referring to one person), however, is not quite as expected. It is '-ku-'. So:

'The book? It hit <u>you</u>' *(hitting one person)*	*is*	*'Kitabu? Kili̱kupiga'*
'To see'	*is*	*'Kuona'*
'I saw <u>you</u>' (seeing one person)	*is*	*'Niliku̱ona'*

NB: 'hit' is also 'gonga'

You remember that '-ku-' also means the opposite of '-li-', for example 'Niliona' is 'I saw', and 'sikuona', is 'I did not see'. You might imagine that also using '-ku- to mean 'you' would bring confusion. However, when it is used to mean 'you', its place in the word will be further down. It will always follow the two letters code for saying whether something is past, present or future, (na, li, ta, ja, etc). So, when saying 'I saw him', then, ('nilikuona'), the -ku- follows the -li- and so must mean 'you'.

When '-ku-' means the opposite of '-li-', by contrast, (and says that something did not happen in the past), it is the second bit of the word, right after the letter(s) saying who did not do the action, (eg 'sikuona', 'I did not see').

The words for you (more than one person), and him/her, are also not quite as expected:
- him/her' is '-m-' (but '-mw-' before a vowel).
- you (more than one person), is '-wa-', exactly the same as the word for 'them'!

'The book? It hit <u>him or her</u>'	*is*	*'Kitabu? Kili<u>m</u>piga'*
'The book? It hit <u>you</u>' (>one)	*is*	*'Kitabu? Kili<u>m</u>piga'*
'I saw the man'	*is*	*'Niliona mwanaume'*
'I saw <u>you</u>' (more than one)	*is*	*'Nili<u>wa</u>ona'*
'I saw <u>them</u>'	*is*	*'Nili<u>wa</u>ona' (same word)*
'I saw <u>him</u>'	*is*	*'Nili<u>m</u>wona'*
'To see <u>him</u>'	*is*	*'Ku<u>m</u>wona'*
'To see <u>them</u>'	*is*	*'Ku<u>wa</u>ona'*

The use of '-wa-' for both 'you' (plural) and 'they' is slightly more open to confusion. Often the context will clarify the meaning. Where is does not, you can add the word for 'you' or 'they', (see Chapter 7), as a way of saying <u>you</u> or <u>them</u> with stress: 'ninyi' and 'wao'. So, when seeing more than one of you, I could say 'I saw you' ('Niliwaona'); but if it were not clear whether I were saying 'I saw you' or 'I saw them', then you could say, "Niliwaona ninyi" – "I saw you", or "Niliwaona wao" – "I saw them".

Note that the 'wa' did not merge with the 'ona'. None of these me/him/her/you/them words merge with the action word that follows, when it begins with a vowel. However, in the case of the word for him or her, ('m', pronounced 'mmm'), if it is followed by a vowel, a 'w' is inserted to make the 'm' longer, like 'mmm', eg 'I saw her', is 'Nilimwona'.

You might remember that when talking about the past you use 'li', and that when the action word is very short, the 'ku' is retained: eg 'to give to' is 'kupa'. 'I gave' is 'Nilikupa', (not 'nilila'). However, you cannot just say 'I gave' – you have to say who to, and so you need to add 'm' or 'tu' of 'wa' etc. Importantly, when you add this, you drop the 'ku'. (Just as happened with 'might' and 'if').

So 'I gave-' is 'Nilikupa', but I gave him' is 'Nilimpa'. 'I gave us' is 'Nilitupa'. In this way, you can know that any 'ku' following 'li' is never just the beginning of a short action word, and always refers to 'you'.

SUMMARY:
M-Wa class
'I'	'You' (one)	'S/he'	is	'-ni-'	'-ku-'	'-m-' (mw before a vowel)
'Us'	'You' (2 or more)	'Them'	is	'-tu-'	'-wa-'	'-wa-'

M-Mi class
'It'	'Them'		is	'-u-'	'-i-'

Ki-Vi class
'It'	'Them'		is	'-ki-'	'-vi-'

Exercise 23:
Translate:
The plants? I will cook them soon
The children will come soon. I will give them food
The teachers have not yet taught the pupils. They might teach them soon
The dirty bags are not ready. I will come with them
Those dirty bags? I have them
My dirty bags? I will burn (-unguza) them soon
Those books are clean now. I will see them in the village
His teacher is very good. He will give him a plant

24. Nicely, badly, fairly – descriptions of actions

'Nice'		is	'-zuri'
'Nicely'	or 'well'	is	'Vizuri'
'Bad'		is	'-baya'
'Badly'		is	'Vibaya'
'Brief'		is	'-fupi'
'Briefly'		is	'Kifupi'
'Little		is	'-dogo'
'Fairly', 'Quite'		is	'Kidogo'

Points to note:

In English, when talking about a thing, we can say that it is 'nice'. However, when describing an action, (for instance saying how someone behaves), you would have to say 'nicely' – e.g. 'he is playing nicely', not 'he is playing nice'. In other words, when a descriptive word in English is being used to say how something happens, or how something was done, we add '-ly' to the end of the describing word.

In Swahili, (as you might expect!), the change is at the front end of the word. So, for instance, nice, ('-zuri-), becomes 'nicely, ('vizuri'). The good news with this type of word is that it does not change according to context: 'vizuri' is always 'vizuri', no matter what action it is talking about. I do not know why they chose 'vi' to be the front-end change for this type of word, but it has little to do with Ki-Vi words. However, the front-end change is not always 'vi' for words that describe actions. It is sometimes 'ki', despite the fact that in neither case is this change directly to do with Ki-Vi words.

Therefore, 'brief' ('-fupi') becomes 'briefly', ('kifupi'), but it is always 'kifupi'. In short, to convert from a word describing a thing, to a word describing an action, you add 'vi' or 'ki' to the front end. These same changes apply to many words. The bad news is that there is no rule for knowing which one you add. You just need to learn them one by one, (but if you were to guess, you would have a 50:50 chance of being right!)

You will have noticed that the word for 'nicely', ('vizuri'), can also mean 'nice' if applied to a word like Vitabu, (books): 'vitabu vizuri' – 'nice books'. However, there is no confusion, because it is clear that 'vitabu vizuri' is talking about the books, whereas 'Vitabu viliwaka vizuri' means 'the books burnt nicely'. (Or 'the books burnt well'.) In this example, it is clear that the 'vizuri' word is describing the action of burning, not the books, because it follows in the sentence the word for 'burning', not the word for 'books'. So, in Ki-Vi situations, simply look at the word before 'vizuri' to work out what it is describing – sometimes a thing; sometimes an action.

When you are not dealing with a Ki-Vi word, there is no confusion – e.g. 'Miti minawaka/inaungua vizuri' – 'the trees are burning well'.

Adding 'ki' or 'vi' is not, however, the only way to make words which describe actions. 'Briefly', for example, can either be 'kifupi', or it can be '**kwa** kifupi', where 'kwa' sort of means 'of that type'.

'Brief'	*is*	*'-fupi'*
'Briefly'	*is*	*'Kifupi'*
'Briefly'	*is also*	*'Kwa kifupi'*
'Truth'	*is*	*'Kweli'*
'Truthfully'	*is*	*'Kwa kweli'*
'On purpose'	*is*	*'Kwa kusudi'*
'Usually'	*is*	*'Kwa kawaida'*
'Luckily	*is*	*'Kwa bahati'*
'Sound'	*is*	*'Sauti'*
'Loudly'	*is*	*'Kwa sauti'*

Some words describing actions do not have either 'kwa' or 'ki/vi' at the beginning – e.g. 'early' – 'mapema'. These words do not change in any context.

'Gently'	*is*	*'Pole pole'*
'Early' or 'Soon'	*is*	*'Mapema'*
'Especially'	*is*	*'Hasa'*
'Ready'	*is*	*'Tayari'*
'Clearly'	*is*	*Waziwazi'*
'Hastily'	*is*	*'Haraka haraka'*

Summary : Descriptions of actions:
Some start with vi- or ki-, e.g.:
Nice = -nuzuri   Nicely = Vizuri
Brief = -fupi   Briefly = Kifupi

Some use 'kwa', e.g.:
Loudly = Kwa sauti
Some are always the same:
Gently = pole pole

Exercise 24:

Translate:
I have travelled for a purpose
I was travelling on purpose
The village was burning badly
He was speaking truthfully
Luckily, I was in the river
They cooked the food quite nicely ('vizuri kabisa')
I am travelling briefly towards ('kuelekea') the village

We were travelling gently to the right
We especially wanted to travel soon

25.   When?

'Still', 'Not yet'	is	'Bado'
'Quite'	is	'Kidogo'
'Not quite yet'	is	'Bado kidogo'
'Later'	is	'Baadaye'
'Early'	is	'Mapema'
'Now'	is	'Sasa'
'The'	is	'Kisha'
'Possibly'	is	'Labda/Yawezekana'
'Already'	is	'Tayari'
'Recently'	is	'Majuzi' or 'Hivi karibuni'
'Quickly'	is	'Upesi' or 'haraka'
'Since'	is	'Tangu'
'Until'	is	'Mpaka/hadi'
'Always'	is	'Sikuzote' / 'Mara kwa mara'
'Near'	is	'Karibu'
'Nearly'	is	'Karibuni'
'All day'	is	'Kutwa'
'Daily'	is	'Kwa kutwa' / Kila siku'
'Suddenly'	is	'Ghafula'

Points to note:

All these descriptions relating to time stay the same in whatever context they are used. There are no rules to learn about them – only the job of remembering them. This is much easier when you listen to them repeatedly – either in real life or on a CD or MP3. Do not be afraid to learn like a child – listening to something over and over again. When you do this, your brain eventually stores it in a deep memory, where it pops into your head when you need it, and where you do not forget it, as long as you access it from time to time.

The same comments apply to the parts of the day:

'Day'	is	'Siku' / 'Mchana'
'Morning'	is	'Asubuhi'
'Daytime'	is	'Mchana'
'Afternoon'	is	'Alasiri'
'Night'	is	'Usiku'
'Week'	is	'Wiki' / 'Juma'
'Long ago'	is	'Zamani'
'The other day'	is	'Juzijuzi'
'The day before yesterday'	is	'Juzi'
'Yesterday'	is	'Jana'
'Last night'	is	'Jana usiku'
'Last night'	is also	'Usiku wa jana'

'Today'	is	'Leo'
'This morning'	is	'Asubuhi hii/ ya leo'
'Tonight'	is	'Usiku wa leo'
'Tomorrow'	is	'Kesho'
'Next week'	is	'Wiki ijayo'
'Date'	is	'Tarehe'
'The third' (of the month)	is	'Tarehe tatu'
'The tenth' (of the month)	is	'Tarehe kumi'
'Friday' (first day of the week)	is	'Ljumaa'

'Saturday'	is	'Jumamosi' (J1 or first day after)
'Sunday '	is	'Jumapili' (J2 or second day after)
'Monday'	is	'Jumatatu' (J3 or third day after)
'Tuesday	is	'Jumanne' (J4 or fourth day after)
'Wednesday	is	'Jumatano (J5 or fifth day after)
'Thursday'	is	'Alhamisi
(Al or Day of Preparation)		

The same comments apply to some of the words dealing with description of time:

'Early'	is	'Mapema'
'Later'	is	'Baadaye'
'Afterwards'	is	'Halafu'
'Before'	is	'Kabla ya'
'Always'	is	'Sikuzote'
'Daily'	is	'Kwa kutwa/kila siku'
'... just...'	is	'...tu...'

('tu' comes at the end of the phrase to mean '... just' as in 'just after the town')

'Briefly'	is	'Kwa kifupi'
'Quickly'	is	'Upesi/haraka'
'Speedily'	is	'Kwa kasi'
'Suddenly'	is	'Ghafula'
'Slowly'	is	'Polepole'
'Gently!'	is	'Taratibu/Polepole!'
'Usually'	is	'Kwa kawaida'

Telling the time, on the other hand, does require some explanation. Before that, we need to know the numbers in Swahili.

Exercise 25:

Translate

Now	Early	Later	Not quite yet	Afterwards	Before
Then	Since	Until	Always	Nearly	Usually
Already	Suddenly	Quickly	Slowly	Possibly	

Day	Today	Tomorrow	Yesterday	Morning	Afternoon
Night	Tonight	Last night	Long ago		

26. Numbers and telling the time

'One'	is	'-moja'
'Two'	is	'-wili' or '-mbili'
'Three'	is	'-tatu'
'Four'	is	'-nne'
'Five'	is	'-tano'
'Six'	is	'Sita'
'Seven'	is	'Saba'
'Eight'	is	'-nane'
'Nine'	is	'Tisa'
'Ten'	is	'Kumi'
'Eleven'	is	'Kumi na -moja'
'Twelve'	is	'Kumi na -mbili' etc
'Zero'	is	'Sifuri'
'Twenty'	is	'Ishirini'
'Thirty'	is	'Thelathini'
'Forty'	is	'Arobaini'
'Fifty'	is	'Hamsini'
'Sixty'	is	'Sitini'
'Seventy'	is	'Sabini'
'Eighty'	is	'Themanini'
'Ninety'	is	'Tisini'
'One hundred'	is	'Mia' (mia moja)
'One thousand'	is	'Elfu' (elfu moja)
'Thousands!'	is	'Maelfu!'

('Ma-' means 'lots of')

'One million'	is	'Milioni'(milioni moja)
'One half'	is	'Nusu'
'One third'	is	'Theluthi' (theluthi moja)
'One quarter'	is	'Robo'

'One tree'	is	'Mti mmoja'
'Two trees'	is	'Miti miwili'
'Two tables'	is	'Meza mbili'
'Eleven trees' (ten plus one)	is	'Miti kumi na moja'
'One book'	is	'Kitabu kimoja'
'Two books'	is	'Vitabu viwili'
'Eleven books' (ten plus one)	is	'Vitabu kumi na moja'
'Eleven men'	is	'Wanaume kumi na moja'
'Twenty-two men'	is	'Wanaume ishirini na wawili'
'Three hundred and 22 men'	is	'Wanaume mia tatu ishirini na wawili'

For some reason, four of the numbers from one to ten never change when applied to the things they are numbering. With the remainder, the normal changes occur – for instance '–moja' can become 'mmoja' or 'kimoja', etc; '-wili' can become 'wawili', 'miwili', 'viwili', 'mbili', etc.

Sita, saba, tisa and kumi, however, all stay the same in any context. Sita, saba and tisa are converted to 'sixty' 'seventy' and 'ninety' by changing the last letter to 'ini'. The ending '-ini' is common to all the multiples of ten, from twenty to ninety.

Note that anything denoting quantity is always the last word in the phrase, so 'two good children' would be 'watoto wazuri wawili'.

Note that when saying 'eleven', it is translated as 'ten plus one', so the '-moja' part changes as if there were just one of the thing. So 'Eleven children' is 'Watoto kumi na mmoja', not 'watoto kumi na wamoja'. The '-moja' means 'one', and so only ever has a singular front-end change.

In order to turn these numbers into the time, it needs to be appreciated that the Swahili clock is based on sunrise and sunset. (On the equator, these are at 6am and 6pm respectively). The first hour is therefore one hour after sunrise or sunset; the second is two hours after; etc:

'... O'clock'	*is*	*'Saa /kamili...'*
'... hour...'	*is*	*'Saa ...'*
'First hour' (7)	*is*	*'Saa moja'*
'Second hour' (8)	*is*	*'Saa mbili'*
'Third hour' (9)	*is*	*'Saa tatu'*
'First hour am' (7 o'clock am/morning)	*is*	*'Saa moja asubuhi'*
'Second hour am' (8 am)	*is*	*'Saa mbili asubuhi'*
'Third hour am' (9 am)	*is*	*'Saa tatu asubuhi'*
'First hour pm' (7 o'clock pm)	*is*	*'Saa moja ya usiku'*
'Second hour pm' (8 pm)	*is*	*'Saa mbili ya usiku'*
'Third hour' (9 pm)		*is 'Saa tatu ya usiku'*
'Plus'		*is 'Na'*
'9.15pm' (ie third hour + quarter)	*is*	*'Saa tatu na robo ya usiku'*
'9.30pm' (ie third hour + half)	*is*	*'Saa tatu na nusu ya usiku'*
'Minus'	*is*	*'Kasoro'*
'9.45pm' (ie fourth hour - quarter)	*is*	*'Saa nne kasoro robo ya usiku'*
'Minute'	*is*	*'Dakika'*
'9.10pm' (ie third hour + ten mins)	*is*	*'Saa tatu na dakika kumi usiku'*
'9.50pm' (ie fourth hour - ten mins)	*is*	*'Saa nne kasoro dakika kumi*
usiku'		

'On the dot'	*is*	*'Kamili'*
'9.10pm' (ie third hour + ten mins)	*is*	*'Saa tatu na dakika kumi usiku'*

The order of the words when telling the time is important: firstly, the word 'saa' says that you are about to say the time, (the hour). Then comes which hour it is; then any plus or minus; then finally whether it is day or night. Bear in mind that most Swahili-speaking countries are located around the Equator, where there is precisely a twelve-hour day, and so 'mchana' will be daylight', and 'usiku' darkness.

The word 'ya' is inserted before the word 'mchana' or 'usiku'. It means 'belonging to' – ie 'belonging to the day', or 'belonging to the night'. Some people omit it, which is acceptable.

'How many?'	*is*	*'Ngapi?'*
'How many minutes?'	*is*	*'Dakika ngapi?'*
'What is the time?'	*is*	*'Saa ngapi?'*
'What is the time now?'	*is*	*'Saa ngapi sasa?'*
'It's about…'	*is*	*'Ni kama…'*
'It's about nine o'clock' (about the third hour)	*is*	*'Ni kama saa tatu'*
'A period of…'	*is*	*'Muda wa …'*
'A period of nine hours'	*is*	*'Muda wa saa tisa'*

Finally, in order to say the order of a number, (first, second, third, etc), you simply put '-a' as a word before the number. From number three on, the numbers remain the same as normal, but the words for 'first' and 'second' are slightly different:

'First'	*is*	*'-a kwanza/ mosi'*
'Second'	*is*	*'-a pili'*
'Third'	*is*	*'-a tatu'*
'Fourth'	*is*	*'-a nne'*
'Fifth'	*is*	*'-a tano'*
'Sixth'	*is*	*'a sita'*
'Seventh'	*is*	*'a saba'*
'Eighth'	*is*	*'-a nane'*
'Ninth'	*is*	*'a tisa'*
'Tenth'	*is*	*'a kumi' etc*

The '-a' is preceded by the agreement for whatever it is you are talking about:

M-Wa class:

'First man'	*is*	*'Mwanaume wa kwanza'*

M-MI class:

'First tree'	*is*	*'Mti wa kwanza'*

Ki-Vi class:
'First book'   *is*   *'Kitabu cha kwanza'*
Ji-Ma class:
'First answer'   *is*   *'Jibu la kwanza'*
N class:
'First house   *is*   *'Nyumba ya kwanza'*

Exercise 26:

Count 1 – 12 for men; trees; books; answers
Translate:
1, 2, 3 & 4 both am and pm
6th, 7th, 8th and 9th man; tree; book; answer

27. How many? Quantity

'How many?'	is	'ngapi?' or '-ngapi?'
'How many?' (stand-alone)	is	'Ngapi?'
'It costs'	is	'Inagharimu'
'How much does it cost?'	is	'Inagharimu Shilingi ngapi?'
'How much does it cost?'	is	(short) 'Shilingi ngapi?'
'How many trees?'	is	'Miti mingapi?'
'How many men?'	is	'Wanaume wangapi?'
'Few'	is	'-chache'
'Many, much'	is	'-ingi'
'Plenty'	is	'Tele'
'Plenty'	is	also 'Wingi'
'Some' (i.e. part of something)	is	'-kadhaa'
'Another'	is	'-ingine'
'Whole' (ie all of something)	is	'-zima'
'Every, each'	is	'Kila'
'Everything'	is	'Kila kitu'
'A few trees'	is	'Miti michache'
'A few men'	is	'Wanaume wachache'
'Many trees'	is	'Miti mingi'
'Many men'	is	'Wanaume wengi'
'Much bread'	is	'Mkate mwingi'
'Many books'	is	'Vitabu vingi'
'Plenty of books'	is	'Vitabu vingi'
'Plenty of men'	is	'Wanaume wengi'
'Some bread'	is	'Mkate kiasi/baadhi'
'Another tree'	is	'Mti mwingine'
'A whole (loaf of) bread'	is	'Mkate mzima'
'A whole book'	is	'Kitabu chote/kizima'
'Each book'	is	'Kila kitabu'
'Each tree'	is	'Kila mti'
'Each person'	is	'Kila mtu'
'Every person'	is	'Kila mtu'
'Everybody'	is	'Kila mtu'

Points to note:

'Ngapi' can be a question by itself: 'How many?' However, when it is asking 'how many of' something, it undergoes the normal front-end change to the word. Like any word dealing with quantity, it comes at the end of the phrase, (whereas we in English usually put quantity at the beginning).

Similarly, the words for 'few' and 'whole' undergo the normal front-end changes.

The words for 'many', (ingi); and 'some/another', (-ingine); both start with a vowel, so when receiving their front-end changes, there is a merging of vowels, exactly as seen with describing words. So wa-ingi becomes 'wengi'; m-ingi becomes 'mwingi'; mi-ingi becomes 'mingi'; ki-ingi becomes 'kingi'; etc.

There is one exception to the rule that anything dealing with quantity comes at the end of the word – 'kila' always comes at the front.

Exercise 27:
Translate:

How many trees?	How many men?
A few trees	A few men
Many trees	Man men
Plenty of books	Plenty of men
Each book	Each tree

28.   All and any: '-ote' and '-o -ote'

'All'	is	'-ote'
'All of us'	is	'Sisi sote'
'All of you'	is	'Ninyi nyote'
'All of them' (M-Wa class)	is	'Wao wote'
'All the trees' (M-Mi class)	is	'Miti yote'
'All the books' (Ki-Vi class)	is	'Vitabu vyote'
'We all went'	is	'Tulikwenda sote'
'They all went'	is	'Walikwenda wote'
'They all went' (M-Mi class)	is	'Ilikwenda yote'
'They all went' (Ki-Vi class)	is	'Vilikwenda vyote'
'Whole' (means both 'whole' and 'all') is		'-ote'
'The whole tree' (M-Mi class)	is	'Mti wote'
'The whole book' (Ki-Vi class)	is	'Kitabu chote'
'The whole (loaf of) bread is mine'	is	'Mkate wote ni wangu'
'All the loaves are mine'	is	'Mikate yote ni yangu'
'The whole book is mine'	is	'Kitabu chote ni changu'
'All of the books are mine'	is	'Vitabu vyote ni vyangu'
'Any'	is	'-o -ote'
'Any of them' (M-Wa class)	is	'Wao wowote' (plural)
'Any of the trees' (M-Mi class)	is	'Miti yoyote' (plural)
'Any of the books' (Ki-Vi class)	is	'Vitabu vyovyote' (plural)
'Anyone' (M-Wa class)	is	'Mtu yeyote' (singular)
'Any of the bread' (M-Mi class)	is	'Mkate wowote' (singular)
'Any of the book' (Ki-Vi class)	is	'Kitabu chochote' (singular)

Points to note:

The main thing to notice about these descriptions is that they have slightly different agreements to normal – e.g. 'kitabu chote' rather than 'kitabu kiote'. This is because both '-ote' and '-o -ote' begin with a vowel, and, as we have seen, the agreements at the front of the word are slightly modified when this happens.

The agreements, although not the normal ki- vi- etc, are not random: we often see that the second-line preference for agreement with 'ki-' is 'ch-'; and the second-line preference for agreement with 'vi-' is 'vy-'. Similarly, 'y-' and 'w-' crop up from time to time as agreements for the singular and plural in the M-Wa class of words.

Note: '-o -ote' in the plural means 'any', but in the singular it can mean 'any bit of'.

Finally, we should note that as descriptions of quantity, these words would always come at the end of a phrase, e.g. 'any of the good bread' is 'mkate mzuri wo wote'.

SUMMARY:
M-Wa class
All of us = Sisi sote   *All of them = Wao wote*
Anyone = (Mtu) yeyote   *Any of them = Yeyote kati yao*

M-Mi class
The whole (of it) = wote   *The whole (of them) = yote*
Any of it = yoyote   *Any of them = zozote*

Ki-Vi class
The whole (of it) = chote   *The whole (of them) = vyote*
Any of it = cho chote   *Any of them = vyo vyote*

Exercise 28:

Translate:

All of us	All of you	All of them (people)
The whole book is mine	All the books are mine	
Any of the book	Any of the books	

86

29.　Actions to, at, or for someone or something

'To bring'	*is*	*'Kuleta'*
'To bring <u>to</u>'	*is*	*'Kuletea'*

'They are going to town to bring food'
　　　　　　is　*'Wanakwenda mjini kuleta chakula'*
'They are going to town to bring <u>me</u> food'
　　　　　　is　*'Wanakwenda mjini ku<u>ni</u>let<u>e</u>a chakula'*
　　　(i.e. 'to bring food to me': Ku= to; ni= me; let<u>e</u>a= bring <u>to</u>)

'To answer	*is*	*'Kujibu'*
'To answer <u>to</u>' (or for)	*is*	*'Kujibia/kuwajibika kwa....'*

'They are coming to town to answer'
　　　　　is　*'Wanakuja mjini kujibu'*
'They are coming to town to answer me'
　　　　　is　*'Wanafika mjini ku<u>ni</u>jibu*

'To return'	*is*	*'Kurudi'*
'To return for'	*is*	*'Kurudia'*
'They are returning to town'	*is*	*'Wanarudi mjini'*
'They are returning to town for bread'	*is*	*'Wanarudia mkate mjini'*

Points to note:

Whenever something is being done to someone, or for someone, the action word undergoes a change at the end, instead of adding the word 'to' or 'for'. You can bring something, ('to bring' is 'kuleta'), or you can bring something <u>to</u> someone, ('kuletia'). The addition of the letter 'i' near the end of the word changes the meaning to 'bring <u>to</u>'. (Though it can be spelled 'kuletea', because it is pronounced identically.)

As long as the action is directed at something, a similar change occurs: return <u>for</u>; cook <u>for</u>; wash <u>for</u>; give <u>to</u>; read <u>to</u>; etc. The insertion is sometimes 'e' and sometimes 'i', and is always just before the last letter. Which of these it is depends on the vowel in the syllable which comes before, but as they are pronounced very similarly, it is not critical to know the rule.

In the case where the action word already ends in two vowels, (eg kuondoa, to remove; kuchukua to carry), an extra 'l' is used so as to prevent making three vowels in a row: kuondo<u>le</u>a; kuchuku<u>li</u>a. Again, whether '-le- or '-li-' is added depends on the previous syllable. With the Arabic action words that end in '-u', the '-u' is replaced with '-ia', e.g. 'kujibu' becomes 'kujibia'.

However, the exception to this is when one of these words is always implied – for instance 'kutafata', 'to search'. If you are searching, you are always searching for, and in Swahili, the word 'for' is implied in 'kutafata'.

Some action words do not undergo this change, as they always imply 'to', 'at' or 'for':
'To give (to)'   is   'Kupa/kutoa'
'To search (for)'   is   'Kutafuta'
'To look (at or for)'   is   'Kutazama/kuangalia'

For a few particular words, this change at the end can mean a complete change in meaning, and in these cases the change has nothing to do with 'being done to' etc:

'To smell bad'   is   'Kunuka'
'To smell good'   is   'Kunukia'   (The opposite!)

'To bring'   is   'Kuleta'
'To bring to'   is   'Kuletea'
'To answer'   is   'Kujibu'
'To answer to' (or for)   is   'Kujibia'
'To carry'   is   'Kuchukua'
'To carry for'   is   'Kuchukulia/kubebea'
'To give'   is   'Kupa/kutoa'
'To give to'   is   'Kupa' (Same – you always say, 'to give to')
'To smell bad'   is   'Kunuka'
'To smell good'   is   'Kunukia'

Exercise 29:

Translate:
The are going to town to bring food
They are going to town to bring me food
They are coming to town to answer
They are coming to town to answer me
You (plural) are returning to town for bread

30.   Making an action reciprocal – another use of '-na'

'To wash'	is	'Kuosha/kufua/kuoga'
'To wash one another'	is	'Kuoshana/kuogeshana'
'To see'	is	'Kuona/kutazama'
'To see one another'	is	'Kuonana'
'To answer'	is	'Kujibu'
'To answer one another'	is	'Kujibiana/kujibizana'

NB: -bu- changes to -bia-.

Points to note:

If you want to get across the sense of an action happening reciprocally – looking at one another, washing one other, etc, then '-na' is added to the end of the action word.

We have already noted that 'na' has many uses. It means 'is-currently' eg a<u>na</u>pika = s/he is currently cooking. When used to mean 'is-currently', it is within a word, soon after the beginning. When used to mean 'and', it is a separate word: 'beds and books' – 'vitabu <u>na</u> vitanda'. When it is used as 'with', it is at the end of a very short word: 'She is cooking <u>with</u> a thing' = 'anapikia ana kitu'.

When it is used to mean that an action is reciprocal, then it is on the end of an action word – eg 'kuosha<u>na</u>'.

Note that with some examples, you have to first make the change to the action word to signify that something is happening <u>to</u> someone. So 'to answer' is 'kujibu'. To answer <u>to</u>, however, is 'kujibia'. Therefore 'to answer <u>to</u> one another' is 'kujibi<u>a</u>na'.

This change is only necessary where you would need to put 'to' or 'for' in English. When you see one another, or wash one another, you do not say 'see to' or 'wash for', and so no change of the end of the action word before adding the '-na-' is needed.

SUMMARY:

'To wash'	is	'Kuosha/kuoga'
'To wash <u>one another</u>' is		'Kuosha<u>na</u>/kuogeshana' (add -na)
'To answer'	is	'Kuji<u>bu</u>'
'To answer <u>one another</u>'	is	'Kujib<u>ia</u>na' (kujibishana)

NB: -bu- changes to -bia-.

89

Exercise 30:

Translate:

The are going to the river to wash one another

We are going to the town to see one another

We went to the village to answer one another

31.   Doing things to oneself – '-ji-'

'to teach'	is	'Kufunza' (Kufundisha);
'to learn' (ie teach <u>onesself</u>)	is	'Ku<u>ji</u>funza' (or 'Ku<u>ji</u>fundisha')

'to see'	is	'Kuona'

(to see can also be 'kutizama' 'kutazama' or 'kuangalia')

'to see onesself'	is	'Ku<u>ji</u>ona'

'to beat'	is	'Kupiga'
'to beat onesself'	is	'Ku<u>ji</u>piga'

'He taught himself'	is	'Alijifunza'
'They beat themselves'	is	'Walijipiga'
'We have seen ourselves'	is	'Tumejiona' /'Tumejiangalia'

Points to note:
The insertion of '-ji-' immediately before the main stem of an action word makes the action refer to one's self. There are no variations, and only a few actions can come into this category. The insert is still '-ji-' whether it refers to myself, himself, themselves, etc.

Sometimes, there is a need for more emphasis that the action is done <u>by</u> the person(s) <u>to</u> the person. In this case, it is possible to add in a word emphasising 'oneself', 'ourselves', or 'themselves'. In Chapter 15, mention was made of the insert '-enye-', which signifies this possession. And so:

'We taught ourselves'	is	'Tulijifunza'
'We taught <u>ourselves</u> this book'		
	is	'Tulijifunza <u>wenyewe</u> kitabu hiki'

SUMMARY
Doing to one's self – '-ji-'

'He taught himself'	is	'Alijifunza (or 'Alijifundisha')
'We have seen ourselves'	is	'Tumejiona' (or 'Tumejiangalia')
'They beat themselves'	is	'Walijipiga wenyewe'

Exercise 31:
Translate:
We will teach ourselves this book
They were beating themselves with a stone ('stone' is 'jiwe' – a Ji-Ma word)
We will see ourselves within this book

32.   Connecting words

'Therefore'	is	'Kwa hiyo'
'The same, equal'	is	'Sawa'
'Equally'	is	'Sawasawa'
'After'	is	'Baada ya'
'Concerning ...'	is	'Habari ya / kuhusu...'
'Perhaps'	is	'Labda'
'Thus'	is	'Hivyo/ hivyo basi'
'Also'	is	'Pia'
'Also, too', 'Likewise'	is	'Vilevile'
'Instead of'	is	'Badala ya'
'Together'	is	'Pamoja'
'Formerly'	is	'-a-zamani'
'Otherwise'	is	'Vinginevyo'
'In the same way'	is	'Vivihivi/sawasawa'
'Exactly so'	is	'Vivyo hivyo' or 'Vivyo hasa'
'Although'	is	'Ingawa' or 'Ijapokuwa'
'Especially'	is	'Hasa'

Points to note:

These connecting words do not change according to context. The position they occupy in the phrase is subject to certain rules and customs, but these are complex, and mainly putting them in the same place as they would be in formal English will readily convey the meaning.

There are of course subtle alterations in usage when dealing with sophisticated Swahili, but in each case, the word is easily recognisable, as the front end of the main word does not change.

Examples:

'Therefore, he came...'	is	'Kwa hiyo, alikuja...'
'... instead of me'	is	'... badala yangu'
'His book is the same as theirs'	is	'Kitabu chake ni sawa na chao'
'I will go after eating'	is	'Nitakwenda baada ya kula'
'to Tell'	is	'Kuambia' or 'Kusema'
'I am telling him about the town'	is	'Ninamwambia habari ya mji'
'to Want'	is	'Kutaka'
'to Need'	is	'Kuhitaji'
'Perhaps he might want to go'	is	'Labda anataka kwenda'
'Perhaps he might need to go'	is	'Labda anahitaji kwenda'
'We will also go together'	is	'Tutakwenda pamoja pia'

A small subtlety that will help you sound more like a native speaker, is that sometimes, instead of saying: 'after he arrived, he did ...', you can say: 'After

<u>to</u> arrive, he did ...' In English, we use the word 'he' twice, even though it is obvious from the first use whom we are talking about. Eg:

'After he arrived, he said ...   *is 'Baada ya kufika, alisema ...'*

SUMMARY:
These connecting words are vital to learn by heart at an early stage, as they convey so much meaning to the sentence.

When you forget to talk in the past instead of the present, people understand you. When you say 'before' instead of 'after', they do not!!

Exercise 32:
Translate:
Perhaps they will travel together
Therefore, you will cook instead of me
The trees will burn equally
After he arrived, he told us about the plants
Perhaps they will come also
Thus, he will want to go

33. Which, whom, whose, and other questions

'Who?'	*is*	*'Nani?'*
'Which?'	*is*	*'Gani?' or 'Ipi?'*
'Where?'	*is*	*'Wapi?'*
'How much /many?'	*is*	*'Ngapi?'*
'When?'	*is*	*'Lini?'*
'What?'	*is*	*'Nini?'*
'Why?'	*is*	*'Kwa nini?' (For what?)*
'By what means?'	*is*	*'Vipi or kivipi?'*

Or: 'Kwa namna ipi? 'Kwa namma gani?' 'Kwa njia ipi?' 'Kwa njia gani?'

'How?'	*is*	*'-aje' or '-vipi'*

Points to note:

The only one of these questions which needs to take an agreement is 'How'. All the rest stay the same, without needing to agree with any other word in the sentence.

We have already noted that the word for 'where?' tends to go at the end of the phrase: eg 'Where is the town?' is 'Mti uko wapi?'. This perhaps relates to the fact that in Swahili, the speaker first has to clarify that s/he is talking about the general location – 'uko' – and then the question can be formed. ('The town is in the general location of ..where?). This relates back to the general tendency in Swahili to convey the meaning in more than one way in the words of the sentence.

The words 'Why?', 'When?' and 'Who?', however, are much more likely to be found as the first word in the sentence:

'Who will come?'	*is*	*'Nani atafika/atakuja?'*
'Why will he come?'	*is*	*'Kwa nini atafika/aje/atakuja?'*
'When will she come?'	*is*	*'Lini atafika/atakuja?'*

'Which' always relates to a choice, and so follows the word for thing the question is about:

'Which man will come?'	*is*	*'Mwanaume gani atafika?*
'Which man will come?'	*also*	*'Mwanaume gani atakuja?'*

The word 'what?' typically relates to an action, and so follows the action word:

'What did you cook?'	*is*	*'Ulipika nini?'*

The question 'How', (which in Swahili is simply '-je'), also relates to an action, but instead of following the action word is actually added to the end of it:

'How did you cook?' 'Well!'   is   *'Ulipika<u>je</u>?' 'Vizuri!'*

Note: In English, we might have instead said 'How was your cooking?', but that passive formulation does not work well in Swahili. As we have seen in many cases, the action word is a central focus of the grammar, and needs to be expressed in the active format, rather than saying 'He was doing' or 'I was cooking'. Instead, in Swahili, you say 'He did' or 'I cooked', and choose between the '-li-' and '-ja-' forms to convey whether the action was continuous, or whether you are describing something done and dusted.

SUMMARY:

'<u>Who</u> will come?'	*is*	*'<u>Nani</u> atafika / atakuja?'*
'<u>Why</u> will he come?'	*is*	*'<u>Kwanini</u> atafika / atakuja?'*
'<u>When</u> will she come?'	*is*	*'<u>Lini</u> atafika / atakuja?'*
'<u>Which</u> man will come?'	*is*	*'Mwanaume <u>gani</u> atafika?'*
'<u>What</u> did you cook?'	*is*	*'Ulipika <u>nini</u>?'*
'<u>How</u> did you cook?' 'Well!'	*is*	*'Ulipika<u>je</u>?' 'Vizuri!'*

Exercise 33:

Translate:
Who will burn the tree? (use 'kuunguza' for 'to burn')
Why will they burn the tree?
When will they burn the tree?
Which man will burn the tree?
What did you burn?
The tree? How did you burn it?

34.   Who, which and whom as explanations – 'amba'. When as explanation.

'The man <u>whom</u> I hit'	*is*	*'Mwanaume <u>ambaye</u> nilimpiga'*
'The man <u>who</u> is smelling bad'	*is*	*'Mwanaume <u>ambaye</u> ananuka'*
'The men <u>who</u> are smelling bad'	*is*	*'Wanaume <u>ambao</u> wananuka'*
'The tree <u>which</u> is smelling bad'	*is*	*'Mti <u>ambao</u> unanuka'*
'The trees <u>which</u> are smelling bad'	*is*	*'Miti <u>ambayo</u> inanuka'*
'The thing <u>which</u> is smelling bad'	*is*	*'Kitu <u>ambacho</u> kinanuka'*
'The things <u>which</u> are smelling bad'	*is*	*'Vitu <u>ambavyo</u> vinanuka'*
'The things <u>which</u> I burned'	*is*	*'Vitu <u>ambavyo</u> niliunguza'*

NB: 'bad' = 'vibaya' (optional in the Swahili sentences above)

Points to note:

The words 'who', 'whom' and 'which' are not always questions. Sometimes they can be part of an explanation, as in the sentences above. In these cases, there is no difference between these three words in Swahili, and they are translated as 'amba-'.

They will always be referring to something or someone, and so they follow that word in the sentence, and the end of the word 'amba' is changed to produce agreement with the thing(s) it is referring to.

Unusually, in this case we come across irregularities for producing these agreements. With M-Wa words it is much as expected. For the singular, the agreement is '-ye', and for the plural it is '-o'. (Actually, it would be the familiar '-ao', but the two 'a's merge.):

'The man <u>who</u> is smelling bad'	*is*	*'Mwanaume <u>ambaye</u> ananuka'*
'The men <u>who</u> are smelling bad'	*is*	*'Wanaume <u>ambao</u> wananuka'*

However, for M-Mi words it is unexpected: 'ambao' in the singular, and 'ambayo' in the plural:

'The tree <u>which</u> is smelling bad'	*is*	*'Mti <u>ambao</u> unanuka'*
'The trees <u>which</u> are smelling bad'	*is*	*'Miti <u>ambayo</u> inanuka'*

For Ki-Vi words, it is the second-line choice we have already encountered – '-cho' and '-vyo':

'The thing <u>which</u> is smelling bad'	*is*	*'Kitu <u>ambacho</u> kinanuka'*
'The things <u>which</u> are smelling bad'	*is*	*'Vitu <u>ambavyo</u> vinanuka'*

By the way, '-vyo' also creeps into expressions where it does not seem to add much meaning, eg:

'*I went*'	*is*	'*Nilikwenda*'
'*I went*'	*is also*	'*Nilivyokwenda*'

In English we also sometimes have part of a sentence which does not add much, but which sounds better and is more technically correct, – eg 'He went <u>away</u> to sea', says it slightly better than 'He went to sea'.

One important point on the use of question words as explanations is that in formal English, it is correct to say, 'The tree which I burnt', ('Mti ambao niliwasha/nilichoma/niliunguza'); or 'The book which I read', ('Kitabu ambacho nilisoma'); or 'The person whom I met', ('Mtu ambaye nilikutana/nilionana nae'). However, in common speech in English, we often leave out the 'which' or 'whom' word – e.g. 'the book I read'. This is not permissible in Swahili.

The word 'when' can also be an explanation rather than a question, and in this case there are various ways to translate it, according to context, eg 'Wakati' (the time) … '-po-' (when) …:

'*When I went…*'	*is*	'*Wakati nili<u>po</u>kwenda*'

SUMMARY:

'*The man <u>whom</u> I hit*'	*is*	'*Mwanaume <u>ambaye</u> nilimpiga*'
'*The man <u>who</u> is smelling bad*'	*is*	'*Mwanaume <u>ambaye</u> ananuka*'
'*The men <u>who</u> are smelling bad*'	*is*	'*Wanaume <u>ambao</u> wananuka*'
'*The tree <u>which</u> is smelling bad*'	*is*	'*Mti <u>ambao</u> unanuka*'
'*The trees <u>which</u> are smelling bad*'	*is*	'*Miti <u>ambayo</u> inanuka*'
'*The thing <u>which</u> is smelling bad*'	*is*	'*Kitu <u>ambacho</u> kinanuka*'
'*The things <u>which</u> are smelling bad*'	*is*	'*Vitu <u>ambavyo</u> vinanuka*'
'*The things <u>which</u> I burned*'	*is*	'*Vitu <u>ambavyo</u> niliunguza*'

Exercise 34:

Translate:
The pupil whom they beat
The pupil who is beating the plant
The tree which is burning
The trees which are burning
The books which are burning are smelling bad

35.   'With it' – Na + it

Exactly, the same endings as have just been used for 'amba', are used with 'na', when wanting to express 'with it/them'. Because there is no fixed word for 'it' or 'them', the endings which have been chosen to accompany 'na', are:

'With it & with them

M-Wa class:	with me = nami	with us = nasi
M-Wa class:	with you (1) = nawe	with you (>1) = nanyi
M-Wa class:	with him/her = naye	with them = nao
M-MI class:	with it = nao	with them = nayo
Ki-Vi class:	with it = nacho	with them = navyo
Ji-Ma class:	with it = nalo	with them = nayo
N class:	with it = nayo	with them = nazo

As previously mentioned, 'with it' is translated exactly the same as 'and it', so these words also mean 'and it' or 'and them'.

Exercise 35:

Translate:

The man? I have travelled with him

The men? I have travelled with them

The bread? I am traveling with it

The loaves of bread? I am traveling with them

The book? I have travelled with it

The books? I have travelled with them

The water? I travelled with it

The dogs? I travelled with them. ('Dog' is 'Mbwa', an N-class word)

36.   The way things are done – jinsi; kama; kadiri

'How, the way in which'	is	'Jinsi (ya)'
'To know'	is	'Kujua' (or kufahamu / kuelewa)
'They knew how to cook'	is	'Walijua jinsi ya kupika'
'I know the way to clean'	is	'Ninajua jinsi ya kusafisha'

Points to note:

We have just dealt with the use of 'which' as an explanation rather than a question. Another use of 'which' as an explanation rather than a question is the phrase: 'The way in which'. This is translated as 'jinsi', (or more commonly 'jinsi ya'. 'Ya' is a common connecting word, when one thing belongs to or pertains to something else. It is a bit similar to the word 'of' in English, which often denotes possession, but sometimes can be an almost spare word in a sentence – e.g. 'the way of doing things').

In the same way that the word 'which' can be either a question or part of an explanation, so can the word 'how' – e.g. 'to know how to do something'. In this sense, it is translated as 'kama':

'As, like, in the same way that'	is	'Kama'
'A long time ago'	is	'Zamani'
'They do not know ...'	is	'Hawajui...
'...how to cook...'	is	'...jinsi ya kupika...'
'...like they cooked...'	is	'...kama walipika/walivyopika...'
'...a long time ago'	is	'...zamani'.
'I am cooking like you cook'	is	'Ninapika kama unavyopika'

Within the same group of words which explain things is the phrase: 'as much as...', or 'as far as...'. This is translated as 'kadri'. Like 'jinsi and kama, its form is always the same – it does not change any of its letters to produce agreement with any other word:

'I will help...'	is	'Nitasaidia...'
'...as much as I can'	is	'...kadri ninavyoweza'/kadri niwezavyo
'As far as I have gone'	is	'Kadri nilivyokwenda'

Exercise 36:

Translate:
They knew how to cook
They do not know how to cook
I am cooking like they cooked long ago
I will help as much as I can
The dog has gone with me as far as I have gone

37.   N class words

'Rain'	is	'Mvua';
'Shorts'	is	'Kaptula'
'Trousers'	is	'Suruali'
'Soap'	is	'Sabuni'
'Butter'	is	'Siagi'
'Trash'	is	'Takataka'
'Meat'	is	'Nyama'
'Money'	is	'Pesa'
'Clothes'	is	'Nguo/mavazi'
'News'	is	'Habari'
'Fever'	is	'Homa'
'Beer'	is	'Bia'
'Alcohol'	is	'Pombe'
'Bird'	is	'Ndege'
'Aeroplane	is also	'Ndege'

Points to note:

So far, we have only considered M-Wa, M-Mi and Ki-Vi types of word for people or things. However, there are other classes, and this section deals with the 'N class'. In fact, this class has more words in it than any other class, so it might seem strange only to come across it now. Indeed, the names of many relations and animals are in the class. However, it would be a confusing collection of words and agreements if you came across it right at the start, and so is best addressed when already familiar with the normal.

This class includes many of the words for which we do not usually use a separate word for the plural. (See above). Many of them did not originate in Swahili.

Curiously, however, even in many N-class words which clearly have singular and plural forms in English, (e.g. 'animal', 'animals'), there is no separate word for the plural in Swahili. Thus:

'Cat' or 'Cats'	is	'Paka'
'Dog' or 'Dogs'	is	'Mbwa'
'Mother' or 'Mothers'	is	'Mama'
'Father' or 'Fathers'	is	'Baba'
'Journey' or 'Journeys'	is	'Safari'
'Car' or 'Cars'	is	'Motokaa'
'House' or 'Houses'	is	'Nyumba'

Normally, of course, the sense of whether you are talking about just one of these, or more than one, will come from the context.

The agreements, however, are irregular; (as opposed to the agreements of m-, mi-. ki-, vi-, etc, which are normally constant and helpful). In general, the agreement of descriptive words with N-class words is 'n-', (thus the name N-class!); eg 'good' – 'nzuri'

'Good car'	*is*	*'Motokaa nzuri'*

However, if the describing word begins with certain consonants, (those which are softer in their pronunciation – B, V and sometimes P), the agreement is 'm-'. (E.g.:

'Good father'	*is*	*'Baba mzuri/mwema'*
'Bad'	*is*	*'-baya'*
'Bad car'	*is*	*'Motokaa <u>m</u>baya'*
'Bad cars'	*is also*	*'Motokaa <u>m</u>baya'*

Furthermore, if the describing word begins with a vowel, (eg '-eusi' – 'black'), then the agreement is 'ny-', so as to allow a slightly longer 'nnn' sound. (Eg:

'Black car'	*is*	*'Motokaa <u>ny</u>eusi'*

There are also some common exceptions to all of these rules: the commonest are for the word 'good' ('-ema'), as in 'good news', (the agreement is 'nj-'); and the word for 'long', ('-refu') – with an N-class word, this becomes 'ndefu':

'Good news'	*is*	*'Habari njema'*
'Long car'	*is*	*'Motokaa ndefu'*

SUMMARY:
Agreement of descriptions with N-class words:

'Good car'	*is*	*'Motokaa <u>n</u> zuri'*
'Bad car'	*is*	*'Motokaa <u>m</u> baya'*
'Black car'	*is*	*'Motokaa <u>ny</u> eusi'*
'Long car'	*is*	*'Motokaa <u>nd</u> efu'*
'Good news'	*is*	*'Habari <u>nj</u> ema'*

Exercise 37 A:

Translate:
I am going to town in the black car
They went to town in the black cars

I want to travel with the good car
I like the long car
I like long cars
We will travel in the bad car
We will travel in the bad cars

37B: More on N-class words

'The rain has arrived'	*is*	*'Mvua imefika'*
'The plane/flight has arrived'	*is*	*'Ndege imefika'*
'The flights have arrived'	*is*	*'Ndege zimefika'*

Points to note:

Other types of word, (eg this, that, location, possession, etc), will need to agree with the N-class word. It can be seen that in general the agreements for N-class words use 'i-' (or 'y') for singular, and 'z-' or 'zi-' for plurals. The possessive words of mine, yours, his, etc, (-angu; -ako; -ake; -etu; -enu; and -ao), therefore begin with a 'y' for the singular, and a 'z' for the plural.

The words for 'this' and 'these', as for any other class of word, start with the letter 'h'. (Remember 'h' for 'here'.) So 'this' is 'hii', and 'these' is 'hizi'. Similarly, as for other classes of word, the words for 'that' and 'those' end in '-le'. Thus 'that' is 'ile', and 'those' is 'zile'.

'This flight has arrived'	*is*	*'Ndege hii imefika'*
'That flight has arrived'	*is*	*'Ndege ile imefika'*

Annoyingly, sometimes the agreeing words with animals such as 'dog' are not translated as being an N-class word, but an M-Wa word. (see next chapter). So:

'The dog has arrived'	*should be*	*'Mbwa imefika'*
'The dog has arrived'	*but is*	*'Mbwa amefika'*
'The dogs have arrived'	*should be*	*'Mbwa zimefika'*
'The dogs have arrived'	*but is*	*'Mbwa wamefika'*

More of this later.

A special mention needs to be made of counting N-class things. You may remember that the numbers 1 to 10 are:

'One'	is	'-moja'	'Six'	is	'Sita'
'Two'	is	'-wili' or '-mbili'	'Seven'	is	'Saba'
'Three'	is	'-tatu'	'Eight'	is	'-nane'
'Four'	is	'-nne'	'Nine'	is	'Tisa'
'Five'	is	'-tano'	'Ten'	is	'Kumi'

With N-class nouns, there are no agreeing letters at the start of the number, even for those numbers that normally have them, and so counting N-class things is:

'One'	*is*	*'Moja/mosi'*
'Two'	*is*	*'Mbili'*
'Three'	*is*	*'Tatu'*

'Four'	is	'Nne'
'Five'	is	'Tano'
'Six'	is	'Sita'
'Seven'	is	'Saba'
'Eight'	is	'Nane'
'Nine'	is	'Tisa'
'Ten'	is	'Kumi'
'Two cars'	is	'Motokaa mbili'
'Three beers'	is	'Bia tatu'
'Bird'	is	'Ndege'

Please note that when in English we use the 'it' to mean something unspecified, (eg 'it is possible'), the N-class beginning of the action word is used: 'i-'.

'It is possible'	is	'Inawezekana'

SUMMARY:
Agreement with N-class words:

'The rain has arrived'	is	'Mvua imefika'
'The plane /flight has arrived'	is	'Ndege imefika'
'The planes /flights have arrived'	is	'Ndege zimefika'
'This plane has arrived'	is	'Ndege hii imefika'
'These planes have arrived'	is	'Ndege hizi zimefika'
'That plane has arrived'	is	'Ndege ile imefika'
'Those planes have arrived'	is	'Ndege zile zimefika
'Where is the bird / plane /flight?'	is	'Ndege iko wapi?'
'My bird / plane / flight'	is	'Ndege yangu'
'My flights'	is	'Ndege zangu'
'Two flights'	is	'Ndege mbili'
'It is possible'	is	'Inawezekana'

Exercise 37B:
Translate:
It is possible that those planes have arrived
These three planes will soon arrive (or arrive early)
Where are the flights that arrived after me?
Perhaps the rain will arrive soon
My news is good
These three beers are mine

'Grandfather' (also term of great respect) is			*'Babu '*
'Grandmother'		*is*	*'Bibi' or 'Nyanya'*
'Father'		*is*	*'Baba'*
'Mother'		*is*	*'Mama'*
'Father's sister' (aunt)		*is*	*'Shangazi'*
'in-law'		*is*	*'shemeji/ mkwe'*
'Daughter'	*is*		*'Binti' or Mtoto wa kike'*
'Son'	*is*		*'Mwana' or Mtoto wa kiume'*
'Older sister'		*is*	*'Dada'*
'Older brother		*is*	*'Kaka'*
'Sibling'		*is*	*'Ndugu'*
'Friend'		*is*	*'Rafiki'*
'Neighbour'		*is*	*'Jirani'*
'Cousin'		*is*	*'Binamu'*
'Relative'		*is*	*'Jamaa'*

Points to note:

In most Swahili-speaking people, the family is hugely important, and great respect is paid to people older than oneself. The older a person, and the more generations above you, the more you must respect that person, irrespective of what you might believe to be his or her social standing, (and yours!).

It is also normal to use familiar family terms towards people who are not family, and so, for instance, the word 'ndugu', (for 'brother' or 'sister'), might be commonly used to address people of about the same age as oneself. When speaking to a woman old enough to be your mother, it can be deferential to refer to her as 'Mama'. Similarly, you might address a grandfatherly figure as 'Babu'.

All of these words, despite referring to human beings, are 'N' class words. (The only exception is 'mwana', meaning 'son'.) As Class N words, they have no separate plural form – 'jirani' means 'neighbour' or 'neighbours'; 'rafiki' means 'friend' or 'friends'.

However, here is a very important point, already mentioned in relation to dogs: **When dealing with just one thing, the agreements of all living things, even though they might be N-class words, are M-Wa agreements.** This applies even to an N-class animal:

'The daughter is cooking'	*is*	*'Binti anapika'*
'The dog is coming'	*is*	*'Mbwa anakuja'*
'Your dog is coming'	*is*	*'Mbwa wako anakuja'*

As already pointed out, the exception to this use of M-Wa agreements is either in describing words, (eg little, black, long). These are considered to be part of the N-class word, and so take N-class agreements, (e.g. nzuri instead of mzuri, or 'yangu' instead of 'wangu').

'The good daughter is cooking'	*is*	*'Binti mzuri anapika'*
'The good dog is coming'	*is*	*'Mbwa nzuri anakuja'*
'My daughter is cooking'	*is*	*'Binti yangu anapika'*

Note that when making the N-word 'daughter' into the plural 'daughters', the word for 'my' changes, as expected, to the N-word plural – zangu. The action being undertaken, however, continues to be expressed as if done by an M-Wa word:

'My daughter is cooking'	*is*	*'Binti yangu anapika'*
'My daughters are cooking'	*is*	*'Binti zangu wanapika'*
'My woman is cooking'	*is*	*'Mwanamke wangu anapika'*
'My women are cooking'	*is*	*'Wanawake wangu wanapika'*

SUMMARY

The agreements of N-class words to do with family and relations:

'Rafiki nzuri'	is	*'good friend' or 'good friends'*
'Our friend has arrived'	is	*'Rafiki yetu amefika/amewasili'*
'Our friends have arrived'	is	*'Rafiki zetu wamefika'*
'Our flight has arrived'	is	*'Ndege yetu amefika'*
'Our flights have arrived'	is	*'Ndege zetu zimefika'*
'Our nice flights have arrived'	is	*'Ndege zetu nzuri zimefika'*

My/your/his/her/our/their person (just one)	begins with 'y'
My/your/his/her/our/their animal (just one)	begins with 'w'
My/your/his/her/our/their people (>1)	begins with 'z/w'
My/your/his/her/our/their animals (>1)	begins with 'z/w'

Exercise 37C:

Translate:
Your (one person) nice grandfather has good news
Your (one person) nice grandfathers have good news
Your nice journey has good news
Your nice journeys have good news
Perhaps my grandfather will arrive with the dog
It is possible that my grandmother has arrived
These friends will burn the trees
Soon I will travel with those neighbours
My daughter will go to town in her black car

38.   Ji-Ma Class of words

We now have to deal with the remaining classes of word not already covered. We have seen that M-Wa words include most direct names of people, such as mwanamume, (man) and mwalimu, (teacher). The second class of word we dealt with was M-Mi, which were amost all things, such as mti, (tree), and mji, (town).

Ki-Vi words were also almost all words for things, such as kijiji, (village), and vitabu, (books). N-Class words included both things and people, especially family members. This class has unusual rules relating to the plurals.

There are three remaining classes to deal with, (although there are still one or two further grammatical complexities beyond the scope of this book).

The Ji-Ma group of words also mainly comprises things – especialy plants and plant produce – but it also includes some conceptual words, such as many of the well-recognised professions. The typical front-end change is, (self-evidently!) from ji- to ma- when changing from talking of one, to talking of more than one Ji-Ma thing. For instance, the stem for 'eye' is '-cho': one eye is 'jicho', and 'eyes' is 'macho'.

To form the plural, you normally drop the 'ji-', and add 'ma-'.

'Eye'   *is*   **'Jicho'**   **'Eyes'**   *is*   **'Macho'**

However, there are more irregularities in this class than in M-Mi or Ki-Vi. Someimes, for instance, dropping the 'ji' does not happen in the plural:

'Answer' is   **'Jibu'**   **'Answers'** is   **'Majibu'**
'Name'   is   **'Jina'**   **'Names'**   is   **'Majina'**

Another irregularity can be a plural form of 'me-' instead of 'ma-':

'Tooth'   *is*   **'Jino'**   **'Teeth'**   *is*   **'Meno'**

In some cases, the front-end letter code is just 'j-' or 'm-':

'Matter'   *is*   **'Jambo'**   **'Matters'**   *is*   **'Mambo'**

(By the way, you can use this as a one-word question: "Jambo?" – i.e. "What's up?". It is a common informal greeting).

A further irregularity is that for many of the Ji-Ma words, the singular does not even have the 'ji-' as the starting letters! (But when forming sentences, etc, these words still need the Ji-Ma agreements). E.g. 'maduka' is 'shops', but 'shop' is 'duka' not 'jiduka'. 'Mayai' is 'eggs', but 'egg' is 'yai' not 'jiyai'.

'Shop'	is	'Duka'	'Shops'	is	'Maduka'
'Window';	is	'Dirisha'	'Windows'	is	'Madirisha'
'Egg'	is	'Yai'	'Eggs'	is	'Mayai'
'Orange'	is	'Chungwa'	'Oranges'	is	'Machungwa'
'Flower'	is	'Ua'	'Flowers'	is	'Maua'
'Clerk'	is	'Karani'	'Clerks'	is	'Makarani'
'Employer'	is	'Mwajiri'	'Employers'	is	'Waajiri'

Some words are only used in the plural form, and so the only version of the word begins with 'ma-':

'Knowledge'	is	'Maarifa'
'Milk'	is	'Maziwa'
'Water'	is	'Maji'.

(Strangely, you can also do the front-end addition of 'ma-' to some words of other classes, instead of using their normal plural forms, and the resulting word implies a massive version of the thing! E.g. 'nyumba' is an N-class words which means house or houses. 'Majumba', however, means 'massive house/mansions'.)

When using descriptions of Ji-Ma words, the agreements at the front end of the describing word as mainly as you would imagine: 'j-' or ji-' for the singular; 'm-' or 'ma-' for the plural:

'New'	is	'-pya'
'New eye'	is	'Jicho jipya'
'New eyes'	is	'Macho mapya'
'New answer'	is	'Jibu jipya'
'New answers'	is	'Majibu mapya'
'One shop'	is	'Duka moja'
'Two shops'	is	'Maduka mawli'
'Black tooth'	is	'Jino jeusi'
'Black teeth'	is	'Meno meusi'
'Dirty'	is	'-chafu'
'Dirty milk'	is	'Maziwa machafu'
'Dirty water'	is	'Maji machafu'.

Note that the word for black, ('-eusi'), because it starts with a vowel, has the agreements 'j-' and 'm-' (not 'ji' and 'ma'), – exactly comparable to what we have seen in other classes.

For words like 'maziwa' and 'maji', which only exist in the plural form, clearly the agreement will always be 'ma-'.

There is a further exception to these Ji-Ma agreements, however, and that is when the describing word is more than one syllable, and starts with a consonant. In this case, no 'ji-' is used in the singular form. The plural takes 'ma-' as usual. This group – descriptions of more than one syllable, beginning with a consonant – covers a large number of common words. Note the absence of 'ji-' on the describing word in the singular, but the presence of 'ma-' in the plural:

'Big'	*is*	*'-kubwa'*
'Big eye'	*is*	*'Jicho kubwa'*
'Big eyes'	*is*	*'Macho makubwa'*
'Big answer'	*is*	*'Jibu kubwa'*
'Big answers'	*is*	*'Majibu makubwa'*
'Big tooth'	*is*	*'Jino kubwa'*
'Big teeth'	*is*	*'Meno makubwa'*

We now come to yet another, but this time minor, irregularity with Ji-Ma words. You will remember right at the beginning that in Swahili you do not say 'The book is burning', but rather 'The book it-is-burning. 'It-is-burning is 'kinawaka/kinaungua', when 'it' refers to a book, (kitabu). The 'ki-' means 'it'. 'The books are burning' is 'Vitabu vinawaka/vinaungua'. ''Vi-' means 'they'. So the action word begins with a couple of letters forming an agreement or emphasis of who is doing the action. In Ki-Vi words, these agreements are ki and vi, which are very memorable! Unfortunately, with the other classes, the agreements are not always so obvious. With M-Mi words, the starting letters for 'it' and 'they' are 'i' and u'. For N class words they are 'i-' and 'zi-'.

When it comes to actions involving Ji-Ma words, the agreements involving are not 'ji-' and 'ma-', but are instead 'li-' and 'ya-':

'It is burning'	*is*	*'Linawaka/li-/ki-naungua'*
'They are burning'	*is*	*'Yanawaka/yanaungua'*
'It is not burning'	*is*	*'Haliwaki/haliungui'*
'They are not burning'	*is*	*'Hayawaki/hayaungui'*
'The egg? I am burning it'	*is*	*'Yai? Ninaliunguza'*
'The eggs? I am burning them'	*is*	*'Mayai? Ninayaunguza'*

As with M-Wa, Ki-Vi, and other classes of word, the words for 'this'/'that' etc; PKM location words; and 'mine'/'yours', need to agree with the Ji-Ma word. These all use the 'li-' and 'ya-':

'This eye'	*is*	*'Jicho hili'*
'These eyes'	*is*	*'Macho haya'*
'That eye'	*is*	*'Jicho lile/hilo'*
'Those eyes'	*is*	*'Macho yale'*
'Where is the answer'	*is*	*'Jibu liko wapi?'*

'The tooth is in the bag'		is		'Jino limo mfukoni'
'The teeth are in the bag'		is		'Meno yamo mfukoni'
'The tooth is in the kitchen'		is		'Jino liko jikoni
'The teeth are in the kitchen'		is		'Meno yako jikoni'
'My eye'		is		'Jicho langu'
'My eyes'		is		'Macho yangu'.

Singular words for possessing – i.e. you only possess one of the Ji-Ma things:

Mine, yours, his/hers	are	langu, lako, lake
Ours, yours, theirs	are	letu, lenu, lao

Plural words for possessing – ie you possess more than one of the Ji-Ma things:

Mine, yours, his/hers	are	yangu, yako, yake
Ours, yours, theirs	are	yetu, yenu, yao

SUMMARY:
Ji-Ma Class of words:

'Eye'	is	'Jicho'	'Eyes'	is	'Macho'
'Shop'	is	'Duka'	'Shops'	is	'Maduka'

'Water'	is	'Maji'.
'New eye'	is	'Jicho jipya'
'New eyes'	is	'Macho mapya
'Big eye'	is	'Jicho kubwa'
'Big eyes'	is	'Macho makubwa'
'Black eye'	is	'Jicho jeusi'
'Black eyes'	is	'Macho meusi'

'This eye'	is	'Jicho hili'
'These eyes'	is	'Macho haya'
'My eye'	is	'Jicho langu'
'My eyes'	is	'Macho yangu'.

'The egg? I am eating _it_'	is	'Yai? Nina_li_la'
'The eggs? I am eating _them_'	is	'Mayai? Nina_ya_la'

Exercise 38:

Translate:
Perhaps I am burning the eggs
The eggs? They are in the kitchen on the table
Those eyes are big and black

Where is my water?
Their shops will be dirty later
Those new answers are arriving soon

'Goodness'	*is*	*'Uzuri'*
'Badness'	*is*	*'Ubaya'*
'Clean-ness'	*is*	*'Usafi'*
'Dirtiness'	*is*	*'Uchafu'*
'Size'	*is*	*'Ukubwa'*
'Love'	*is*	*'Upendo/mpenzi'*
'Wealth '	*is*	*'Utajiri/mali'*
'Length'	*is*	*'Urefu'*

Points to note:

When you want to turn a word for a description, (eg good, bad), into an actual topic or subject or thing, (eg goodness or badness), you simply add 'u-' to the beginning. It then becomes a U-class word.

Many other conceptual words, (ie words that deal with a concept, rather than with something that can be seen and touched), also come into this category, (eg size, love, wealth, length). It is also the class of word for names of countries, and for some other things which you mainly come across in the singular:

'France'	*is*	*'Ufaransa'*
'Electricity'	*is*	*'Umeme'*
'Sleep'	*is*	*'Usingizi/lala'*
'Porridge'	*is*	*'Uji/ugali'*
'Cooked rice'	*is*	*'Wali'*

NB: Hard/stiff porridge = Ugali

(Note that occasionally, the starting letter is 'w', not 'u'. This hardly alters the pronunciation at all.) By definition, there is no plural form for such words. The agreement in the singular is often 'u', thus the name U-class. For instance, the agreements for 'this' and 'that' are 'u-'.

'This length'	*is*	*'Urefu hu<u>u</u>'*
'This love'	*is*	*'Upendo hu<u>u</u>/mpenzi huyu'*
'That length'	*is*	*'Urefu <u>u</u>le'*
'That love'	*is*	*'Upendo <u>u</u>le'*

This is also the agreement for talking about actions:

'This love has arrived'	*is*	*'Upendo hu<u>u</u> <u>u</u>mefika'*
'That love has arrived'	*is*	*'Upendo <u>u</u>le <u>u</u>mefika'*

'u' is also the word for 'it', when talking about a U-class word:

'This porridge? <u>It</u> has arrived'	*is*	*'Uji/ugali huu? <u>U</u>mefika'*
'That porridge? He has burned <u>it!</u>'	*is*	*'Ugali ule? Ameu̱unguza'*

The words for 'mine', 'your', his/hers/its, our, your, their, could not easily begin with 'u', as the stem is a vowel, and so all begin with 'w': wangu, wako, wake, wetu, wenu, wao:

'My love has arrived'	*is*	*'Upendo wangu umefika'*
'Their love has arrived'	*is*	*'Upendo wao umefika'*
'Their love? It has arrived'	*is*	*'Upendo wao? Umefika'*

The main irregularity with U Class words is that the agreement for describing words is not 'u', but is instead the same as for M-MI words – ie 'm-', (or 'mw-' before a vowel):

'Long length'	*is*	*'Urefu mrefu'*
'Nice love'	*is*	*'Upendo mzuri'*
'Important love'	*is*	*'Upendo mkuu/muhimu'*
'New love'	*is*	*'Upendo mpya'*
'Bad dirtiness'	*is*	*'Uchafu mbaya'*
'Black dirtiness'	*is*	*'Uchafu mweusi'*
'Dirty rice'	*is*	*'Wali mchafu'*
'Little sleep'	*is*	*'Usingizi kidogo'*
'Big sleep'	*is*	*'Usingizi mkubwa'*
'Big size'	*is*	*'Ukubwa mkubwa'*
'Tall size'	*is*	*'Ukubwa mrefu'*

Unfortunately, the U-class is not purely of things which are singular, and does contain some words which have a plural version. In each case, the singular word starts with a 'u', but start of the plural has a number of options – eg no letter; 'ny-'; 'nd-'; or even occasionally 'm-':

'Wind'	*is*	*'Upepo'*	*'Winds'*	*is*	*'Pepo'*
'Wall'	*is*	*'Ukuta'*	*'Walls'*	*is*	*'Kuta'*
'Key'	*is*	*'Ufunguo'*	*'Keys'*	*is*	*'Funguo'*
'Face'	*is*	*'Uso'*	*'Faces'*	*is*	*'Nyuso'*
'Fork'	*is*	*'Uma'*	*'Forks'*	*is*	*'Nyuma'*
'String'	*is*	*'Uzi'*	*'Faces'*	*is*	*'Nyuzi'*
'Tongue'	*is*	*'Ulimi'*	*'Tongues'*	*is*	*'Ndimi'*
'Board'	*is*	*'Ubao'*	*'Boards'*	*is*	*'Mbao'*

The agreement for the singular words is as for all U-class words:

'This wind'	*is*	*'Upepo huu'*
'Big wind'	*is*	*'Upepo mkali'*

'That face'	is	'Uso ule'
'Black face'	is	'Uso mweusi'
'My face'	is	'Uso wangu'

Annoyingly, however, the agreements for the plural versions is as for N-class words, which, you might remember, vary according to the first letter of the rest of the describing word. The agreeing letter is typically 'n', but can be 'ny-' in front of a vowel. It is 'nd-' in the specific case of 'ndefu', meaning 'long'.

'Nice faces'	is	'Nyuso nzuri'
'Black faces'	is	'Nyuso nyeusi'
'Long faces'	is	'Nyuso ndefu'

With some descritions, there is no agreeing letter:

| 'Dirty faces' | is | 'Nyuso chafu' |
| 'Clean faces' | is | 'Nyuso safi' |

When the stem of the description begins with b or v, (or sometimes p), the agreement is not 'n-', but is instead 'm-':

| 'Bad faces' | is | 'Nyuso mbaya' |
| 'Two faces' | is | 'Nyuso mbili' |

The other agreements, for plural U-class words are also as for N-class. They are all based on the letter 'z': 'zi-' for 'they' or 'them'; 'hizi' for 'these'; 'zile' for 'those'; and 'zangu', 'zako', etc for 'mine', yours', etc:

'These faces'	is	'Nyuso hizi'
'Those faces'	is	'Nyuso zile'
'Those boards are burning'	is	'Mbao zile zinawaka/zinaungua'
'Their boards are burning'	is	'Mbao zao zinawaka'
'My boards? They are burning'	is	'Mbao zangu? Zinawaka'
'My boards? He is burning them'	is	'Mbao zangu? Anaziunguza'

There is one final strange case to mention, to do with the words for 'quarrel' and 'disease'. In the singular, they are normal U-class words. However, in the plural, the beginning of the word becomes 'ma-'. The reason for this is that the 'ma-' beginning can be used in any situation where you want to really emphasise the bigness or seriousness, and, conventionally, you always do this with the plural of these words.

'Quarrel'	is	'Ugomvi'
'Disease'	is	'Ugonjwa'
'Quarrels'	is	'Magomvi/mgogoro'
'Diseases'	is	'Magonjwa'

This means also that these words, in the plural, function like Ma-class words, and their agreements are based on 'ma-' and 'ya-':

'Some diseases are coming'	is	'Magonjwa baadhi yanakuja'
'Those diseases are coming'	is	'Magonjwa yale yanakuja'
'These diseases are coming'	is	'Magonjwa haya yanakuja'
'These diseases are not coming'	is	'Magonjwa haya hayaji'
'Dirty diseases are coming'	is	'Magonjwa machafu yanakuja'
'Big diseases are coming'	is	'Magonjwa makubwa yanakuja'
'Black diseases are coming'	is	'Magonjwa meusi yanakuja'
'Their diseases are coming'	is	'Magonjwa yao yanakuja'

SUMMARY:
U Class of words:

'That love has arrived'	is	'Upendo ule umefika'
'Their love? It has arrived'	is	'Upendo wao? Umefika'
'This porridge? It has arrived'	is	'Ugali huu? Umefika'
'That porridge? He has burned it!'	is	'Uji ule? Ameuunguza'
'Nice love'	is	'Upendo mzuri'
'Black dirtiness'	is	'Uchafu mweusi'
'Dirty rice'	is	'Wali mchafu'
'Dirty face'	is	'Uso mchafu'
'Dirty faces'	is	'Nyuso chafu'
Bad faces'	is	'Nyuso mbaya'
'Some diseases are coming'	is	'Magonjwa baadhi yanakuja'
'Those diseases are coming'	is	'Magonjwa yale yanakuja'
'Black diseases are coming'	is	'Magonjwa meusi yanakuja'

Exercise 39:
Translate:
Some diseases arrive with black dirtiness
Those quarrels perhaps will be here later
Your face is very dirty
Their new porridge is in the kitchen
Goodness and love have arrived in the village

40.   Pa Class, plus more on location

'Place' or 'places'	*is*	*'Mahali'*
'A good place'	*is*	*'Mahali pazuri'*
'A bad place'	*is*	*'Mahali pabaya'*
'Some bad places'	*is also*	*'Mahali pabaya'*
		(baadhi ya mahali pabaya)
'The place with trees'	*is*	*'Mahali palipo na miti'*
'The place has trees'	*is also*	*'Mahali pana miti'*
'This place'	*is*	*'Mahali hapa'*
'That place'	*is*	*'Mahali pale'*
'My place with trees'	*is*	*'Mahali pangu palipo na miti'*
		(mahali pangu penye miti)
'Their place with trees'	*is*	*'Mahali pao palipo na miti'*
		(mahali pao penye miti)

The Pa class of words only has one word in it!: Mahali, meaning 'place', or 'places'. As can be seen above, the agreements are regular, being 'pa-'. 'Pa-' also means 'it' when referring to 'mahali':

'My place? It is smelling bad'	*is*	*'Mahali pangu? Pananuka'*
'My place? I like it!'	*is*	*'Mahali pangu? Ninapapenda'*

The 'p' we see in this agreement is the same 'p' we have already come across to describe precise location:

'My place is in the village'	*is*	*'Mahali pangu papo kijijini'*

This is a good point to say a little more about the 'k' (for indefinite location), and the 'M' (within something). The word for a definite place is 'mahali'. However, when referring to an indefinite place, ('that place vaguely over there', 'that general area'), then you do not use 'mahali'. You simply drop the word for the place altogether and just use the describing word and rest of the sentence. So instead of saying 'That good general area is green', you simply say 'that good…is green'.

The idea that you are talking about a general area is given away by the agreement you put on the word 'good'. Whereas 'that good (precise) place' would be 'mahali pazuri', 'That good general area' would be:

'That good (general) area'	*is*	*'… kuzuri kule (eneo lile zuri)*
'That large (general) area'	*is*	*'… kukubwa kule (eneo lile kubwa)*

The 'ku-' agreement to the words 'that', 'good' and 'large' imply that you are talking about an ill-defined place. (The agreement is 'kw-' in some cases, eg in front of a vowel).

'That (ill-defined) large place has trees' is *'... Mahali pale pa<u>ku</u>bwa*
<u>ku</u>na/pana miti' (eneo lile kubwa lina miti)
'My (ill-defined) place has trees' is *'... <u>kw</u>angu <u>ku</u>na miti'*
'His (ill-defined) place is burning' is *'...<u>kw</u>ake <u>ku</u>nawaka/kunaungua'*

Note: Because you completely drop the word for 'place', you therefore need some sort of describing word in such sentences – you cannot just say '<u>the</u> ill-defined place is burning' – it has to be 'mine' or 'large' or some other description. However, when dealing with the PKM location issues, it was mentioned that 'pana' means 'there is/are' in a specific place; 'kuna' means the same but for a general place; 'mna' means 'there is/are inside'. The 'ku' of 'kuna' is enough to say that you are talking of an indefinite place, and so can be the main subject of the sentence:

'There are trees here, (in this ill-defined place)' is *'Kuna miti huku'*
(pana miti hapa)

(Note that 'here' is 'hu<u>ku</u>', to agree with 'ku'). The K or 'ku' agreement therefore may be used in sentences talking of ill-defined location. Similarly, the 'M/N/K' agreement for 'within' can be used in sentences where you do not specify within what:

'Nice (ill-defined) inside' is *'... m-/nzuri ndani/kwa ndani'*
'The nice rice inside is burning is *'(wali) mzuri ndani unaunga'*
'Inside my (village) there is a tree' is *'... mwangu mna mti'*
'Inside my village there is a tree' is *'Kijijini m-/kwangu mna mti'*
'<u>Inside</u> this village there is a tree' is *'Kijiji<u>ni</u> hu<u>mu</u> <u>m</u>na/kuna mti'*
'<u>Inside</u> (this) good (village) it smells' is *'... <u>m</u>zuri <u>m</u>nanuka'*

The '-ni' at the end of 'kijiji' implies that the sentence is about location, and tells you to look out for a P, K or M agreement. Just as with 'kuna', so 'mna' can be used as the subject of a sentence:

'There is bread in the kitchen' is *'Mna mkate jikoni'*

There is another word for 'inside':

'Inside' or *'within'* is *'Katika'*

However, when you use this way of saying 'inside', you do not use 'M' agreements – you use whatever other agreements are in the sentence, e.g.:

'Inside this good village it smells'
is *'Katika <u>kijiji</u> hiki <u>ki</u>zuri, <u>ku</u>nanuka'*

117

Note that if you are not using the PKM system for talking about location, but instead use 'katika', you do not add the '-ni' to the end of the word for the place you are talking about.

SUMMARY:
Pa Class, plus more on location

'Place' or 'places' (specific)	*is*	*'Mahali'*
'A good (specific) place'		*is* *'Mahali pazuri'*
'A bad (specific) place'	*is*	*'Mahali pabaya'*
'The (specific) place with trees'	*is*	*'Mahali palipo na miti'*
'My (specific) place with trees'	*is*	*'Mahali pangu penye miti'*
'My place? I like it!'	*is*	*'Mahali pangu? Ninapapenda'*
'My place is in the village'	*is*	*'Mahali pangu papo kijijini' (kwangu ni kijijini)*

Pa Class, plus more on location (continued)

'That good (general) area'	*is*	*'... kuzuri kule*
'That large (general) area'	*is*	*'... kukubwa kule*
'My (ill-defined) place has trees'	*is*	*'... kwangu kuna miti'*

'The nice rice inside is burning'	*is*	*'... mzuri ndani unaungua' (Wali mzuri ndani unaungua)*
'Inside my (village) there is a tree'	*is*	*'... changu mna mti'*
'Inside (this) good (village) it smells'	*is*	*'... mzuri mnanuka'*
'Inside this good village it smells'	*is*	

'Katika kijiji hiki kizuri kunanuka'

Exercise 40:
Translate:
Some bad places perhaps have goodness
The place with trees is smelling bad
I like my place
That good area is burning and smelling
Inside my village there is a good place

41.   W: Being done to you, rather than doing it

'to hit'	is	'kupiga';	'to <u>be</u> hit'	is	'kupig<u>wa</u>'
'to see'	is	'kuona';	'to <u>be</u> seen'	is	'kuon<u>wa</u>'
'to bring'	is	'kuleta';	'to <u>be</u> brought'	is	'kulet<u>wa</u>'
'to use'	is	'kutumia';	'to <u>be</u> used	is	'kutumi<u>wa</u>'
'to cut	is	'kukata';	'to <u>be</u> cut'	is	'kukat<u>wa</u>'

'I will hit'	is	'Nitapiga'	'I will be hit'	is	'Nitapigwa'
'I will see'	is	'Nitaona'	'I will be seen'	is	'Nitaonwa'
'I will bring'	is	'Nitaleta'	'I will be brought'	is	'Nitaletwa'

'The tree used the water'	is	'Mti ulitumia maji'
'The tree was used'	is	'Mti ulitumiwa'

Points to note:

This section deals with when the sentence describes what has happened <u>to</u> the person or thing involved in the action, (e.g. he was seen), rather than describing what the subject <u>did</u>, (e.g. he saw). To create this sense, the letter 'w' is inserted just before the end of the action word.

When the action word ends in a double vowel, then the 'w' cannot simply be inserted before the last letter, or it will not be heard: If, for instance, the last letters are '-ua', then this would be pronounced the same as '-uwa', so the sense would not come out. In such cases, then instead of just ionserting 'w', you insert '-liw-' or '-lew-':

'to open'	is	'kufungua'
'to <u>be</u> opened'	is	'kufungu<u>liwa</u>'
'to carry'	is	'kuchukua'
'to be carried'	is	'kuchuku<u>liwa</u>'
'to give birth'	is	'kuzaa/kujifungua'
'to be born'	is	'kuza<u>liwa</u>'
'to put out'	is	'kutoa';
'to <u>be</u> put out'	is	'kuto<u>lewa</u>'
'I will carry'	is	'Nitachukua'
'I will be carried'	is	'Nitachukuliwa'

If the action word ends in an 'i' or an 'u', (as do some words of Arabic origin – the normal ending for action words is 'a'), then '-wa' or 'liwa' is added to the end, so as to make the word end in 'wa'.

'To answer'	is	'kujibu'
'to be answered'	is	'kujibi<u>wa</u>'
'To forget'	is	'kusahau'
'to be forgotten'	is	'kusahau<u>liwa</u>'

The same principle applies to very short action words such as 'kula' – to eat. Inserting only a 'w' might interfere with the clarity of meaning, so (e.g.) '-iw-' is inserted:

'To eat'	is	*'kula'*
'to be eaten'	is	*'kuli<u>wa</u>'*

In this section, then, we have dealt with the situation where the action is being done <u>to</u> the subject, rather than <u>by</u> the subject. But someone or something must be doing that action. To form sentences, there needs to be a link to the person or thing who is doing the action to the subject it is being done to. When the action is being done by a human, the connecting word is 'na'. When it is being done by a thing or things, the connecting word is 'kwa':

'The tree was used by the man'	is	**'Mti ulitumiwa na mwanaume'**
'The tree was used by the dog'	is	**'Mti ulitumiwa na mbwa'**
'The tree was cut by the man'	is	**'Mti ulikatwa na mwanaume'**
'The tree was cut by the knife'	is	**'Mti ulikatwa kwa kisu'**
'The tree was cut with a knife'	is	**'Mti ulikatwa kwa kisu' (same)**

It is really important to note that the insertion of 'w' to describe what was done to something or someone, only occurs when the sentence is dealing with the <u>action</u>, (for instance who was doing it – e.g. it was cut by the man; it was used by the dog; etc). As long as the purpose of the sentence is to talk about the action that happened to something or someone, then you still use the 'w' insertion – eg when saying 'it was cut yesterday'; or 'it was used recently'. If, however, you are just describing the <u>state</u> that the thing was in – eg the state it was in was that it was cut; it was used – then you use the letter 'k' – see below!

SUMMARY:
Inserting '-w-': an action ending in '-wa' means passive: eg 'is cut', 'was done', 'will be carried':

'To cut	is	*'Kukata';*
'To <u>be</u> cut'	is	*'kukat<u>wa</u>'*
'I will cut'	is	*'Nitakata'*
'I will <u>be</u> cut'	is	*'Nitakat<u>wa</u>'*
'I will carry'	is	*'Nitachukua'*
'I will <u>be</u> carried'	is	*'Nitachuku<u>liwa</u>'*
'I will answer'	is	*'Nitajibu'*
'I will <u>be</u> answered'	is	*'Nitajib<u>iwa</u>'*
'I will eat'	is	*'Nitakula'*
'I will be eaten'	is	*'Nitaliwa'*

'The tree was cut by the man'	is	'Mti ulikatwa na mwanaume'
'The tree was cut by the knife'	is	'Mti ulikatwa kwa kisu'
'The tree was cut with a knife'	is	'Mti ulikatwa kwa kisu' (same)

Exercise 41

Translate:

Their dogs will be forgotten

They will be answered soon

The man was cut with a knife

The bag will be opened in that place over there

We will be carried to the village

42.   K: more on the passive

If you want to describe the state something is in, without specifying who made it into that state, then instead of an insertion based on the letter 'w', you use one based on the leter 'k':

'to hit'	*is*	*'kupiga';*
'to be hit'	*is*	*'kupigika'*
'to see'	*is*	*'kuona';*
'to be seen'	*is*	*'kuonekana/kuonwa'*
'to bring'	*is*	*'kuleta';*
'to be brought'	*is*	*'kuleteka/kuletwa'*
'to cut	*is*	*'kukata';*
'to be cut'	*is*	*'kukatika/kukatwa'*
'to open'	*is*	*'kufungua'*
'to be opened'	*is*	*'kufunguka/kufunguliwa'*
'to carry'	*is*	*'kuchukua'*
'to be carried'	*is*	*'kuchukulika/kubebwa'*
'to put out'	*is*	*'kutoa/kuweka nje'*
'to be put out'	*is*	*'kutoka/kutolewa'*
'to use'	*is*	*'kutumia'*
'to be used	*is*	*'kutumika'*
'to give birth'	*is*	*'kuzaa'*
'to be born'	*is*	*'kuzalika/kuzaliwa'*
'To answer'	*is*	*'kujibu'*
'to be answered'	*is*	*'kujibika/kujibiwa'*
'to forget'	*is*	*'kusahau'*
'to be forgotten'	*is*	*'kusahaulika/kusahauliwa'*

Note, then, that where there are two vowels at the end of the action word, (eg kutoa), then just a 'k' is inserted to make it 'kutoka'. (The exceptions are words ending in double 'a'. In this case, 'lik' is inserted).

For the remaining words, the insertion is based on 'k', eg 'ik', 'ek', or 'lik'. For the action words of Arabic origin, 'lika' is added to the end.

When forming sentences using these words describing the state of something, you use it with the '-me-' tense. You may remember that the insertion of 'me' talks about the past, using the word 'has /have': 'I have hit' is 'nimepiga'; 'I have seen' is 'nimeona'; etc. In describing the state of something, then, you say, for example:

'I have been (have become) seen'	*is*	*'Nimeonekana'*
'I have been cut'	*is*	*'Nimekuwa nimekatika'*
'The tree? It is (has become) burnt'	*is*	*'Mti? Umewakeka'*
'The book? It is open'	*is*	*'Kitabu? Kimefunguka'*
'The bag? It is put out'	*is*	*'Mfuko? Imetoka'*

To clarify then, there are two sorts of 'something-being-done-to-you' situations: one uses insertions based on 'w', and deals with the action; the other uses insertions based on 'k' and deals with the state resulting from that action.

The sentences above deal with the state resulting from an action – e.g. someone cut me; now I am cut – being cut is the state I am in.

In a slightly confusing extension of these thoughts, these sentences denoting the state something is in, might also imply that the state is a possibility and not yet happened! The meaning will be given by the context, e.g.:

'I have seen'	is	*'Nimeoneka'*
'I can be seen'	is	*'Nimeoneka'*
'I have been seen'	is	*'Nimeonekana'*

When describing the state some things are in, some action words already have the 'k' built in, because they naturally describe a state, eg:

'To smell bad'	is	*'Kunuka'*
'The bag? It smells bad	is	*'Mfuko? Unanuka'*

Finally, it should be noted that some specific words describe a state without using the 'k' insertion. These words will not be derived by turning an active word into a passive one, (He cuts – he was cut). Instead they are just words in their own right, describing certain specific states:

'to be mistaken	is	*'kukosea/kuchanganywa'*
'to be tired'	is	*'kuchoka'*
'to be angry'	is	*'kukasirika'*
'to be lost'	is	*'kupotea'*

SUMMARY:
Describing the state things are in – inserting '-k-'

'to cut	is	'kukata';
'to **be** cut'	is	'kuka<u>t</u>ika/kukatwa'
'to see'	is	'kuona';
'to **be** seen'	is	'kuon<u>e</u>kana/kuonwa'
'I have been seen'	is	'Nimeonekana/nimeonwa'
(i.e. 'I have become seen')		
'I have become /been cut'	is	'nimekuwa/Nimekatwa'
'I am cut'	is also	'Nimekatika/Nimekatwa'
'The tree? It is/has been burnt'	is	'Mti? Umewaka/Umeungua'

'*I can be seen*'	*is*	'*Ninaweza kuonekana*'
The tree? It can be burnt'	*is*	'*Mti? Unaweza kuwaka/kuungua*'

'*to be mistaken*	*is*	'*kukosea*'
'*to be tired*'	*is*	'*kuchoka*'
'*to be angry*'	*is*	'*kukasirika*'
'*to be lost*'	*is*	'*kupotea*'

Exercise 42:

Translate:

The children will be born in the town

The fire in the village is put out now

The tooth can be seen in the bag

We will be tired and angry when we arrive in the village

The dogs are lost in that place

43.   Causing things to happen – '-isha'; '-esha'; and '-za'

'to go'	is	'kuenda/kwenda';
'to _cause to_ go' (i.e. drive)	is	'kuend_esha_'
'to _borrow_'	is	'kukopa';
'to _cause to_ borrow' (i.e. lend)	is	'kukop_esha_'
'to rot'	is	'kuoza';
'to _cause to_ rot'	is	'kuoz_esha_'
'to be tired'	is	'kuchoka';
'to tire'	is	'kuchok_esha_'

Points to note:

Swapping the last letter of a word for '-esha' or '-isha' typically implies that you are now talking about a <u>cause</u> – e.g. the change above from 'kuoza' to 'kuozesha' changes the meaning from 'to rot' into 'to cause to rot'.

Sometimes the change is '-isha', (typically when the word in question does not contain an 'o' or an 'e'):

'to eat'	is	'kula'
'to feed'	is	'kulisha'
'to arrive'	is	'kufika';
'to reach'	is	'kufik_isha_/kufik_ia_'

It can be seen that the use of this ending extends beyond what is strictly a cause, but always deals with an action which <u>leads to</u> doing something or being something. It is not only action words which can be dealt with in this way, but also descriptions, eg:

'ready'	is	'tayari';
'to make ready'	is	'kutayar_isha_'
'right'	is	'sawa';
'to put right'	is	'kusawaz_isha_/kurekeb_isha_'

Swapping the last letter of a word for '-esha' or '-isha' therefore deals with actions that produce a result. There are of course exceptions, and sometimes the ending used is '-za' or '-eza' or '-iza' or -isha:

'to like'	is	'kupenda';
'to please'	is	'kupend_eza_/kufurah_isha_'
'to be loose'	is	'kulegea'
'to loosen'	is	'kulegeza'
'to be lost'	is	'kupotea'
'to lose'	is	'kupoteza'
'to be filled'	is	'kujaa/kujazwa'
'to fill'	is	'kujaza'

'to enter'	is	kuingia'
'to insert'	is	'kuingiza'
'to be clear'	is	kuelewa/kueleweka'
'to explain'	is	'kueleza/kuelezea'

Note that sometimes an extra letter such as an 'l' is inserted to make the word easier on the tongue:

'to hear'	is	'kusikia'
'to listen'	is	'kusikiliza'
'to wear'	is	'kuvaa';
'to put on clothes'	is	'kuvalisha/kuvaa'

SUMMARY
Causing things to happen – '-isha'; '-esha'; and '-za'

'to go'	is	'kuenda/kwenda'
'to cause to go' (i.e. drive)	is	'kuendesha'
'to be tired'	is	'kuchoka';
'to tire'	is	'kuchokesha'

'to eat'	is	'kula'
'to feed'	is	'kulisha'
'to arrive'	is	'kufika';
'to reach'	is	'kufikisha/kufikia'

'to like'	is	'kupenda';
'to please'	is	'kupendeza/kufurahisha'
'to be loose'	is	'kulegea'
'to loosen'	is	'kulegeza'

'to hear'	is	'kusikia'
'to listen'	is	'kusikiliza'
'to wear'	is	'kuvaa';
'to put on clothes'	is	'kuvalisha/kuvaa'

Exercise 43:

Translate:
It is possible that they have driven to the town
I will lend my book to the house with the clean books
They are making ready to travel to his place
They will feed their children well
It will please them to burn the trees at their place

The teachers will explain to the pupils, but the pupils will tire
I will get dressed before I go to their place
She has listened to her grandparents and likes to please them

Please note that, as in English, there is often more than one way to express the meaning. Where there is a commonly used alternative, this is also given, for completeness.

The alternative is not always grammatically pure, but then neither is our use of English always precisely as it should be!

Sometimes you will notice that the letter 'w' creeps in towards the end of the word. This signifies the passive situation, and is dealt with in chapter 41. Sometimes, this makes a better translation, especially when the sentence is less about the action which took place, and more about what happened as a result.

Exercise 1A: 'Na'= Currently happening

The child is visiting the town.
The children are visiting the town.
The children are visiting the towns.

> *Mtoto anazuru/anatembelea mji.*
> *Watoto wanazuru/wanatembelea mji.*
> *Watoto wanazuru/wanatembelea miji.*

Exercise 1B M-Wa

The pupils are baking bread.
The teachers are hiding the bag.

> *Wanafunzi wanaoka mkate.*
> *Walimu wanaficha mfuko.*

Exercise 1C More on M-Wa

You (plural) are beating the men.
We are currently arriving.
The women are currently cooking

> *Mnapiga wanaume.*
> *Tunafika/tunawasili.*
> *Wanawake wanapika.*

Exercise 2 M-Mi

The bread is arriving
The smoke is sufficient
The mango trees are smelling (bad)
The hands are touching

Mkate unafika.
Moshi unatosha.
Miembe inanuka
Mikono inagusa/inapapasa.

Exercise 3 Ki-Vi and Ch-Vy

The toilet is coming
The books are growing
The things are arriving
The book is burning

Choo kinakuja.
Vitabu vinakua.
Vitu vinafika.
Kitabu kinawaka/kinaungua.

Exercise 4 Na & possession

The village has mango trees and crops
Men and women have hands and are beating
The teacher and pupils have food and are hiding.

Kijiji kina miembe na mimea/mazao.
Wanaume na wanawake wana mikono na wanapiga.
Mwalimu na wanafunzi wana chakula na wanaficha.

Exercise 5 Ni = am /are. Si = am not /are not

The books and beds are good.
The toilets and villages are good.
We are good.
You are good. (one person)
The book is not good
The book is with me
The trees are with them
The trees are not with them

Vitabu na vitanda ni vizuri.
Vyoo na vijiji ni vizuri.
Sisi ni wazuri/wema.
Wewe ni mzuri/mwema.
Kitabu si kizuri.
Nina Kitabu /kitabu ninacho mimi.
Wana miti/Miti wanayo wao.

Exercise 6 Si & Ha: Negatives

The pupils are not eating the plants
The villages are not feeding the teachers
The teachers and the pupils have no books
The villages have no toilets and no mango trees.

Wanafunzi hawali mimea.
Vijiji havilishi/haviwalishi walimu.
Walimu na wanafunzi hawana vitabu.
Vijiji havina vyoo na miembe.

Exercise 7 Ndiyo & Siyo

Are the pupils growing? – Yes!
Are the pupils growing? – No!
Are the teachers eating? – Yes!
Are the teachers not eating? –They are not!
Is the tree burning? Yes, that is so.
Is the tree not burning? Yes, that is so.

Wanafunzi wanakua? Ndiyo! /ndivyo
Wanafunzi wanakua? Siyo!/sivyo
Walimu wanakula? – Ndiyo! /ndivyo
Walimu hawali? Ndiyo! /ndivyo
Mti unawaka/unaungua? Ndiyo! /ndivyo
Mti hauwaki? Ndiyo!/ndivyo

Exercise 8 PKM: location

He is located somewhere …
They are located somewhere …
He is (precisely) located …
I am (precisely) located …
The books are not approximately located …
The books are not within…
Where are the children?
The children are within…

(Yeye) yuko …
(Wao) wako …
(Yeye) yupo …
(Mimi) nipo ….

Vitabu haviko …
Vitabu havimo…
Watoto wako wapi?
Watoto wamo…

Exercise 9 Ni: in or near to

Where is the book? It is on the table
Where are the children? They are at the town
Where are the teachers? They are in the river

Kitabu kiko wapi? Kiko mezani.
Watoto wako wapi? Wapo mjini.
Walimu wako wapi? Wamo mtoni.

Exercise 10 Here = Hapa or Huku. There = Pale or Kule.

The teachers do not have bread here.
The bread is there in the house (somewhere).
Where are the books? They are right here.
The river there has no water.
The books are over there in the river.
The students are not here.

Walimu hawana mkate hapa.
Mkate uko (kule) nyumbani.
Vitabu viko wapi? Vipo hapa.
Mto ule pale hauna maji.
Vitabu viko kule mtoni. (or 'Vitabu vimo mle mtoni')
Wanafunzi hawapo hapa. (or 'hawako hapa')

Exercise 11: There is /There are = Pana, kuna, mna

There are mango trees right here in the village
There are teachers over there in the river somewhere
There are some books on the table.
Some books are somewhere in the kitchen.
There is water over there somewhere.

131

Pana miembe hapa kijijini.
Kuna walimu kule mtoni.
Pana vitabu mezani. (or 'Baadhi ya vitabu viko mezani')
Vitabu viko jikoni. (or 'Baadhi ya vitabu viko jikoni')
Kuna maji kule. (or 'kuna maji fulani hapa')

Exercise 12: h-: this/these; -le: that/those

Where is that child?
Where are those children?
Those books are in the river.
These books are right there on the table in the kitchen.
That is not so! They are in the bag.

Mtoto yule yuko wapi?
Watoto wale wako wapi?
Vitabu vile vimo/viko mtoni.
Vitabu hivi vipo pale mezani jikoni.
Siyo! Vimo/viko mfukoni.

Exercise 13: More on location

Where is that man? He is in front of the river.
Where are the women? They are among the trees.
That book is beside the bed.
Those toilets are hereabouts. They are within the village.
That is so! They are behind us.
The bread is hereabouts. That is so! It is under the bed.

Mwanaume yule yuko wapi? Yupo mbele ya mto.
Wanawake wako wapi? Wako kati ya miti.
Kitabu kile kipo/kiko kando ya kitanda.
Vyoo vile viko huku. Vimo/viko kijijini.
Ndiyo! Vipo nyuma yetu.
Mkate uko huku. Ndiyo! Upo chini ya kitanda.

Exercise 14: Other directions

I am cooking near the river
We are travelling to the left as far as the town
We are going far from the river
They are travelling straight on by the river
He is going in there

He is travelling to the right towards the village

Ninapika karibu na (kando ya) mto.
Tunasafiiri kuelekea upande wa kushoto mpaka mjini.
Tunakwenda mbali na mto.
Wanasafiri moja kwa moja mtoni.
(or 'Wanasafiri moja kwa moja kupitia mtoni.)
Anakwenda mle/humo.
Anasafiri upande wa kulia kuelekea kijijini.

Exercise 15: More on possession

Where are my books? They are beside you.
The student's bread is under the bed
Where is your village? Mine is over there somewhere.
Those trees just there are theirs.
I am cooking my food
The teacher's plants are beside the river.
Your pupils are here somewhere

Vitabu vyangu viko wapi? Vipo kando/pembeni yako.
Mkate wa mwanafunzi upo chini ya kitanda.
Kijiji chako/chenu kiko wapi? Kijiji change/chetu kiko kule.
Miti ile pale ni yao.
Ninapika chakula changu.
Mimea ya walimu iko kando ya mto.
Wanafunzi wako wako huku (or 'Wanafunzi wako mahali fulani huku').

Exercise 16: Agreement of descriptions

Some dangerous black foods are under the bed
I am cooking some very black bread
The very big child is in the kitchen
The bad old toilet is in the village
The best child has my book
My clean child is ready
The big woman is cold but the child is hot. ('But' is 'lakini')

Baadhi ya vyakula hatari vyeusi vipo chini ya kitanda.
Ninapika mkate mweusi sana.
Mtoto yule mkubwa sana yupo jikoni.
Choo kibaya na kikuukuu kipo kijijini.
Mtoto bora ana kitabu changu.
Mtoto wangu msafi yuko tayari.
Mwanamke mkubwa ni wa baridi lakini mtoto mdogo ni wa moto.
('mdogo' means 'little', or 'little one')

Exercise 17: Greetings

From a child to an adult polite greeting:
Response from the adult to a child
Greet the child's parent as he arrives
Ask if he is well
Ask about his family and home
Say 'Thanks. Safe journey. Goodbye'

Shikamoo!
Marahaba!
(e.g.) Hujambo! Or Habari za asubuhi, bwana!
U hali gani? Or U mzima/hujambo/mambo?
Habari ya nyumbani?
Asante. Safiri salama. Kwaheri!

Exercise 18: -li- : The completed past;   -me- : 'have' + the past

I have eaten the black bread
I ate the black bread
That very big man went
This very clean book succeeded
That big tree has started
Those crops did grow over there somewhere
Hi! How are you? Have you already succeeded?

Nimekula mkate mweusi.
Nilikula mkate mweusi.
Mwanaume yule mkubwa sana alikwenda.
Kitabu kisafi sana hiki kilifaulu /kilifanikiwa.
Mti ule mkubwa umeanza.
Mimea ile imekua kule.
Jambo! Mzima? Tayari umefaulu /umefanikiwa?

Exercise 19: -ku- & -ja- : The negatives of the past

Translate:
Those plants did not arrive
He has not come yet – he is somewhere in the village
He did not talk and they did not succeed
The big child has not yet eaten
The very clean toilets over there somewhere did not shut
The men did not eat in the village
The trees have not yet succeeded in the town

Mimea ile haikufika.
Hajaja bado (or hajafika or hajawasili) – yuko kijijini.
Hakuongea na (wao) hawakufanikiwa.
Mtoto mkubwa bado hajala.
Vyoo visafi sana kule havikufungwa
Wanaume hawakula kijijini.
Miti haijafanikiwa/haijastawi mjini.

Exercise 20: -ta- : The future

The very big children will not eat in the town
The big black tree just there will not burn
These teachers will eat these plants
Those pupils are in the town somewhere. They will come.
My big clean bag will open in the kitchen.
Good morning! I will come to the town early ('early' or 'soon' = 'mapema')
The men? They will not speak. They have already spoken

Watoto wakubwa sana hawatakula mjini.
Mti mkubwa mweusi pale hautawaka/hautaungua.
Walimu watakula mimea hii.
Wanafunzi wale wako mjini. Watakuja. (or watafika).
Mfuko wangu msafi mkubwa utafunguka jikoni.
Habari za asubuhi! Nitakuja mjini mapema.
Wanaume? Hawataongea. Tayari wameongea.

Exercise 21A: Commands and requests

Translate (to one person and to two):
Do not burn the plant! Cook it!
Come! We are going to the village over there.
Speak! We will listen. ('listen' is 'kusikiliza')
Might you go with me and my child?

Would you cook this plant?
(Could you (pl) cook this plant?)
<u>Please</u> can you come to the village?
Would you kindly burn that plant?
Would you not go to the village?

Usiunguze mmea! Upike!
(Msiunguze mmea! Upikeni!)
Njoo! (or Kuja!) Tutakwenda kijijni pale.
(Njooni! Tutakwenda kijijini pale).
Ongea! Tutasikiliza.
(Ongeani! Tutasikiliza.)
Uende nami na mtoto wangu (or unaweza kwenda nami na mtoto wangu)
(Mwende nami na mtoto wangu)
Ungepika mmea huu?
(Mnaweza kupika mmea huu?)
Tafadhali unaweza kuja kijijini?
(Tafadhali mnaweza kuja kijijini?)
Unaweza kuungua mmea ule?
(Mnaweza kuungua mmea ule?)
Unaweza usiende kijijini?
(Mnaweza msiende kijijini?)

Exercise 21B: Hopes and aspirations

I am going so that he might succeed
Might you eat this bread so that I won't cook?
It's best that you eat this food now ('Now' is 'sasa')
They will be succeeding in order that you (more than one) might eat
They succeeded in order that you (one person) might eat
We have not yet gone so that we can cook
The trees over there will not burn now – it is best that they do not burn

Nitakwenda ili afanikiwe.
Unaweza kula mkate huu ili nisipike.
Bora ule chakula hiki sasa.
Watafanikiwa ili mle.
Walifanikiwa ili ule.
Hatujaenda ili tupike.
Miti ile haijaungua sasa …
… bora isiwake/isiungue.

Exercise 22: -ki- : If

Those big black trees? We saw them burning
If I come to the village, I might cook the food
Those little children will come to the town if we give them food (To give to = kupatia…)
Come here! (to one). If you come, I will give you some books
The toilets over there by the river are opening
Those big dirty toilets in the town are closing
If the tree burns, I will go over there
If I cook the food, will the teachers eat it?
If I cook the foods, will the teachers eat them?

Miti ile mikubwa myeusi ile? Tuliiona ikiwaka.
Nikija kijijini, nitapika chakula.
Wale watoto wadogo watakuja mjini, kama tukiwapatia chakula.
Njoo hapa! Ukija, nitakupatia baadhi ya vitabu.
Vyoo kule mtoni vinafungua/vinafunguka.
Vile vyoo vikubwa vichafu mjini vinafunga.
Mti ukiungua, nitaenda kule.
Nikipika chakula, walimu watakila?
Nikipika vyakula, walimu watavila?

Exercise 23: To me, to you, to it, to them

The plants? I will cook them soon
The children will come soon. I will give them food
The teachers have not yet taught the pupils. They might teach them soon
The dirty bags are not ready. I will come with them
Those dirty (trash) bags? I have them
My dirty bags? I will burn them soon
Those books are clean now. I will see them in the village
His teacher is very good. He will give him a plant

Mimea? Nitaipika hivi karibuni.
Watoto watakuja mapema. Nitawapa chakula.
Walimu hawajafundisha wanafunzi. Watawafundisha hivi karibuni.
Mifuko michafu haiko tayari. Nitakuja nayo.
Ile mifuko michafu? Mimi ninayo.
Mifuko yangu michafu? Nitaiunguza mapema.
Vitabu vile ni visafi sasa. Nitaviona kijijini.
Mwalimu wake ni mzuri sana. Atampatia mmea.

Exercise 24: Vi- Ki- and kwa: Describing an action

I have travelled for a purpose
I was travelling on purpose
The village was burning badly
He was speaking truthfully
Luckily, I was in the river
They cooked the food quite nicely ('vizuri kabisa')
I am travelling briefly towards (kuelekea) the village
We were travelling gently to the right
We especially wanted to travel soon ´

Nimesafiri kwa kusudi
Nilikuwa nasafiri kwa kusudi.
Kijiji kilikuwa kinawaka vibaya.
Alikuwa anasema ukweli.
Kwa bahati nzuri, nilikuwa mtoni.
Walipika chakula vizuri kabisa.
Ninasafiri kwa kifupi kwenda kijijini
Tulisafiri pole pole kuelekea kulia.
Tulipenda hasa kusafiri mapema/hivi karibuni.

Exercise 25: Expressions of time

Now	Early	Later	Not quite yet	Afterwards	Before
Then	Since	Until	Always	Nearly	Usually
Already	Suddenly	Quickly	Slowly	Possibly	
Day	Today	Tomorrow	Yesterday	Morning	Afternoon
Night	Tonight	Last night	Long ago		

Sasa	*Mapema*	*Baadaye*	*Bado*	*Halafu*	*Kabla*
Kisha	*Tangu*	*Mpaka*	*Sikuzote*	*Karibia*	*Kwa*
kawaida	*Tayari Ghafula*	*Kwa haraka*	*Polepole*	*Yawezekana*	
Siku	*Leo*	*Kesho*	*Jana*	*Asubuhi*	*Alasiri*
Usiku	*Usiku wa leo*	*Jana usiku*	*Zamani*		

Exercise 26: Numbers and clocks

Count 1 – 12 for men; trees; books; answers
1, 2, 3 & 4 both am and pm
6th, 7th, 8th and 9th man; tree; book; answer

Mmoja; Wawili; Watatu; Wanne; Watano; Sita; Saba; Wanane; Tisa; Kumi; Kumi na mmoja; Kumi na wawili.

Mmoja; Miwili; Mitatu; Minne; Mitano; Sita; Saba; Minane; Tisa; Kumi; Kumi na mmoja; Kumi na miwili.

Kimoja; Viwili; Vitatu; Vinne; Vitano; Sita; Saba; Vinane; Tisa; Kumi; Kumi na kimoja; Kumi na viwili.

Moja; Mbili; Tatu; Nne; Tano; Sita; Saba; Nane; Tisa; Kumi; Kumi na Moja; Kumi na mbili.

Saa saba ya mchana; Saa nane ya mchana; Saa tisa ya mchana; saa kumi ya mchana

Saa saba ya usiku; Saa nane ya usiku; Saa tisa ya usiku; saa kumi ya usiku

wa sita; wa saba; wa nane; wa tisa;
wa sita; wa saba; waa nane; wa tisa;
cha sita; cha saba; cha nane; cha tisa;
la sita; la saba; la nane; la tisa;

Exercise 27: Quantities

How many trees?	How many men?
A few trees	A few men
Many trees	Many men
Plenty of books	Plenty of men
Each book	Each tree

Miti mingapi?   *Wanaume wangapi?*
Miti michache   *Wanaume wachache.*
Miti mingi   *Wanaume wengi*
Vitabu vingi   *Wanaume wengi*
Kila kitabu   *Kila mti.*

Exercise 28: -ote and -o –ote: All and any

All of us	All of you	All of them (people)
The whole book is mine	All books are mine	
Any of the book	Any of the books	

Sisi sote   *Ninyi nyote*   *Wao wote*
Kitabu chote ni changu   *Vitabu vyote ni vyangu*
Kitabu chochote   *Vitabu vyovyote*

Exercise 29: -i- -li- etc: Actions to, at or for

They are going to town to bring food
They are going to town to bring me food
They are coming to town to answer
They are coming to town to answer me
You (plural) are returning to town for bread

Wanakwenda mjini kuleta chakula.
Wanakwenda mjini kuniletea chakula.
Wanakuja mjini kujibu.
Wanakuja mjini kunijibu.
Mnarudia mkate mjini.

.

Exercise 30: -na : Reciprocal actions

They are going to the river to wash one another
We are going to the town to see one another
We went to the village to answer one another

Wanakwenda mtoni kuoshana.
Tunakwenda mjini kuonana.
Tulikwenda kijijini kujibizana.

Exercise 31: -ji- : Action to one's self

We will teach ourselves this book
They were beating themselves with a stone ('stone' is 'jiwe' – a Ji-Ma word)
We will see ourselves within this book

Tutajifunza wenyewe kitabu hiki/tutajifundisha kitabu hiki.
Walijipiga wenyewe kwa jiwe.
Tutajiona wenyewe ndani ya kitabu hiki.

Exercise 32: Connecting words

Perhaps they will travel together
Therefore, you will cook instead of me
The trees will burn equally
After he arrived, he told us about the plants
Perhaps they will come also
Thus, he will want to go

Labda wata safiri pamoja.
Kwa hiyo utapika badala yangu.
Miti itawaka/itaungua sawasawa.
Baada ya kufika, alitueleza juu ya mimea.

Labda watakuja pia.
Kwa hiyo atataka kwenda.

Exercise 33: Questions

Who will burn the tree? (use 'kuunguza' for 'to burn')
Why will they burn the tree?
When will they burn the tree?
Which man will burn the tree?
What did you burn?
The tree? How did you burn it?

Nani ataunguza mti?
Kwa nini wataunguza mti?
Lini wataunguza mti?
Mwanaume yupi ataunguza mti?
Uliunguza nini?
Mti? Uliuunguzaje?

Exercise 34: -amba- : Who and which as explanations

The pupil whom they beat
The pupil who is beating the plant
The tree which is burning
The trees which are burning
The books which are burning are smelling bad

Mwanafunzi ambaye walimpiga.
Mwanafunza ambaye anapiga mmea.
Mti ambao unawaka.
Miti ambayo inawaka.
Vitabu ambavyo vinawaka na vinanuka.

Exercise 35: Nayo etc: With it/them

The man? I have travelled with him
The men? I have travelled with them
The bread? I am traveling with it
The loaves of bread? I am traveling with them
The book? I have travelled with it
The books? I will travel with them
The water? I travelled with it
The dogs? I travelled with them. ('Dog' is 'Mbwa', an N-class word)

Mwanaume? Nimesafiri naye.
Wanaume? Nimesafiri nao.
Mkate? Ninasafiri nao.
Mikate? Ninasafiri nayo.
Kitabu? Nilisafiri nacho.
Vitabu? Nitasafiri navyo.
Maji? Nilisafiri nayo.
Mbwa? Nilisafiri nao.

Exercise 36: Jinsi Kama Kadiri: The way things are done

They knew how to cook
They do not know how to cook
I am cooking like they cooked long ago
I will help as much as I can
The dog has gone with me as far as I have gone

Walijua jinsi ya kupika.
Hawajui jinsi ya kupika.
Ninapika kama walivyopika zamani.
Nitasaidia kwa kadri ninavyoweza.
Mbwa amekwenda nami kadri nilivyokwenda

Exercise 37A: N-class words

I am going to town in the black car
They went to town in the black cars
I want to travel with the good car
I like the long car
I like long cars
We will travel in the bad car
We will travel in the bad cars

Ninakwenda mjini ndani ya gari nyeusi.
Walikwenda mjini ndani ya gari nyeusi.
Ninataka kusafiri na gari nzuri.
Ninapenda gari ndefu.
Ninapenda gari ndefu.
Tutasafiri ndani ya gari mbaya.
Tutasafiri katika gari mbaya.

Exercise 37B: More on N-class words

It is possible that those planes have arrived
These three planes will soon arrive (or arrive early)
Where are the flights that arrived after me?
Perhaps the rain will arrive soon
My news is good
These three beers are mine

Inawezekana kuwa ndege zile zimefika.
Ndege hizi tatu zitafika mapema.
Ziko wapi ndege ambao zilifika baada yangu?
Labda mvua itanyesha hivi karibuni.
Habari yangu ni njema.
Bia hizi tatu ni zangu.

Exercise 37C: The family

Your (one person) nice grandfather has good news
Perhaps my grandfather will arrive with the dog
Your (one person) nice grandfathers have good news
It is possible that my grandmother has arrived
Your nice journey has good news
These friends will burn the trees
Your nice journeys have good news
Soon I will travel with those neighbours
My daughter will go to town in her black car

Babu yako mzuri ana habari njema.
Inawezekana babu yangu atafika/atakuja na mbwa.
Babu zako wazuri wana habari njema.
Inawezekana bibi yangu amefika.
Safari yako nzuri ina habari njema.
Rafiki hawa wataunguza miti.
Safari zako nzuri zina habari njema.
Hivi karibuni nitasafiri na jirani wale.
Binti yangu atakwenda mjini katika gari yake nyeusi.

Exercise: 38 Ji-Ma class

Perhaps I am burning the eggs
The eggs? They are in the kitchen on the table
Those eyes are big and black
Where is my water?
Their shops will be dirty later
Those new answers are arriving soon

Labda ninaunguza mayai.
Mayai? Yapo jikoni mezani.
Macho yale ni makubwa na meusi.
Maji yangu yako wapi?
Maduka yao yatakuwa machafu badaaye.
Yale majibu mapya yatafika hivi karibuni.

Exercise 39: U-class

Some diseases arrive with black dirtiness
Those quarrels perhaps will be here later
Your face is very dirty
Their new porridge is in the kitchen
Goodness and love have arrived in the village

Magonjwa mengine hufika/huja na uchafu mweusi.
Labda magomvi yale yatafika badaaye.
Uso wako ni mchafu sana.
Uji wao mpya upo jikoni.
Uzuri na upendo zimefika kijijini.

Exercise 40: Mahali; Pa class; Location

Some bad places perhaps have goodness
The place with trees is smelling bad
I like my place
That good area is burning and smelling
Inside my village there is a good place

Labda mahali pabaya pana uzuri.
Mahali palipo na miti pananuka.
Ninapenda mahali pangu.
Lile eneo zuri linawaka na kunuka.
Ndani ya kijiji changu mna mahali pazuri.

Exercise 41: -w- : It being done to you

Their dogs will be forgotten
They will be answered soon
The man was cut with a knife
The bag will be opened in that place over there
We will be carried to the village

Mbwa wao watasahauliwa.
Watajibiwa hivi karibuni.
Mwanaume alikatwa kwa kisu.
Mfuko utafunguliwa mahali pale/mfuko utafunguliwa kule.
Tutachukuliwa mpaka kijijini.

Exercise 42: -k- : The state things are in

The children will be born in the town
The fire in the village is put out now
The tooth can be seen in the bag
We will be tired and angry when we arrive in the village
The dogs are lost in that place

Watoto watazalika mjini.
Moto kijijini umetoka sasa.
Jino limeokeka limo mfukoni.
Tutakuwa tumechoka na kukasirika tutakapofika kijijini.
Mbwa wanapotea katika mahali pale.

Exercise 43: –isha –esha –za : Causing things to happen

It is possible that they have driven to the town
I will lend my book to the house with the clean books
They are making ready to travel to his place
They will feed their children well
It will please them to burn the trees at their place
She has listened to her grandparents and likes to please them

Inawezekana kuwa wameendesha kuelekea mjini.
Nitakopesha kitabu changu kwa nyumba yenye vitabu safi.
Wanajitayarisha kusafiri kuelekea kwake.
Watawalisha watoto wao vizuri.
Itawapendeza kuunguuza miti mahali pao.
Amewasikiliza babu na bibi zake na anapenda kuwafurahisha.

Section 2

This section is a concise revision of the first section, using the same paragraph numbering. It now contains the grammatical detail for those who like the technical terms. It repeats the rules briefly, but without painstaking explanation where this has already been covered in the first section. It sometimes adds more technical detail or deals with the topic more deeply.

It is constructed for those who feel that they now have a working understanding of the first section. It is important in this section both to listen and to read. The purpose is to allow the language simply to sink in, without too much effort. Listen often to the recording of the sentences written in bold, and their translation. (These are re-written in list form at the end of the Section.) Just by listening on your device in spare moments, then reading the text when you feel the need, the language (but not yet all the vocabulary), will arrive in your head without forcing it. This written + spoken section is the secret weapon of this course: the visual and listening materials go together to allow the grammar to sink in painlessly. The place where most language learning crashes is the brain-curdling confusion which happens when you get past being a raw beginner, trying to learn an entire language from books. This section of the course will get you through this.

Listening repeatedly, plus re-checking the book when you do not understand, will in a surprisingly short time, allow you readily to translate all the sentences in this section. Once you can do that – and know why they translate as they do – then you will have a fully functional grasp of the way the Swahili language works. These sentences have been carefully selected and crafted, and between them cover all the grammar you need to know for a good working knowledge of Swahili.

To begin, cover up answers, and try to transate the words and phrases at the beginning of each chapter. Then check if you are right or wrong, and why. Then listen to the same exercise. Listen to the recordings over and over again, both to test yourself, and to painlessly drive the learning into your long-term memory. (That's how children learn to speak a language fluently, even though they are not as clever as you are now!) When you do not understand, or when you want to revise, re-read the section.

Using a dictionary for the vocabulary is fine – this is about understanding how the language works, which is more than just remembering words.

1. '-na-' Present continuous. M-Wa nouns

'The child is currently visiting the town'	*is*	*'Mtoto anazuru mji'*
'The children are visiting the town'	*is*	*'Watoto wanazuru mji'*
'The children are visiting the towns'	*is*	*'Watoto wanazuru miji'*
'The teacher is cooking bread'	*is*	*'Mwalimu anaoka mkate'*
'The teachers are cooking bread'	*is*	*'Walimu wanaoka mkate'*
'The pupil is hiding the bag'	*is*	*'Mwanafunzi anaficha mfuko'*
'The pupils are hiding the bag'	*is*	*'Wanafunzi wanaficha mfuko'*
'The pupils are hiding the bags'	*is*	*'Wanafunzi wanaficha mifuko'*
'The man is arriving'	*is*	*'Mwanaume anafika'*
'The women are arriving''	*is*	*'Wanawake wanafika'*
'I am currently coming'	*is*	*'(Ni)nakuja'*

(When the meaning is obvious, the 'ni' part if often omitted in the spoken language)

'You are currently coming' (one person)	*is*	*'Unakuja'*
'S/he is currently coming'	*is*	*'Anakuja'*
'We are currently coming'	*is*	*'Tunakuja'*
'You are currently coming' (>1 person)	*is*	*'Mnakuja'*
'They are currently coming'	*is*	*'Wanakuja'*

Grammatical notes:

'To arrive' is 'kufika'. Such 'infinitive' forms of verbs almost always begin with 'ku-', which is normally dropped when specifying who is doing the action – e.g. 'The child is arriving' is Mtoto anafika'.

The 'ku' is not dropped with very short verbs like 'kuja' – 'to come'. (i.e. verbs which without the 'ku-' would be monosyllabic.)

'A-na-fika' means 'S/he-is currently-arriving'.
In Swahili, then, you say 'The child she is currently arriving'. In technical terms, the verb begins with a pronoun, even though it is already clear who is doing the action.
The pronouns in the M-Wa class are:
I = Ni; You= U; S/he = A; We = Tu; You (plural) = M; They = Wa.

'Child' is 'Mtoto'. 'Children' is 'Watoto'. This front-end change when moving from singular to plural is typical of an M-Wa noun. The M-Wa class of nouns deals mainly with people.

2. M-Mi nouns

'The bread is burning' (i.e. aflame) is		'Mkate unawaka/unaungua'
'The bag is sufficient'	is	'Mfoko unatosha'
'The smoke is smelling'	is	'Moshi unanuka'
'The body is smelling'	is	'Mwilii unanuka'
'The bodies are smelling'	is	'Miili inanuka'
'The hands are touching'	is	'Mikono inagusa'
'The plants are arriving'	is	'Mimea yanafika'
'The trees are burning'	is	'Miti inawaka'
'The mango trees are burning'	is	'Miembe inawaka'
'The tree? It is burning'	is	'Mti? Unawaka'
'The trees? They are burning'	is	'Miti? Inawaka'

Grammatical notes:

'Tree' is 'Mti', and 'Trees' is 'Miti'. This front-end change is typical of M-Mi Class nouns.

This class of noun does not include people, and so has no need of the pronouns I, you, or we.

Nevertheless, as for M-Wa nouns, every verb used next to an M-Mi word must begin with a pronoun, which would be either 'u-' ('it'), or 'i-', ('they') – even when the subject is already clearly stated. This is a common tendency in Swahili – to reinforce the meaning in several ways within the same sentence.

By the way, note that the pronoun 'u' means 'you' (singular) in M-Wa words, but means 'it' in M-Mi words. Therefore 'Unakuja' when applying to an M-Wa word means 'you are coming'. When applied to an M-Mi word, it means 'it is coming'.

3. Ki-Vi and Ch-Vy nouns

'The things are touching'	is	'Vitu vinagusa'
'The food is growing	is	'Chakula kinaongeza'
'The village is growing	is	'Kijiji kinaongeza'
'The man is bringing beds'	is	'Mwanaume analeta vitanda'
'The beds are arriving'	is	'Vitanda vinafika'
'The toilet is smelling'	is	'Choo kinanuka'
'The toilets are smelling'	is	'Vyoo vinanuka'
'The villages are burning'	is	'Vijiji vinawaka/vinaungua'

Grammatical notes:

'Book' is 'Kitabu' and 'Books' is 'Vitabu'. This front-end change is typical of Ki-Vi Class nouns.

Like the M-Mi class of words, the Ki-Vi class comprises only names of things, never of types of people.

The words for the pronouns are 'ki' (it) and 'vi', (they). The Ch-Vy class of words are really just a sub-group of the Ki-Vi words, and so exactly the same words are used for 'it' and 'they' – ki and vi.

4. Na = To have

'Is-currently'	is	'Na'
'And'	is	'Na'
'With'	is	'Na'
'Have'	is	'Na'
'It has' (M-Mi class)	is	'Una/ina'
'They have' (M-Mi class)	is	'Ina/wana'
'It has' (Ki-Vi class)	is	'Kina'
'They have' (Ki-Vi class)	is	'Vina'
'I have a book'	is	'Nina kitabu'
'You have a book' (one)	is	'Una kitabu'
'S/he has a book'	is	'Ana kitabu'
'We have a book'	is	'Tuna kitabu'
'You (>1) have a book'	is	'Mna kitabu'
'They have a book'	is	'Wana kitabu'
'The villages have no food'	is	'Vijiji havina chakula'
'The village has no beds'	is	'Kijiji hakina vitanda'
'The village has beds'	is	'Kijiji kina vitanda'
'The child has a tree'	is	'Mtoto ana mti'
'The child has some trees'	is	'Mtoto ana miti baadhi'
'I have a bed and a book'	is	'Nina kitanda na kitabu'

'The villages have food'	is	'Vijiji vina chakula'
'The villages with food'	is	'Vijiji chenye chakula'

(note 'chenye' agrees with 'chakula', not with 'vijiji')

'The villages without food'	is	'Vijiji bila chakula'

'The child has a bed and a book'   is 'Mtoto ana kitanda na kitabu'
'The child with a bed and a book'   is 'Mtoto chenye kitanda na kitabu'
'The child without a bed and a book' is 'Mtoto bila kitanda na kitabu'

'The village is increasing and has beds'
          is   'Kijiji kinaongezeka na kina vitanda'
'The books and beds are burning'
          is   'Vitabu na vitanda vinawaka/vinaungua'
'I have food and books. They are sufficient'
          is   'Nina chakula na vitabu. Vinatosha'
'The child has no bed and no book'
          is   'Mtoto hana kitanda wala kitabu (na hana kitabu)'

Grammatical notes:

When 'na' is used to mean 'is-currently', it is within a word, soon after the beginning – eg anapika.

When used to mean 'and', it is a separate word: 'beds and books' – 'vitabu na vitanda'.

When it is used as 'with', it is at the end of a short word: 'She is cooking with a thing' = 'anapika ana kitu'.

There is no special verb for 'to have'. You just say e.g. 'he-with book': ana kitabu.

The opposite of 'na' is created by putting 'ha-' at the beginning of the '-na' word – eg 'vina' = 'has' and 'havina' = 'has not'.

Another means of expressing 'to have' is the use of '-enye', which could be translated as 'with'. It says that the person or thing mentioned before it in the sentence has, or owns, or is with, the thing mentioned immediately after it. Technically, it is an adjective describing the second thing, and so has to have a front-end change to make it agree. The agreements are:

M-Wa class:	M + -enye = mwenye	Wa + -enye = wenye
M-Mi class:	U + -enye = wenye	I + -enye = yenye
Ki-Vi class:	Ki + -enye = chenye	Vi + -enye = vyenye

The opposite of '-enye' ('with') is 'bila' – without. 'bila', Bila does not change in any situation.

5. The verb 'To be'

'The man is good'	*is*	*'Mwanaume ni mzuri/mwema'*
'You are good'	*is*	*'Wewe ni mzuri/mwema'*
'You are not good'	*is*	*'Wewe si mzuri'*
'I am good'	*is*	*'Mimi ni mzuri'*
'I am not good'	*is*	*'Mimi si mzuri'*
'The tree is good'	*is*	*'Mti ni mzuri'*
'The book is good'	*is*	*'Kitabu ni kizuri'*
'The book is not good'	*is*	*'Kitabu si kizuri'*
'The food and the beds are good'	*is*	*'Chakula na vitanda ni vizuri'*
'The food and the beds are not good'	*is*	*'Chakula na vitanda si vizuri'*

Grammatical notes:

'Ni', as a separate word, means 'is' or 'are'. It is the same word whether talking of 'I', 'You', 'We', etc.
The opposite of 'ni' is 'si'.

When needing to emphasise or clarify, or when the person is otherwise unclear, the following 'subject pronouns' can be used:

mimi=I/me;
wewe=you, (one only);
yeye=s/he
sisi=we;
ninyi=you, (more than one);
wao=they

These are different from the pronouns which go at the front of verbs. They are only used for people, and only then for clarification or emphasis. Thus 'John is cooking' is 'John anapika'. 'John? He is cooking' is 'John? Anapika'. But 'He is cooking', (emphasising 'he'), is 'Yeye anapika'. Both the 'yeye' and the 'a-' are subject pronouns, and mean the same thing, but they perform different functions.

These pronouns give rise to the amalgamated words, where they are combined with 'na-' meaning 'with':

With me	= nami
With you (one)	= nawe
With him/her	= naye
With us	= nasi
With you (>one)	= nanyi
With them	= nao

6. Expressing the negative of verbs

'I-not'	*'You-not'*	*'S/he-not'*	*is*	*'Si-'*	*'Hu'*	*'Ha'*
'We-not'	*'You-not'*	*'They-not'*	*is*	*'Ha-tu'*	*'Ha-m'*	*'Ha-wa'*
'It-not'	*'They-not'*	*(M-Mi class)*	*is*		*'Ha-u'*	*'Ha-i'*
'It-not'	*'They-not'*	*(Ki-Vi class)*	*is*		*'Ha-ki'*	*'Ha-vi'*

'The pupils do not come'	*is*	*'Wanafunzi hawaji'*
'He does not feed and does not wash'	*is*	*'Halishi/hali na haoshi'*
'He does not feed and does not wash'	*is*	*'Yeye halishi na haoshi'*
'The tree, it is not burning'	*is*	*'Mti hauwaki/hauungui'*
'The plant does not feed'	*is*	*'Mmea haulishi/hauli'*
'The plants do not feed'	*is*	*'Mimea hailishi/haili'*
'The toilet does not shut'	*is*	*'Choo hakifungi'*
'I do not have water'	*is*	*'Sina maji'*
'We do not have trees'	*is*	*'Hatuna miti'*

Grammatical notes:

Note that in turning an action in the present into the negative, you lose the 'na', (which means 'is/are currently'). Additionally, changing the last letter to an 'i' lets the hearer know clearly that you are saying 'not'. In the case of very short verbs, this can leave very little of the original verb, e.g. 'They are not coming' is 'hawaji'. The verb 'kuja' has lost the 'ku-' and has had the last letter changed to 'i'. Only the '-j-' and the context will tell you what you are talking about. Surprisingly, that is normally plenty!

Some action words of Arabic origin, however, end in 'u', and they lose meaning if you change this to an 'i', so the u remains.

To make 'not' into 'have not', just add 'na':

'I have not'	'You have not'	S/he has not'	is
'sina'	'huna'	'hana'	

'We have not'	'You have not'	'They have not'	is
'hatuna'	'hamna'	'hawana'	
'It has not'	'They have not'	(M-Mi class)	is
'hauna'	'haina'		
'It has not'	'They have not'	(Ki-Vi class)	is
'hakina'	'havina'		

7. Agreement & disagreement with statements

'That is so!'	*is*	*'Ndiyo/ndivyo!'*
'That is not so!'	*is*	*'Siyo! (or sivyo)*
'No'	*is*	*'La' or can be 'Hapana'*
'Are the bodies smelling?' – 'Yes!'	*is*	*'Miili inanuka?' – 'Ndiyo!'*
'Are the hands touching?' – 'Yes!'	*is*	*'Mikono inagusa?' – 'Ndiyo!'*
'Are the plants arriving?' – 'No!'	*is*	*'Mimea yanafika?' – 'Siyo!' or 'La!'*
'Are the trees burning?' – 'They are!'	*is*	*'Miti inawaka?' – 'Ndiyo!'*
'The trees are not burning?' – 'They are!'	*is*	*'Miti haiwaki?' – 'Siyo!'*

Grammatical notes:

The terms 'Ndiyo' and 'Siyo' do not mean 'Yes' and 'No'. They express either agreement or disagreement with the sentence just stated.

8. Location – the PKM system

'The children are located hereabouts ...'	is	'Watoto wa<u>k</u>o ...'
'The children are located precisely...'	is	'Watoto wa<u>p</u>o ...'
'The children are located within..'	is	'Watoto wa<u>m</u>o...'
'The children are not located precisely...'	is	'Watoto hawapo ...'
'The book is located precisely .. .'	is	'Kitabu kipo ...'
'The books are located precisely ...'	is	'Vitabu vipo ...'
'The books are within ...'	is	'Vitabu vimo ...'
'Where?'	is	'Wapi?'
'Where are the children?'	is	'Watoto wako wapi?'
'Where are the books?'	is	'Vitabu viko wapi?'
'The books? They are not located ...'	is	'Vitabu? Havipo ...'
'The books? They are not within ...'	is	'Vitabu? Havimo ...'
'The children are not located within..'	is	'Watoto hawamo...'

Grammatical notes:

'Wapi?' means 'Where?' This word is usually at the end of the sentence. The p, k, and m, in words such as wapo, kipo, wako, kiko, wamo and kimo, indicate, respectively, precise, approximate, and within location. This rule is repeated wwith numerous location-related words.

The front-end agreement is with the person or thing which is located. It is mainly regular, though you would expect 's/he is located...' to be 'apo...' but it is 'yupo'. Other agreements are:
M-Wa words re precise location:
I am: Nipo;
You are: Upo:
S/he is: Yupo
We are: Tupo;
You are: Mpo;
They are: Wapo

M-Mi words:	It is:	Upo;	They are: Ipo
Ki-Vi words:	It is:	Kipo;	They are: Vipo

Remember that these beginnings (ni; wa; etc), are for when you are translating <u>subjects</u> (eg I am; <u>they</u> are). When translating objects – eg 'me', 'them' – we will see later a slightly different set of pronouns: ni; ku; m or mw; tu; wa; wa.

Regarding <u>NOT</u> being precisely located somewhere:
M-Wa:
'S/he is not...'   is   'Hayupo...'
'They are not...'   is   'Hawapo...'

M-Mi class

| 'It is not…' | is | 'Haupo…' |
| 'They are not…' | is | 'Haipo…' |

Ki-Vi class
| 'It is…' | is | 'Hakipo…' |
| 'They are…' | is | 'Havipo…' |

9. Location – In; on; nearby = -ni.

'Where is the bread? It's on the table'
        is   **'Mkate uko wapi? Upo mezani'**
'Where are the children? They're in the village'
        is   **'Watoto wako wapi? Wapo/wako kijijini'**
'By the river'	is	**'Mtoni'**
'By the good river'	is	**'Katika mto mzuri'**
'By the rivers'	is	**'Mitoni'**
'By the good rivers'	is	**'Katika mito mizuri'**
'On the good bed'	is	**'Katika kitanda kizuri'**
'On the beds'	is	**'Katika vitanda/vitandani'**

Grammatical notes:

'In, on, by' is '-ni'
Another way of saying '-ni', meaning 'in, on, by', is 'katika'. This is the only way to say it, if the thing you are talking about has a describing word attached. Thus 'by the river' can be: 'Mtoni'; or 'Katika mto'. But 'by the good river' can only be 'katika mto mzuri'.

10.   Location – Here = Hapa or Huku. There = Pale or Kule.

'The children are (located) right here'	is	**'Watoto wapo hapa'**
'The children are right there'	is	**'Watoto wapo pale'**
'The books are somewhere round here'	is	**'Vitabu viko huku'**
'The rivers are somewhere there'	is	**'Mito iko kule'**
'Where is the doctor?'	is	**'Mganga yuko wapi?'**
'The doctor is here somewhere'	is	**'Mganga yuko huku'**
'The doctor is not around here'	is	**'Mganga hayuko huku'**
'Is the doctor right here?'	is	**'Mganga yupo hapa?'**
'The doctor is not here.	Is	**'Mganga hayupo hapa…**
…He is in the village'	is	**Yuko kijijini'**
'The doctor is not there	is	**'Mganga hayupo pale…**
…He is in the town somewhere'	is	**Yuko mjini'**
'The books? They are not here'	is	**'Vitabu? Havipo'**
'The children? They are not here'	is	**'Watoto? Hawapo hapa'**
'Up there'	is	**'Huko'**

Grammatical notes:

Not-very-sure location – huku & kule – have got the characteristic letter 'k' in them.
Precise location – hapa & pale – have got a 'p'.
The two words dealing with 'here' both start with h.
The two words dealing with 'there' both end in -le.

11. Location – (In that place) there is; there are: Pana, Kuna & Mna

'There are books right here'	is	'Pana vitabu hapa'
'There are books right there'	is	'Pana vitabu pale'
'There are some books hereabouts'	is	'Kuna vitabu baadhi huku'
'There are some books thereabouts'	is	'Kuna vitabu baadhi kule'

'There are books somewhere in the kitchen'
          is   'Kuna vitabu mahali fulani jikoni'
'The books are somewhere in the kitchen'
          is   'Vitabu viko mahali fulani jikoni'

'There are no books exactly here'	is	'Hakuna vitabu hapa'
'There are no books hereabouts	is	'Hakuna vitabu huku'
'There are books in the river'	is	'Mna vitabu mtoni'
'There are no books within the river'	is	'Hamna/hakuna vitabu mtoni'

Grammatical notes:

Note that the P or the K is specified both in the 'there is' word, and in the 'here/there' word.
Neither of these words needs to change to accommodate the thing being talked.
Swahili makes no distinction between 'a' book and 'the' book, ('kitabu').
It makes no distinction between 'the' books and 'some' books, ('vitabu').
To convert 'there is/are' (pana) into 'there is not/are not', add 'ha' to the front of the word: 'hapana'.

12. Location – Nearby: this; these: H- Further away: that; those: -le

'This man'	is	'Mwanaume huyu'
'That man'	is	'Mwanaume yule'
'These men'	is	'Wanaume hawa'
'Those men'	is	'Wanaume wale'
'This tree'	is	'Mti huu'
'That tree'	is	'Mti ule'
'These trees'	is	'Miti hii'
'Those trees'	is	'Miti ile'

'This book'	is	'Kitabu hiki'
'That book'	is	'Kitabu kile'
'These books'	is	'Vitabu hivi'
'Those books'	is	'Vitabu vile'

'This nice book is burning'

is   'Kitabu hiki kizuri kinawaka / kinaungua'

'That nice book is burning'

is   'Kitabu kile kizuri kinawaka/kinaungua'.

Grammatical notes:

When talking of things nearby, (this and these), the word in Swahili starts with an H.
When talking of things further away, (that and those), the word in Swahili ends with -le.

'He' is 'a' (e.g. he cooks – anapika), However, 'this' in 'this man' is not (H+a) Ha, but huyu. This use of 'yu' instead of 'a' to represent s/he is the same as is found in other location words, e.g. 'He is precisely located': 'Yupo'; 'He is approximately located': 'Yuko'.

Summary of this/that/location:

'There are these books hereabouts' is		'Kuna vitabu hivi huku'
'There is that child thereabouts'	is	'Kuna mtoto yule kule'
'That book is right here'	is	'Kitabu kile kipo hapa'
'This book is hereabouts'	is	'Kitabu hiki kiko huku'
'This child is right there'	is	'Mtoto huyu yupo pale'

13.   Location – In front of, on top of, behind of, etc.

'Where is the book?'	is	'Kitabu kiko wapi?'
'The book is on top of the tree'	is	'Kitabu kipo juu ya mti'
'The book is in front of the tree'	is	'Kitabu kipo mbele ya mti'
'The book is among 'of' the trees'	is	'Kitabu kiko kati ya miti'
'The book is close to the tree'	is	'Kitabu kipo karibu na mti'
'The book is far from the tree'	is	'Kitabu kipo mbali na mti'
'Beside me'	is	'Kando yangu'
'Beside you' (One person)	is	'Kando yako'
'Beside him'	is	'Kando yake'
'Beside us'	is	'Kando yetu'
'Beside you' (>One person)	is	'Kando yenu'
'Beside them'	is	'Kando yao'

Grammatical notes:

When used with the words above, 'ya' means 'of', in the sense of 'on top <u>of</u>'; 'outside <u>of</u>', etc.

'Ya' implies belonging to something or someone. 'Beside me', it is not 'kando ya mimi', but rather 'kando yangu'. 'Yangu' means not 'me', but 'of me'. 'Kando yangu' means 'Beside of-me'.

'Ya' (or 'y'), often signifies possession, but in this context, means location.

Some explanations of location use 'na' instead of 'ya', for instance 'mbali na vijiji' – 'far from the village'. 'Ya' has other 'connecting' uses, the general theme being to represent a relationship between the preceding word and the following word.

Location – Directions

'Towards'	*is*	*'Kuelekea'*
'To the right'	*is*	*'Kulia' or 'Kwa kulia'*
'He went to the right'	*is*	*'Alikwenda kulia'*
'Right hand'	*is*	*'Mkono wa kulia'*
'To the left'	*is*	*'Kushoto'*
'Near to'	*is*	*'Karibu na'*
'Before ...'	*is*	*'Kabla ya'*
'More than'	*is*	*'Zaidi ya'*
'In here'	*is*	*'Humu'*
'In there'	*is*	*'Mle'*
'Travel straight on...'	*is*	*'Safiri kwa kunyoosha...*
'Travel straight on...'	*is also 'Safiri moja kwa moja ...'*	
... as far as the town'	*is*	*'... mpaka mjini'*
'Morogoro is far from Arusha'	*is*	*'Morogoro ni mbali na Arusha'*

Grammatical notes:

The word for 'right' and 'left' are 'kulia' and kushoto'. When these words are used as adjectives, instead of directions, they need to agree with what they are describing. Thus, when describing a hand, (m-kono), 'kulia' becomes 'wa kulia'. The 'wa' forms an agreement between kulia and mkono, an M-Mi word.

When used as prepositions to give direction, their form remains constant.

14.   Location versus Possession and the possessive

'Beside me'	*is*	*'Kando yangu' (location)*
'Beside you'	*is*	*'Kando yako' (location)*
'My pupil'	*is*	*'Mwanafunzi wangu' (possession)*

'Your pupil' (just one of you) (possession)	*is*	*'Mwanafunzi wako'*
'The pupil of the teacher'	*is*	*'Mwanafunzi wa mwalimu'*
'The pupil of the teachers'	*is*	*'Mwanafunzi wa walimu'*
'The pupils of the teacher'	*is*	*'Wanafunzi wa mwalimu'*
'The tree of the teacher'	*is*	*'Mti wa mwalimu'*
'The trees of the teacher'	*is*	*'Miti ya mwalimu'*
'The thing of the teacher'	*is*	*'Kitu cha mwalimu'*
'The things of the teacher'	*is*	*'Vitu vya mwalimu'*
'The things of the teachers'	*is*	*'Vitu vya walimu'*
'My pupils'	*is*	*'Wanafunzi wangu'*
'My tree'	*is*	*'Mti wangu'*
'My trees'	*is*	*'Miti yangu'*
'My book'	*is*	*'Kitabu changu'*
'My books'	*is*	*'Vitabu vyangu'*

'I am going to my house'
                 is   *'(Ni)nakwenda kwenye nyumba yangu'*
'I am going to my house'
                 Is also '(Ni)nakwenda nyumbani kwangu'

Grammatical notes:

When we were talking about location, 'ya' means 'of' (and 'to' etc), and stays in the same in each context. When talking about possession, however, the connecting word needs to agree with the thing being possessed. It is the thing being possessed which determines this change, not the possessor. For M-Wa words, this will be 'wa', in both singular and plural. For M-Mi words, the connector (meaning 'of') is still 'wa' in the singular. When more than one M-Mi thing is possessed, the word for 'of' is 'ya'. For Ki-Vi words 'of' is 'cha' or 'vya'.

These words, (wa, ya, cha, vya), are used when you are naming the owner. However, when you just say 'mine' or 'yours', (ie 'of me' or 'of you'), there is a specific set of words:

Of (possession):   wa,   ya,   cha,   vya, etc

My /mine: wangu, yangu, changu, vyangu, etc
Your/s (just one of you): wako, yako, chako,   vyako, etc
His/ hers/ its: wake, yake, chake,   vyake, etc
Our/s: wetu, yetu, chetu,   vyetu, etc
Your/s (more than one owner): wenu, yenu, chenu,   vyenu, etc
Their/s: wao, yao, chao,   vyao

Just to clarify: 'Wa', 'ya', 'cha', and 'vya' mean 'of' in sentences like: 'Kitabu cha mwalimu' – 'the book of the teacher'. However, when you say, 'His book', instead of using 'wa', 'ya', 'cha', etc, you use 'wangu', 'yangu' 'changu', etc.

Getting used to all these different ways of saying, 'my', 'their' etc is one of the challenges of Swahili. It is made more complex by the fact that sometimes the rules are seemingly broken – for instance 'My house' should be 'nyumba yangu', as 'house' is a singular N-class word, and 'of', meaning possession of a single N-class thing is 'ya'. However, the substitution of 'kwa' for 'ya' makes 'kwango' instead of 'yango'. 'Kwa' incorporates the idea of 'towards' or 'belonging', and so when applied to one's house, it means not just that you own it, but that it is home!

Listen often to sentences with these connecting words. Only listening often will bed them into your mind – combined only now and then with making sense of them by re-reading the grammar.

15.   Adjectives

'A big man'	*is*	*'Mwanaume mkubwa'*
'Big child'	*is*	*'Mtoto mkubwa'*
'Big trees'	*is*	*'Miti mikubwa'*
'Big book'	*is*	*'Kitabu kikubwa'*
'Big books'	*is*	*'Vitabu vikubwa'*
'A good book'	*is*	*'Kitabu kizuri'*
'A very good book'	*is*	*'Kitabu kizuri sana'*
'An honest child'	*is*	*'Mtoto mwaminifu' (m+a=mwa)*
'Honest children'	*is*	*'Watoto waaminifu' (wa+a=wa)*
'A black child'	*is*	*'Mtoto mweusi' (m+e=mwe)*
'Part of the child'	*is*	*'Mtoto mwingine' (m+i=mwi)*
'Many children'	*is*	*'Watoto wengi' (wa+i=we)*
'Some black teachers'	*is*	*'Walimu baadhi weusi' (wa+e=we)*
'Some black trees'	*is*	*'Miti baadhi myeusi' (mi+e=mye)*
'Many trees'	*is*	*'Miti mingi' (mi+i=mi)*
'A black book'	*is*	*'Kitabu cheusi' (ki+e=che)*
'Black books'	*is*	*'Vitabu vyeusi' (vi+e=vye)*
'Dangerous men'	*is*	*'Wanaume hatari'*
'Dangerous food'	*is*	*'Chakula hatari'*
'Dangerous trees'	*is*	*'Miti hatari'*

Grammatical notes:

The general principle in Swahili is that where two words relate to each other, they often need to agree with each other. This is archetypally the case with adjectives, which are clearly wholly dependent on the noun they are describing, and so need to agree with it.

The agreements are often predictable, but not always. If the stem of an adjective begins with a vowel, then the agreement and the stem get squashed together, sometimes with a 'w' in between. Adjectives that are preceded by '-a' are saying 'as' or 'like'. The -a must agree with the thing being described.

In English, comparisons are made by alteration of the end of the adjective, eg small, smaller, smallest. In Swahili, the word 'kuliko' is used, which effectively 'more'; e.g. 'kidogo kuliko' = smaller; 'nzuri kuliko' = better.

'A bigger man'	*is*	*'Mwanaume mkubwa kuliko'*
'Bigger trees'	*is*	*'Miti mikubwa kuliko''*
'A better book'	*is*	*'Kitabu kizuri kuliko''*
'More dangerous men'	*is*	*'Wanaume hatari kuliko'*

'Hatari kuliko' therefore means 'more dangerous' (than something else). However, in English we have another, slightly different, use of the word 'more', which does not compare anything to anything, but just says that we are talking about an increase. 'More dangerous men' can therefore mean 'Men who are more dangerous'; or it can mean 'An increase in the number of dangerous men'. For the latter sense in Swahili, the word 'zaidi' is used:

'More dangerous men' (comparison)		
	is	*'Wanaume hatari zaidi/kuliko'*
'More dangerous men' (more of them)		
	is	*'Wanaume hatari zaidi'*
'More big trees'	*is*	*'Miti mikubwa zaidi'*
'More of those better books'	*is*	*'Zaidi ya vile Vitabu vizuri'*

The related phrase, 'more than' is 'zaidi ya':

'More than those books'	*is*	*'Zaidi ya vitabu vile'*
'More than three books'	*is*	*'Zaidi ya vitabu vitatu'*

Swahili can also achieve comparison by describing, longhand, the degree to which the thing differs, or is in excess. This cumbersome way uses verbs such as 'kupita', (to pass). In order for this to work, you need to express what it actually is that is being passed. You cannot for instance say that a child is bigger: he has to have 'passed that one':

'This child is bigger'   *is*   *'Mtoto huyu ni mkubwa zaidi/kuliko...'*
'This child is bigger than that one' ('to pass that one')
     is   *'Mtoto huyu ni mkubwa kupita yule/zaidi ya yule'*
'This book is better than that one'   *is*   *'Kitabu hiki ni kizuri kupita kile'*

16.   Greetings

'Hi!'   is   *'Jambo!'*
        Response: 'Jambo!'
'(polite greeting from child)   *is Shikamoo!'*
        Response: 'Marahaba!'
'How's it going?' (to 1 person)   is   *'Hujambo?'*
        Response: 'Sijambo!'; or 'Safi!' (Pure!); or 'Poa!', (Cool!)
'How's it going?' (to 2+)   is   *'Hamjambo?'*
        Response: 'Hatujambo!'

'How are you?' 'Complete!'   is   *'U hali gani?' 'Mzima!'*
'What news?' 'Fine!'   is   *'Habari gani?'   :'Nzuri!' or 'Njema!'*
'How's things?'   is   *'Mambo vipi/Habari?' (i.e. News?')*
'Fine. How's things with you?' is   *'Poa/Nzuri. Habari yako' (Your news?)*

'Good morning, friend'   is   *'Habari za asubuhi, Bwana?'*
(i.e. 'What news of the morning?')
'Good!'   (i.e. good news! – i.e. all OK) is   *'Nzuri' or 'Njema!'*
'What news of the daylight?'   is   *'Habari ya mchana?'*
'Good day, ladies and gentlemen!'   is
                    'Siku njema mabibi na mabwana!'
'God be with you until we meet again!'   is
                    'Mungu awe nanyi mpaka tutakapoonana tena!'
'It's very good to be here!'   is
                    'Ni vizuri sana kuwa hapa!'
'Goodbye!' (end of day)   is   *'Kwaheri!': 'Kwaheri!'*
'Goodbye!' (to 2+)   is   *'Kwaherini!'*
                    (to 2+): 'Kwaherini!'
'May I come in? '   is   *'Hodi'*
'Yes, come in!'   is   *'Karibu!'*
                    (or Karibuni if >1)

Grammatical notes:

'Shikamuu' ('I prostrate myself at your feet') and 'Marahaba' ('How delightful!') are both taken straight from Arabic.

'U hali gani?' uses 'u' as the pronoun for 'you', instead of 'wewe'. 'U' is the normal pronoun at the start of a verb, (e.g. 'unafika' – 'you are coming'). However, 'hali' means 'the state you are in', and is not a verb. As sometimes happens in greetings, then, the verb is omitted. Effectively, instead of saying 'What state are you in?', it is saying 'What state you?'

Note that when replying to 'Habari?', you can say 'Habari yako' – 'Yako' means 'yours' – ie 'what is your news?'

'Jambo' is a Ji-Ma word meaning 'topic' or 'matter' or 'trouble'. If you wanted to say, 'you do not have trouble', then for one person it would be 'huna jambo'; and for more than one it would be 'hamna jambo'. (see Section 4 above, & 19 below). Therefore, shortening the phrase into a word, you end with 'Hujambo' or 'Hamjambo'. The answer is 'No trouble!' – 'Sijambo!' or 'Hatujambo!':

'Hu-' = 'you do not…'
'Si-' = 'I do not…'
'Ham-' = 'You (plural) do not…'
'Hatu-' = 'We do not…'

'Nzuri' and 'Njema' both mean 'good'. The stem for the first is '-zuri', and, starting with a z follows normal patterns. The stem for the second is '-ema', and so the 'nj-' is a customised beginning, otherwise you would have to say just 'nema'.

The addition of '-ni' at the end of a word to imply talking to more than one person, is yet another use of the ubiquitous 'ni'.

17.   The past – to have done something = '-me-'; did something = '-li-'

'We have gone'	*is*	*'Tumekwenda'*
'We went'	*is*	*'Tulikwenda'*
'We have spoken'	*is*	*'Tumesema /Tumeongea'*
'We spoke'	*is*	*'Tulisema /Tuliongea'*
'The teachers have started'	*is*	*'Walimu wameanza'*
'The teachers started'	*is*	*'Walimu walianza'*
'I gave you'	*is*	*'Nilikupa / nilikupatia'*
'I have given you'	*is*	*'Nimekupa'*

Grammatical notes:
In the word 'Tunakwenda', (we are going), the -na- part of the word means 'is/are currently'. To express the past, you simply replace this with either '-me-' or '-li-'.

'-me- corresponds to the 'perfect tense' – where in English we would say 'We have gone'. The word 'perfect' does not mean 'without blemish' in this context. It comes from the Latin 'perficere', meaning 'to finish'. The perfect tense deals with things that are finished, (I have walked, they have eaten) – as compared to the imperfect tense, (eg I was walking, I used to walk, they were eating, they used to eat), in which we have not specified whether you have stopped walking or eating. In the imperfect tense, the action might for all we know be still continuing.

However, when dealing with things that are clearly over, and when telling them for instance in a narrative or history, then we use the 'remote past', or 'past historic' – eg I walked, they ate, etc. This is translated by the substitution of '-li-' for '-na-'.

These arrangements for talking of the past are perhaps the most simple and elegant in any language in the world. When using 'li' or 'me' with an otherwise mono-syllabic verb, the 'ku' is retained: eg 'I gave' is 'nilikupa', not 'nilipa'.

The imperfect ('past continuous') tense of Swahili does exist, as does the pluperfect tense, (I had eaten, we had walked). Both are based on the use of the auxiliary verb 'kuwa', ('to be' or 'to become'). It is entirely possible to find a way of expressing one's self without the need for them, but for the record, they are formed of two words: The first word is: subject pronoun + -li- + kuwa – eg 'nilikuwa' = 'I was' or 'I became'. The second word uses the insertion '-ki-' or '-me-'. The former is for the past continuous, and the latter for the pluperfect.

Thus:

'They are walking'	*is*	*'Wanatembea'*
'They have walked'	*is*	*'Wametembea'*
'They walked'	*is*	*'Walitembea'*
'They were walking'	*is*	*'Walikuwa wakitembea'*
('They became (that) they were walking')		
'They had walked'	*is*	*'Walikuwa wametembea'*
('They became (that) they have walked')		

18.   Negative of the past – '-ja-' and '-ku-'

'I have not gone'	*is*	*'Sijakwenda / Sijaenda'*
'I did not go'	*is*	*'Sikukwenda'*
'You have not gone'	*is*	*'Hujakwenda / Hujaenda'*
'You did go' (ie you went)	*is*	*'Hulikwenda'*
'You did not go'	*is*	*'Hukukwenda'*
'We have not gone'	*is*	*'Hatujakwenda / Hatujaenda'*
'We did not go'	*is*	*'Hatukukwenda'*
'S/he did not go'	*is*	*'Hakukwenda'*
'You did not go' (plural)	*is*	*'Hamkukwenda'*
'They did not go'	*is*	*'Hawakukwenda'*
'The doors have not shut'	*is*	*'Milango haijafunga / haijafungwa'*
'The doors did not shut'	*is*	*'Milango haikufunga'*

Grammatical notes:

The negative subject pronouns are:

I not;	you not;	s/he not	=
si-;	hu-;	ha-	
We not;	you not (>1);	they not	=
hatu-;	ham-;	hawa-	

In most cases, these are formed by adding 'ha-' to the front of the positive personal pronoun, but the first three do not exactly follow the rule.

Additionally, to make -me- into the negative, you change it to -ja-.
To make -li- into the negative, you change it to -ku-.
This insertion of '-ku-' sometimes does not happen in normal speech, which seems to mean that you would be talking in the present tense. However, as in English, sometimes we use the present tense to describe the past, eg: 'So I go in the house, and what do I see? ...etc'

By the addition of ha- to the front of the word, to indicate 'not', plus the change of the insertion, the idea of negativity is expressed twice. This exemplifies the general tendency in Swahili to pack meaning into each word and phrase.

However, when talking about the negative in the past, the final letter change from 'a' to 'i' is not needed. The double negative is already achieved by changing 'ni' to 'si', and by changing 'me' to 'ja'.

The negative form -ja- also implies 'not yet'

19.   The future – '-ta-'

'I will go'	*is*	*'Nitakwenda'*
'I will not go'	*is*	*'Sitakwenda'*
'We will speak'	*is*	*'Tutasema'*
'We will not speak'	*is*	*'Hatutasema'*
'The bag will open'	*is*	*'Mfuko utafunguka'*
'The bag will not open'	*is*	*'Mfuko hautafunguka'*
'The doors will shut'	*is*	*'Milango itafunga'*
'The doors will not shut'	*is*	*'Milango haitafunga'*
'They are wanting/going to go'	*is*	*'Wanataka kwenda'*
'It is wanting/going to rain'	*is*	*'Inataka kunyesha mvua'*
'I am going to fall'	*is*	Nitaanguka / nitadondoka'

Grammatical notes:

In the future tense, the -na- changes to -ta-. With very short action words such as kuja, the 'ku' is retained. When speaking of the negative, the -ta- remains.

When translating 'going to...', (e.g. 'they are going to walk'), you may either use the future tense, ('they will walk'), or, if something less definite is preferred, the verb 'kutaka' plus an infinitive can be used. 'Kutaka' means 'to want'. Thus 'Tunataka' means 'we are wanting'. 'Tunataka kutembea' means 'we are wanting to walk' – or 'we are going to walk'.

20.   The imperative and the subjunctive: Giving orders and making requests

'To cook'	*is*	*'Kupika'*
'Cook! (to one person)	*is*	*'Pika...'*
'Cook! (to 2+ people)	*is*	*'Pikeni...'*
'Would you cook...? (to one person)	*is*	*'Upike...?'*
'Would you cook...? (to 2+ people)	*is*	*'Mpike...?'*
'Would you not cook...? (to one person)	*is*	*'Usipike...?'*
'Would you not cook...? (to 2+ people)	*is*	*'Msipike...?'*
'Please'	*is*	*'Tafadhali'*
'Please would you cook ...?' (Already polite)	*is*	*'Upike...?'*
'<u>Please</u> would you cook ...?' (extra polite!)	*is*	*'Tafadhali upike'*
'Would you cook...? (to one person)	*is*	*'Upike...?'*
'I want you to cook' ('I want that you might cook')	*is*	
		'Ninataka upike'
'It's best that you cook now'	*is*	*'Bora upike sasa'*
'I am cooking in order that you might eat'	*is*	*'Ninapika ili ule'*
'I am cooking in order that he might eat'	*is*	*'Ninapika ili ale'*
'Let him cook' (i.e. 'might he cook?')	*is*	*'Ngoja/acha apike'*
'Let's cook' (ie 'might we cook?')	*is*	*'Ngoja/acha tupike'*
'Let's not cook' (ie 'might we not cook?')	*is*	*'Ngoja tusipike'*
'I might cook'	*is*	*'Nipike/naweza kupika'*
'I might not cook'	*is*	*'Nisipike/naweza nisipike'*
'Am I not to cook?'	*is*	*'Nisipike?' (same)*
'Let me not cook'	*is*	*'Nisipike' (same)*
'Let them not cook'	*is*	*'Wasipike'*
'They might not cook'	*is*	*'Wasipike' (same)*
'Are they not going to cook?'	*is*	*'Hawatapika?' (but with '?')*
'We refused to let them cook'	*is*	*'Tuliwakataza wasipike'*

Grammatical notes:

The imperative is the giving of commands: 'Do this!'

In example 'Clean up!', 'clean!' is the imperative of the verb 'to clean'.

The subjunctive, on the other hand, equates to the use of the word 'might' in formal or old-fashioned English: eg 'I hope you might clean it'. In this example, 'might clean' is the subjunctive form of the verb 'to clean'.

The subjunctive is the correct tense to use when talking about a purpose, a suggestion, a desire, an intention, or even an obligation – anything where there is a possibility it might not happen, and the whole thing is **subject** to cirumstances.

Sometimes, the two overlap. For instance, in English, the subjunctive is used in commands where one wishes to maintain some politeness, rather than being too bossy: 'Might you do this?' 'You might tidy up a little' etc. Swahili follows formal English surprisingly closely in this. A polite command is expressed in the subjunctive, whereas a straightforward, get-on-with-it command is in the imperative.

To form the imperative, drop the 'ku-' at the front of the infinitive of the verb, and do not add a subject pronoun. Thus 'kutembea' (to walk) becomes 'Tembea!' (Walk!) When speaking to more than one person, the final 'a' is replaced with '-eni': 'Tembeni!' ('Walk all of you!')

To form the subjunctive, or to give a polite order or request, drop the 'ku-' at the front, and replace it, in the normal way, with the personal subject pronoun: u- for 'you' (singular); or m- for 'you' (plural). To make the particular subjunctive flavour, you change the last 'a' to an 'e'. Similarly, in stating polite hopes, ('might?'), change the final letter from 'a' to 'e'. In this way, you will be conveying that you are not taking it for granted that it will happen.

This change of the last letter only applies to action words normally ending in -a. For those ending in -u (e.g. kujaulu); or -i, (e.g. kufikiri, to think); there is no final letter change in the polite version.

To turn the imperative or subjunctive, (eg a request), into the negative, simply add '-si-'. Please note therefore, that when talking about refusing that someone might do something, a double-negative is used: 'We refused to let them cook' is 'Tuliwakataza wasipike' – i.e. 'we refused … that they might not cook'.

Of interest in passing: In English, as in other European languages, the use of the subjunctive is dropping away somewhat. Nowadays, we would often say 'I hope to clean it', or 'I hope I'll clean it', not 'I hope I might clean it'.

The verb 'to be' has particular subjunctive forms, which are also being lost. For instance, technically, you should say 'I hope it be' (subjunctive), rather than 'I hope it is', (indicative). The reason is that if it is a hope, then it is too definite, in theory, to say 'it is', so you cannot use the indicative!

Reminder:
Verbs with mono-syllabic stems such as kuja, (to come), or kula, (to eat):

Drop the '-ku-' in:
Subjunctive, (eg Ule = might you eat?);
Ku tense = negative of Li, (e.g. Sikula = I did not eat);
Ja tense = negative of Me, (e.g. Sijala = I have not eaten).

Retain the '-ku-' in:

Imperative, (e.g. Kula! – Eat!);
Present continuous, (e.g. Ninakula = I am eating);
Future, (eg Nitakula = I will eat);
Negative of future, (e.g. Sitakula = I will not eat);
'Li' tense, (e.g. Nilikula = I ate);
'Me' tense, (e.g. Nimekula = I have eaten).

21.   The conditional: If: '-ki-'. If not: 'kama' or 'sipo'

'If I cook...'	*is*	*'Nikipika'*
'If you cook'	*is*	*'Ukipika'*
'If I don't cook' (= if I might not cook)	*is*	*'Kama nikipika*
'If I <u>do not</u> cook'	*is*	*'Ni<u>si</u>popika'*
'Unless I cook'	*is*	*'Nisipopika'*
'We saw them cook<u>ing</u>'	*is*	*'Tuliwaona wa<u>ki</u>pika'*
'If I come'	*is*	*'Nikija'*
'<u>If</u> I come'	*is*	*'Kama nikija'*
'If I (will) come'	*is*	*'Kama nitakuja'*
'If I came'	*is*	*'Kama nilikuja'*
'If I do not come'	*is*	*'Nisipokuja'*
'If I will not come'	*is*	*'Kama nisipokuja'*
'Unless I come'	*is*	*'Nisipokuja'*
'We saw them cooking'	*is*	*'Tuliwaona wakipika'*
'The trees? We saw them burning'	*is*	*'Miti? Tuliiona ikiwaka/ikiungua'*
'The books? They saw them burning'		
	is	*'Vitabu? Waliviona vikiwaka/vikiungua'*

Grammatical notes:

The conditional tense is typified by the word 'would'. E.g. 'I would go'. Such a clause often is linked to the word 'if', e.g.: 'If...., then I would go.'

In English, the first part of the sentence, following the word 'if', deals with something which has not happened, but might. In other words, it is **subject** to circumstances. Because of this, we should use the subjunctive: eg 'If I were to go ...' instead of the indicative, 'If I went ...' (In reality, these days, most people say 'If I went ..., but, technically, that is incorrect!)

You will be very relieved to know that in another elegant Swahili shorthand, you do not need to use the subjunctive after 'If...' The tense for 'if' is simply formed by changing the insertion before the stem of the verb to '-ki-'. This means there is no extra word 'if', which is automatically implied.

'If I cook...'	*is*	*'Nikipika'*
'If you cook'	*is*	*'Ukipika'*

'If I come'   *is*   **'Nikija'**
'If you come'   *is*   **'Ukija'**
'If you come to Dar, you will see the sea'   *is*
                                                  'Ukija Dar, utaona bahari'

You can, however, use the word 'kama' if you want to emphasise the 'if':

'If I come'   *is*   **'Nikija'**
'If I come'   *is*   **'Kama nikija'**
'If you come to Dar, you will see the sea' *is*
                                                  'Kama ukija Dar, utaona bahari'

In the last example, the second part ('you will see the sea'), is expressed in the future tense, ('will'), instead of the conditional tense, ('would'), because the speaker thinks there is nothing left to chance. 'You will see the sea'.

More typically, the whole idea of the conditional is that things are not certain. Therefore, although we use the 'indicative' in both in English and Swahili:

'If I come, I will bring some food'   *is*
                                                  'Kama nikija, nitaleta chakula'

Technically, this should be:

'If I were to come, I would bring some food' *is*
                                                  '(Kama) Nikikuja ningeleta chakula'

The second part of the sentence, ('… I would…') is the conditional. A condition has been stated in the first part, (if I were to come). Thereafter you then express, in the conditional, what you would do. In Swahili, the conditional tense is achieved by the insertion of '-nge-', which therefore translates as 'would':

You can therefore use the '-nge-' (in the present) to imply the whole idea of something conditional. For the negative, add 'si':

'I would bring some food'   *is*   **'Ningeleta chakula'**
'I would like…'   *is*   **'Ningependa…'**
'I would do'   *is*   **'Ningefanya'**
'I would not like…'   *is*   **'Nisingependa…'**
'I would not do'   *is*   **'Nisingefanya'**

If you introduce the verb 'to be' (kuwa) as an auxiliary verb, it helps convey more of a sense of the future, as 'kuwa' also means 'to become'. You therefore get:

'I would be doing (if)…'   is   *'Ningekuwa nikifanya / ninafanya…'*
'They would be coming (if)…'   is   *'Wangekuwa wakija / wanakuja …'*

Note that you have to use the '-ki-' insertion in this construction, to convey the sense of 'if'.

In short, **'-nge-' + '-ki-'** conveys **'would' + 'if'**.

If instead you wanted to say what would have happened in the past, you would insert '-ngali-' instead of '-nge-'. You can still use the 'kuwa' verb to signify 'been' or 'have been'. For the negative, add 'si':

'I would have liked / if I were to have liked…'   is   *'Ningalipenda…'*
'We would have been cooking (if)'   is   *'Tungalikuwa tukipika'*
'I would not have liked'   is   *'Nisingalipenda…'*
'We would not have been cooking (if)'   is   *'Tusingalikuwa tukipika'*

Use of '-sipo-' instead of '-ki-' forms the negative, but can mean 'unless'. With mono-syllabic verb stems such as ku-ja (to come), the 'ku' is dropped in the positive, ('ki'), but not in the negative, ('sipo').

The word 'kama', (which also means 'if'), inserted at the front of the sentence, would either strengthen the idea of 'if' when used with the conditional, or would turn any other tense into an alternative version of the conditional. Some Swahili speakers do not use the 'ki' tense much, and 'kama' for them is the normal way of saying 'if'. (Bear in mind that for many if not most Swahili speakers, it is their second language, and the mother-tongue of the tribal language is spoken at home.)

In addition to its meaning as conveying the conditional tense, the insertion of -ki- before the stem of a verb can turn it into the present participle – ie what we would translate as the verb ending '-ing'. E.g. nikipika' can mean 'if I cooked', or 'I was cooking'.

'I was cooking' is, technically, the imperfect tense, and 'I was cooking', because it uses 'was', (past tense of the verb 'to be – 'kuwa'). It is probably better expressed:

 'I was cooking'   is   *'Nilikuwa nikipika'*

(Literally, 'I became I was cooking').

It is possible to use other double-verb combinations, where '-ki-' in the second verb means '-ing' – e.g.:

'I saw him cooking'   is   *'Nilimwona akipika'*

(Literally: 'I saw him if he cooks'. Notice the insertion of 'mw' to mean 'him'.) Such forms are recognisable by the fact that the 'ki' is in the second of two consecutive verbs. However, in normal speech, in the absence of such complex constructions, hearing '-ki-' implies 'if'.

22. Object pronouns: Me, you, him/her, us, them

'They are giving me the tree'	is	'Wa-na-ni-pa mti'

(wa = they; na = currently; ni = to me; pa = give; mti = the tree)

'They are giving you the tree' (to 1 person)	is	'Wana-ku-pa mti'
'They are giving him/her the tree'	is	'Wana-m-pa mti'
'They are giving us the tree'	is	'Wana-tu-pa mti'
'They are giving you the tree' (>1 person)	is	'Wana-wa-pa mti'
'They are giving them the tree'	is	'Wana-wa-pa mti'
'The book? It hit me'	is	'Kitabu? Kilinipiga'
'The book? It hit you' (hitting one person)	is	'Kitabu? Kilikupiga'
'The book? It hit us'	is	'Kitabu? Kilitupiga'
'The book? It hit you' (>one)	is	'Kitabu? Kiliwapiga'
'The book? It hit them' (people)	is	'Kitabu? Kiliwapiga'
'The book? It hit it' (hit a tree)	is	'Kitabu? Kiliupiga'
'The book? It hit them' (hit trees)	is	'Kitabu? Kiliipiga'
'The book? It hit it' (hit another book)	is	'Kitabu? Kilikipiga'
'The book? It hit them' (hit other books)	is	'Kitabu? Kilivipiga'

Grammatical notes:

The object pronouns are: Me = ni; you (one) = ku; him/her = m; us = tu; you (>1) = wa; and them = wa. The word for you (more than one person), is '-wa-', exactly the same as the word for 'them'. The context will clarify the meaning. Where is does not, you can add 'ninyi' or 'wao'. The word for him/her is '-m-' (but '-mw- before a vowel).

The word for 'you' (referring to one person), is '-ku-', which is the same two letters as forms the infinitive, as well as being the insertion which forms the negative of '-li-'. However, these forms are easily distinguishable: In an infinitive, the word begins with 'ku-'. In the negative of the past, the '-ku-' will be inserted between the subject pronoun, (e.g. 'tu-' = 'we') and the verb stem, (e.g. '–pika' = 'cook') – thus 'tukupika' = 'we did not cook'.

By contrast, 'ku' as a pronoun, (meaning 'you'), will be always after whichever insertion tells you the tense – na, li, me, etc. Thus tukukupika' = 'we did not cook you!'

'It' & 'them' for other noun classes are as expected: -
M-Mi words: "-u-', '-i-',

Ki-Vi words: '-ki-' and '-vi-'.

23.   Adverbs: Descriptions of actions. Prepositions and conjunctions

'Nice'		*is*	*'-zuri'*
'Nicely'	*or 'well'*	*is*	*'Vizuri'*
'Bad'		*is*	*'-baya'*
'Badly'		*is*	*'Vibaya'*
'Brief'		*is*	*'-fupi'*
'Briefly'		*is*	*'Kifupi'*
'Briefly'		*is also*	*'Kwa kifupi'*

Grammatical notes:

To describe a noun, you need an adjective. To describe an action, it is an adverb which is required. In English, typically we add '-ly' – e.g. 'nice' and 'nicely'. To make this change in Swahili, either 'vi-' or 'ki-' is put in front of the adjective stem. There is, unfortunately, no rule for which to apply in each case, so each has to be learnt separately.

Note that the word for 'nicely', ('vizuri'), can also mean 'nice' if applied to a word like Vitabu, (books): 'vitabu vizuri' – 'nice books'. Therefore, in Ki-Vi situations, look at the word before 'vizuri' to work out what it is describing – sometimes a thing; sometimes an action.

The word 'more' can amplify a noun, (in which case it is an adjective), or it can act as an adverb and amplify a verb. In such a case, words of this type demand the use of 'ya' – what follows is then the noun or verb being related to.

'More than...'	*is*	*'Zaidi ya...'*
'Furthermore...'	*is*	*'Zaidi ya....'*

The rest of this chapter continues the idea of relationship between two parts of a sentence.

A preposition, (see later) instead of relating two clauses, tends to relate a thing or a person to a clause – eg a thing is above, beyond, before, beside, etc. Prepositions in Swahili also demand the use of 'ya' to denote relationship.

A conjunction is a word connecting two clauses – eg 'and', (na), or 'but', ('lakini'). A conjuctive adverb also links two clauses, but expresses some qualification – eg 'instead'. As they deal with relationships, such constructions in Swahili can also use 'ya':

'Instead of...'	*is*	*'Badala ya...'*
'After that time...'	*is*	*'Baada ya muda/wakati huo...'*
'Before that time...'	*is*	*'Kabla ya muda...'*

Another way of describing an action is by the use of 'kwa', which, in this case, means 'in the manner of'.

'Truthfully'	*is*	*'Kwa kweli/kiukweli'*
'Usually'	*is*	*'Kwa kawaida'*
'Luckily	*is*	*'Kwa bahati'*
'Therefore'	*is*	*'Kwa hiyo / hivyo'*
'Because...'	*is*	*'Kwa sababu or kwakuwa*

Some constructions need both 'kwa' and 'ya':

'Because of / On account of...'	*is*	*'Kwa ajili ya' ('kwasababu')*
'For the reason that...'	*is*	*'Kwa maana ya' ('kwasababu')*

Some adverbs have neither kwa nor ya:

Sometimes the link between two parts of a sentence uses a combination of link words. If these involve the idea of 'with', then the link is 'na', but 'na' is also used with some other prepositions:

'Together with...	*is*	*'Pamoja na...'*
'Far from...'	*is*	*'Mbali na...'*
'Close to...'	*is*	*'Karibu na...'*

Finally, some adverb linkages just stand on their own, eg:

'Afterwards'	*is*	*'Kisha/halafu/baada ya'*
'In order that...'	*is*	*'Ili...'*
'Gently'	*is*	*'Polepole' / 'Taratibu'*
'Equally'	*is*	*'Sawasawa' (pia/ vilevile)*
'Early' or 'Soon'	*is*	*'Mapema'*
'Especially'	*is*	*'Hasa'*
'So then ...'	*is*	*'Hivyo basi / hivi'*

24. Expressions of relationships in time

'Still', 'Not yet'	*is*	*'Bado'*
'Quite'	*is*	*'Kidogo'*
'Not quite yet'	*is*	*'Bado kidogo'*
'Later'	*is*	*'Baadaye'*
'Early'	*is*	*'Mapema'*
'Now'	*is*	*'Sasa'*
'Afterwards'	*is*	*'Halafu'*

'Before'	*is*	*'Kabla ya'*
'Always'	*is*	*'Siku zote'*
'Always'	*is also*	*'Mara zote' or 'Mara kwa mara'*
'Suddenly'	*is*	*'Ghafula'*
'Day'	*is*	*'Siku'*
'Today'	*is*	*'Leo'*
'Tomorrow'	*is*	*'Kesho'*
'Yesterday'	*is*	*'Jana'*
'This morning'	*is*	*'Asubuhi ya leo' or 'Asubuhi hii'*
'Tonight'	*is*	*'Usiku wa leo'*
'Last night'	*is*	*Jana usiku'*
'Next week'	*is*	*'Wiki ijayo'*
'Long ago'	*is*	*'Zamani'*
'The third' (of the month)	*is*	*'Tarehe tatu'*
'Period of time'	*is*	*'Wakati' or 'Muda'*
'After that time...'	*is*	*'Baada ya muda'*
'Before that time...'	*is*	*'Kabla ya muda'*
'At that time'	*is*	*'Wakati huo'*
'I do not know when they are coming'	*is*	*'Sijui wanakuja muda wakati gani'*
'When we are ready...	*is*	*'Wakati tukiwa tayari...*
...we can begin'	*is*	*... tunaweza kuanza'*
'I will do it...'	*is*	*'Nitafanya/nitaifanya...*
...when I have time'	*is*	*'...wakati nikiwa na muda'*

Grammatical notes:

All these descriptions relating to time stay the same in whatever context they are used. There are no rules to learn about them – only the job of remembering them. The same comments apply to the parts of the day.

'Wakati' means a period of time. ('Muda' is another word meaning much the same.) There is no actual word for 'when' except as a question, and 'wakati' can sometimes perform this function – e.g. 'sijui wanakuja wakati/muda gani'.

'I will do it' should perhaps be 'Nitaifanya' or 'Nitaufanya', but there is difficulty in selecting which pronoun to use for 'it'. One way around this is to say, 'I will do <u>thus</u>. 'Thus' is 'Hivi' or 'Hivyo/ hivyo basi' In Swahili you can say, 'With me, to do thus' – i.e. 'Nami kufanya hivyo'. (This is not the only way to say this phrase, in the same way that in English there would be many ways of expressing 'I will do it', e.g. 'I'll get around to it'.)

The literal translation of 'I will do it when I have time' is therefore: 'With me to do it thus, time me with time'. Reassuringly for the learner, this illustrates the fact that in Swahili, it is sometimes quite acceptable to simply string the words together without too much in the way of tenses and conjugations.

25.   Numbers and telling the time

'One tree'	is	'Mti mmoja'
'Two trees'	is	'Miti miwili'
'Two tables'	is	'Meza mbili'
'Eleven trees'	is	'Miti kumi na m-/moja' (ten + one)
'One book'	is	'Kitabu kimoja'
'Two books'	is	'Vitabu viwili'
'Eleven books' (ten plus one)	is	'Vitabu kumi na ki-/moja'
'Eleven men'	is	'Wanaume kumi na mmoja'
'Twenty-two men'	is	'Wanaume ishirini na wawili'
'322 men' is		'Wanaume mia tatu ishirini na wawili'

'What is the time now?'	is	'Saa ngapi sasa / Ni saa ngapi?'
'First hour am' (7 o'clock am)	is	'Saa moja asubuhi'
'First hour pm' (7 o'clock pm)	is	'Saa moja usiku'
'9.15pm' (i.e. third hour + quarter)	is	'Saa tatu na robo usiku'
'It's about nine o'clock'	is	'Ni kama saa tatu kamili' (about
the 3rd hour)		
'First'	is	'-a kwanza'
'First man'	is	'Mwanaume wa kwanza'
'First tree'	is	'Mti wa kwanza'
'First book'	is	'Kitabu cha kwanza'
'First answer'	is	'Jibu la kwanza'
'First house	is	'Nyumba ya kwanza'

Grammatical notes:

Sita, saba, tisa and kumi, all stay the same in any context. The others act like adjectives, and have to agree with what they are describing. In the case of ordinals, (i.e. the words representing the order of numbers – first, second, etc), it is the '-a' of the phrase '-a kwanza', which is preceded by the agreement for whatever it is you are talking about.

The ordinals beyond 'first' just use the normal cardinal numbers with no change:

'Third man'	is	'Mwanaume wa tatu'
'Third tree'	is	'Mti wa tatu'
'Third book'	is	'Kitabu cha tatu'

When expressing three-figure numbers, only one 'na' is used, and is the penultimate word:

'Four hundred and twenty three'	is	'Mia nne ishirini na tatu'
'Seven hundred and four'	is	'Mia saba na nne'

When expressing thousands, especially when nothing else follows, the number of thousands is said after the word for 'thousand/s':

'Seven thousand'	*is*	*'Elfu saba'*
'Seven thousand and four'	*is*	*'Elfu saba na nne'*

However, when expressing long numbers where there needs to be a 'na' in the thousands, to save confusion, it is easier to put the number of thousands before the word 'elfu'.

'14,403'	*is*	*'Kumi na nne elfu, mia nne na tatu'*

The word for 'month' is 'mwezi'. To say the month, simple cardinal numbers are used, combined with the word 'wa'. The word for 'date' is 'tarehe', and this does not even need the 'wa':

'First month' (January)	*is*	*'Mwezi wa kwanza'*
'Third month' (March)	*is*	*'Mwezi wa tatu'*
'The 1st day of the month'	*is*	*'Tarehe moja'*
'The 3rd day of the month'	*is*	*'Tarehe tatu'*

Anything denoting quantity is always the last word in the phrase.

26.　　Quantity

'How many trees?'	*is*	*'Miti mingapi?'*
'How many men?'	*is*	*'Wanaume wangapi?'*
'A few trees'	*is*	*'Miti michache'*
'A few men'	*is*	*'Wanaume wachache'*
'Many trees'	*is*	*'Miti mingi'*
'Many men'	*is*	*'Wanaume wengi'*
'Much bread'	*is*	*'Mikate mingi'*
'Many books'	*is*	*'Vitabu vingi'*
'Plenty of books'	*is*	*'Vitabu vingi'*
'Plenty of men'	*is*	*'Wanaume wengi'*
'Some bread'	*is*	*'Mkate kiasi'*
'Another tree'	*is*	*'Mti mwingine'*
'A whole (loaf of) bread'	*is*	*'Mkate mzima'*
'A whole book'	*is*	*'Kitabu kizima'*
'Each book'	*is*	*'Kila kitabu'*
'Each tree'	*is*	*'Kila mti'*
'Each person'	*is*	*'Kila mtu'*
'Every person'	*is*	*'Kila mtu'*
'Everybody'	*is*	*'Kila mtu'*

The words for 'many', (ingi); and 'some/another', (-ingine); both start with a vowel, so when receiving their front-end changes, there is a merging of vowels, exactly as seen with adjectives. So, wa-ingi becomes 'wengi'; m-ingi becomes 'mwingi'; mi-ingi becomes 'mingi'; ki-ingi becomes 'kingi'; etc.

There is one exception to the rule that anything dealing with quantity comes at the end of the word – 'kila' always comes at the front.

27.   All and any: '-ote' and '-o -ote'

'All of us'	*is*	*'Sisi sote'*
'All of you'	*is*	*'Ninyi nyote'*
'All of them' (M-Wa class)	*is*	*'Wao wote'*
'All the trees' (M-Mi class)	*is*	*'Miti yote'*
'All the books' (Ki-Vi class)	*is*	*'Vitabu vyote'*
'They all went'	*is*	*'Walikwenda wote'*
'They all went' (M-Mi class)	*is*	*'Ilikwenda yote'*
'They all went' (Ki-Vi class)	*is*	*'Vilikwenda vyote'*
'The whole (loaf of) bread is mine'	*is*	*'Mkate wote ni wangu'*
'All the loaves are mine'	*is*	*'Mikate yote ni yangu'*
'Any of them' (M-Wa class)	*is*	*'Yoyote kati yao' (plural)*
'Any of the trees' (M-Mi class)	*is*	*'Miti yoyote' (plural)*
'Any of the books' (Ki-Vi class)	*is*	*'Vitabu vyovyote' (plural)*
'Anyone' (M-Wa class)	*is*	*'Mtu yoyote' (singular)*
'Any of the bread' (M-Mi class)	*is*	*'Mkate wowote' (singular)*
'Any of the book' (Ki-Vi class)	*is*	*'Kitabu chochote' (singular)*
'Any of the good book'	*is*	*'Kitabu kizuri chochote'*

These descriptions have slightly different agreements to normal – e.g. 'kitabu chote' rather than 'kitabu kiote'. This is because both '-ote' and '-o -ote' begin with a vowel, and, as we have seen, the agreements at the front of the word are slightly modified when this happens.

Note that '-o -ote' in the plural means 'any', but in the singular it can mean 'any bit of'.

Finally, we should note that as descriptions of quantity, these words would always come at the end of a phrase, e.g. 'any of the good bread' is 'mkate mzuri wo wote'.

28. Indirect object pronouns: Actions to, at, or for someone or something

'They are going to town to bring books'
　　　　　　　　　　　　is　　*'Wanakwenda mjini kuleta vitabu'*
'They are going to town to bring me a book'
　　　　　　　　　　　　is　　*'Wanakwenda mjini kuniletea kitabu'*
'They are coming to town to answer'
　　　　　　　　　　　　is　　*'Wanafika mjini kujibu'*
'They are coming to town to answer me'
　　　　　　　　　　　　is　　*'Wanakuja mjini kunijibu'*
'They are returning to town tomorrow'
　　　　　　　　　　　　is　　*'Wanarudi mjini kesho'*
'They are returning to town tomorrow for bread'
　　　　　　　　　　　　is　　*'Wanarudia mkate mjini kesho'*

Grammatical notes:

Indirect object pronouns, (eg 'to me', 'to them'), are translated the same as normal object pronouns - Me = ni; you (one) = ku; him/her = m; us = tu; you (>1) = wa; and them = wa.

It is not in the pronoun itself that the distinction is found between direct and indirect. To make the direct object (eg 'him') into the indirect object, ('to him'), an 'i' or an 'e' is inserted into the <u>verb</u>, typically before the final 'a'. In every situation where the action is directed at something, this change occurs: return <u>for</u>; cook <u>for</u>; wash <u>for</u>; give <u>to</u>; read <u>to</u>; etc. Therefore, the object immediately follows in the sentence.

In the case where the verb already ends in two vowels, 'li' or 'le' is used so as to prevent making three vowels in a row: kuondo<u>le</u>a; kuchuku<u>li</u>a. With the Arabic action words that end in '-u', the '-u' is replaced with '-ia', eg 'kujibu' becomes 'kujibia'.

29.   Making an action reciprocal – another use of '-na'

'They are washing'	is	'Wanaosha/wanafua'
'They are washing one another'	is	'Wanaoshana'
'They will see'	is	'Wataona'
'They will see one another'	is	'Wataonana'
'We are answering'	is	'Tunajibu'

'They are coming to town to answer me' is
                    'Wanakuja mjini kunijibu'
'They are coming to town to answer one another'   is
                    'Wanakuja mjini kujibiana'
'We are answering one another'   is   'Tunajibiana / Tunajibizana'

Grammatical notes:

When 'na' is used to mean that an action is reciprocal, then it is on the end of the verb. In cases of verbs ending in 'u', the verb first has to undergo the same change as when dealing with indirect object pronouns – ie the 'u' becomes 'ia'.

Technically, what has happened in such cases is that the Arabic verb has changed to its prepositional form before the '-na' is added. (i.e. the verb ending first changes from '-u' to '-ia', which changes the meaning from e.g. 'kujaribu', ('to try'), to 'kujaribia', ('to try to/with/for'). The '-na' is then added to the prepositional form, to make 'kujaribiana' = 'to try for one another'.

30.   Doing things to oneself – '-ji-'

'To teach'	is	'Kufunza/kufundisha';
'To learn' (i.e. teach <u>onesself</u>)	is	'Ku<u>ji</u>funza/kujifundisha'
'To see'	is	'Kuona';
'To see onesself'	is	'Kujiona'
'To beat'	is	'Kupiga'
'To beat onesself'	is	'Kujipiga'
'He taught himself'	is	'Alijifunza/alijifundisha'
'They beat themselves'	is	'Walijipiga'
'We have seen ourselves'	is	'Tumejiona'

Grammatical notes:

The insertion of '-ji-' immediately before the main stem of an action word makes the action refer to one's self. The change is the same, irrespective of whether it refers to myself, himself, themselves, etc.

When, by contrast, one wishes to convey the sense of 'I myself', or 'we ourselves', there is a special word for this: '-enyewe':

'I myself have helped'	*is*	*'Mimi mwenyewe nimesaidia'*
'The tree itself has helped'	*is*	*'Mti wenyewe umesaidia'*
'The book itself has helped'	*is*	*'Kitabu chenyewe kimesaidia'*

31. Conjunctions and adverbial connecting words

'Therefore, he came...'	*is*	*'Kwa hiyo alikuja...'*
'... instead of me'	*is*	*'... badala ya mimi / badala yangu'*
'His book is the same as theirs'	*is*	*'Kitabu chake ni sawa na chao'*
'I will go after eating'	*is*	*'Nitakwenda baada ya kula'*
'I am telling him about the town'	*is*	*'Ninamweleza habari ya mji'*
'I am telling him about the town'	*is*	*'Ninamwambia kuhusi mji'*
'Perhaps he might want to go'	*is*	*'Labda atahitaji kwenda'*
'Equally, he might want to go'	*is*	*'Sawasawa atahitaji kwenda'*
	('Equally' can also be:	*'vilevile' or 'pia')*
'Thus, he will want to go'	*is*	*'Hivyo atahitaji kwenda'*
'We will also go together'	*is*	*'Vilevile tutakwenda pamoja'*

Grammatical notes:

Technically, 'perhaps' and 'instead' are adverbs, because they modify the interpretation of the verb. A conjunction is a connector such as 'but' or 'and'. Many times, however, words such as 'perhaps' and 'instead' act as the link between two parts of a sentence. When they do so, as with adverbs, their form is always the same, and does not need to agree with other parts of the sentence.

Their position in the sentence is much the same as for English.

32. Questions

'Where will he come?'	*is*	*'Atakuja wapi?'*
'Who will come?'	*is*	*'Nani atakuja?'*
'Why will he come?'	*is*	*'Kwa nini atakuja?'*
'When will she come/arrive?'	*is*	*'Lini atafika/atawasili?'*
'Which man will arrive?'	*is*	*'Mwanaume gani atafika?'*
'How many men will arrive?'	*is*	*'Wanaume wangapi watafika?'*
'What did you cook?'	*is*	*'Ulipika nini?'*
'In which way will you cook?'	*is*	*'Utapika vipi?' or 'Utapikaje?'*
'How did you cook?' 'Well!'	*is*	*'Ulipikaje?' 'Vizuri!'*

The words for 'where?' and 'in which way' tend to go at the end of the phrase. The words 'Why?', 'When?' and 'Who?', however, are more likely to be found as the first word in the sentence. 'Which' always relates to a choice, and so follows the word for thing the question is about. The word 'what?' typically relates to an action, and so follows the action word. The question 'How', (which in Swahili is simply '-je'), also relates to an action, but instead of following the action word is actually added to the end of it.

The only one of these questions which needs to take an agreement is 'How'. All the rest stay the same, without needing to agree with any other word in the sentence.

33. Relatives: Who, which and whom – 'amba'; 'must'; and the letter 'o'

'The man whom I hit'	is	'Mwanaume ambaye nilimpiga'
'The man who is smelling bad'	is	'Mwanaume ambaye ananuka'
'The men who are smelling bad'	is	'Wanaume ambao wananuka'
'The tree which is smelling bad'	is	'Mti ambao unanuka'
'The trees which are smelling bad'	is	'Miti ambayo inanuka'
'The things which I burned'	is	'Vitu ambavyo niliunguza /nilichoma'
'The thing which is smelling bad'	is	'Kitu ambacho kinanuka'
'The things which are smelling bad'	is	'Vitu ambavyo vinanuka'
'The things which are bad'	is	'Vitu ambavyo ni vibaya'
'The things which were bad'	is	'Vitu ambavyo vilikuwa vibaya'
'The things which had badness'	is	'Vitu ambavyo vilikuwa na ubaya'

Grammatical notes:
The words 'who', 'whom', 'what', 'that', and 'which' can be 'relatives' – i.e. they form part of an explanation. In these cases, there is no difference between these words in Swahili, and they can all be translated as 'amba-'.

Furthermore, although in English we can sometimes omit the relative – e.g. 'The man I hit', instead of 'the man whom/that I hit', in Swahili that is not allowed. The relative must be present in such a sentence.

The relative will always be referring to something or someone. The end of the word 'amba' is changed to produce agreement with the person or thing(s) it is referring to. The 'amba' ending will agree with this person or thing(s), and will follow that word in the sentence.

	singular	plural
For M-Wa words	'ambaye'	'ambao'
For M-Mi words:	'ambao'	'ambayo'
For Ki-Vi words	'ambacho'	'ambavyo'
For Ji-Ma class	'ambalo'	'ambayo'
For N class	'ambayo'	'ambazo'

In each case, the word means 'who' or 'whom' or 'which' or 'that' or 'what'. (E.g. 'the man who/whom/which/that I hit' In English we choose between these four words, according to certain grammatical rules, but in Swahili they are all translated by 'amba' – 'Mwanaume ambaye nilimpiga'.

For the grammatically minded, you might have noticed that, in the sentence "The man who is smelling bad", the subject of the sentence is 'the man'. On the other hand, in the sentence "The man whom I hit", the man is the object, (and 'I' am the subject). In English, this makes a difference: you use 'who' for the subject, and 'whom' referring to the object. For the most part in Swahili, this bit of technical detail does not matter – you say first in the sentence the thing you are referring to, and then the 'amba' word in agreement with it, irrespective of whether it is a subject or an object.

The word 'whose' is also dealt with using 'amba-':

'The person whose things were bad'   *is*
        'Mtu ambaye vitu vyake vilikuwa vibaya/mtu ambaye mambo yake yalikuwa mabaya/-- alikuwa na mambo mabaya/ya ovyo'

('The person whose … his things … they were bad').

A common usage of the relative is in constructions with the word 'must':

'The people who must work now   '
                is   **'Watu ambao lazima wafanye kazi sasa'**
'The trees which must be seen'
                Is   **'Miti ambayo lazima ionwe/ionekane'**
'The books which must be read'
                Is   **'Vitabu ambavyo lazima visomwe'**

The word 'lazima' means 'must', and needs to be followed by the subjunctive, because by definition it is dealing with something which might not happen. So, in Swahili, you have to say, 'The people who might work now', but the 'lazima' adds a sense of having to. Compare:

'The people who come'	*is*	**'Watu ambao huja'**
'The people who came'	*is*	**'Watu ambao walikuja'**
'The people who might come'	*is*	**'Watu ambao wanaweza kuja'**

'The people who must come'   is   **'Watu ambao lazima waje'**

There is another way of expressing the relative, without using the intervening word comprising 'amba+agreement'. In this case, you just use the agreement alone – ie the bit you would have added to the 'amba-' word – but you insert it into the verb after the tense sign:

'The man whom I hit'   is   **'Mwanaume ambaye nilimpiga'**
'The man whom I hit'   is   **'Mwanaume niliyempiga'**
'The tree which is smelling bad'   is   **'Mti ambao unanuka'**
'The tree which is smelling bad'   is   **'Mti unaonuka'**
'The things which I burned'   is   **'Vitu ambavyo niliunguza/nilichoma'**
'The things which I burned'   is   **'Vitu nilivyounguza/nilivyochoma'**

Note that the endings of the amba word, (apart from the first), is always 'o'. When you leave the 'amba' out, you get:

	singular	plural
For M-Wa words	'-ye-'	'-o-'
For M-Mi words:	'-o-'	'-yo-'
For Ki-Vi words	'-cho-'	'-vyo-'
For Ji-Ma class	'-lo-'	'-yo-'
For N class	'-yo-'	'-zo-'

This 'o' ending can also be used instead of the normal ending for the demonstratives ('this'; 'that'). The words for 'these' are:
'hawa' (M-Wa); 'hii', (M-Mi); 'hivi', (Ki-Vi); 'haya' (Ji-Ma); 'hizi', (N and U).

If there is a situation in which you are relating back to something already referred to, then you can change these to:
'hao' (M-Wa); 'hiyo', (M-Mi); 'hivyo', (Ki-Vi); 'hayo' (Ji-Ma); 'hizo', (N and U).

These then mean '**this**', (the thing we are really talking about), as opposed to just 'this'. When used in the 'o' form, the demonstrative can come either before or after the vowel:

'These children are really good'   is   **'Watoto hawa ni wazuri sana'**
'These children are really good'   is   **'Hawa watoto ni wazuri sana'**
'These shops are really good'   is   **'Maduka haya ni mazuri sana'**

You can even use the endings of the relative, (ye, o, cho, etc), added to the end of 'na-', to make the sense of having the thing being referred to, (See Ch. 35)

'A child? I have one'   is   **'Mtoto? Ninaye (mmoja)'**
'Children? I have them'   is   **'Watoto? Ninao'**

'Books? I have them'	*is*	*'Vitabu? Ninavyo'* etc.
'A child? I have come with one'	*is*	*'Mtoto? Nimekuja naye'*
'Children? I have come with them'	*is*	*'Watoto? Nimekuja nao'*
'Books? I have come with them'	*is*	*'Vitabu? Nimekuja navyo'* etc.

You need to look out then, for the letter 'o'. In the same way that a word ending in 'a' might well be a verb, and a word ending in 'e' might be a subjunctive, so it is that a word ending in 'o' might be a 'relative', if it is preceded by 'amba'. But if you spot an 'o' where you were not expecting it, in the middle of a verb, right after the 'na' or 'li' part, (signifiying present or past simple tense), the letter 'o' might represent a relative, meaning 'which', or 'who/m' etc.

One common example of this is with the verb 'kupita', meaning 'to pass'. 'Ilipita' therefore means 'it passed'. If, however, you are talking about the year which passed, then the word for 'year' is mwaka', and being an M-Mi word, the relative is 'o' or 'ambao'. Thus, if you insert the relative in the verb you get:

'The year which passed' (i.e. last year)   is   'Mwaka uliopita'

Thus, the word 'iliopita' means 'last'. However, it is sometimes spelt 'iliyopita', (e.g. 'the last trees'); or 'kilichopita' (the last book); 'zilizopita', (the last dogs); etc, depending on what thing or things is being talked about. (By the way, 'next' is '-a kufuata'. 'Kufuata means 'to follow'.)

If you want to use the 'o' insertion in the future, you have to add the letters 'ka' in front: kaye; kao; kayo; kacho; etc. (The reason for this relates to the resulting 'taka' sound in the middle of the word – 'taka' means 'want'):

'The man whom I hit'	*is*	*'Mwanaume ambaye nilimpiga'*
'The man whom I will hit'	*is*	*'Mwanaume nitakayempiga'*
'The tree which is smelling bad'	*is*	*'Mti ambao unanuka'*
'The tree which will smell bad'	*is*	*'Mti utakaonuka'*
'The things which I burned'	*is*	*'Vitu ambavyo niliunguza'*
'The things which I will burn'	*is*	*'Vitu nitakavyounguza'*

Negative sentences using the relative use the insert '-si-' instead of na, li, ta, etc. The 'si' insert is the same in past present and future, so Swahili makes no distinction between these in the negative:

'The man whom I will hit'	*is*	*'Mwanaume nitakayempiga'*
'The man whom I will not hit'	*is*	*'Mwanaume ambaya sitampiga*
'The tree which will smell bad'	*is*	*'Mti utakaonuka'*
'The tree which will not smell bad'	*is*	*'Mti ambao hautanuka'*

'The things which I will burn'	*is*	*'Vitu nitakavyounguza'*

184

'The things which I will not burn'   is   *'Vitu ambavyo sitaunguza'*
'The things which I am not burning' is   *'Vitu nisivyoununguza' (same)*
'The things which I did not burn'   is   *'Vitu   ambavyo   sitaunguza'*
(same)

The word 'when', (when used as an explanation rather than a question), is also an insert in the same place, but is translated as '-po' in the present and past, and 'kapo' in the future, (again, creating a 'taka' sound in the middle of the word):

'The man whom I will hit'   is   *'Mwanaume nitakayempiga'*
'When I will hit the man...'   is   *'Nitakapompiga mwanaume'*
'When I hit the man...'   is   *'Nilipompiga mwanaume'*

These rules seem weird at first, but are very elegant, and always apply, and so are actually much simpler than the complex and sometimes unpredictable rules of English grammar. In Swahili, simply knowing a short verb – e.g. kupiga = to hit, means that you are immediately able to express all sorts of complex sentences in the past and future, just by knowing how to handle the short prefixes, suffixes and inserts which add so much meaning.

34.   Preposition + object: 'With it' – Na +it

'The tree? I am cooking with it'   is   *'Mti? Ninapika nao'*
'The trees? I am cooking with them'   is   *'Miti? Ninapika nayo'*
'The book? I am cooking with it'   is   *'Kitabu? Ninapika nacho'*
'The books? I am cooking with them' is   *'Kitabu? Ninapika navyo'*
'The tooth? I am cooking with it'   is   *'Jino? Ninapika nalo'*
'The water? I am cooking with it'   is   *'Maji? Ninapika nayo'*
'The egg? I am cooking with it'   is   *'Yai? Ninapika nalo'*
'The eggs? I am cooking with them'   is   *'Mayai? Ninapika nayo'*

Grammatical notes:

When a preposition such as 'with' refers directly to an object or objects, the translation in Swahili typically combines the two to form a single word. Such is the case when expressing 'with it' or 'with them'. The word for 'with' is 'na-'. Because there is no fixed word for 'it' or 'them', exactly the same endings as have just been used for 'amba', are used with 'na-', to express 'with it/them':

M-MI class:	with it = nao	with them = nayo
Ki-Vi class:	with it = nacho	with them = navyo
Ji-Ma class:	with it = nalo	with them = nayo
N class:	with it = nayo	with them = nazo

When adding personal pronouns (I, we, you, etc), to the front of these words, the meaning becomes 'I/we/you have it/some/them':

'The tree? I have it'	*is*	*'Mti? Ninao'*
'Trees? I have some'	*is*	*'Miti? Ninayo baadhi/kiasi'*
'The book? I have it'	*is*	*'Kitabu? Ninacho'*
'Books? I have some'	*is*	*'Vitabu? Ninavyo kiasi/baadhi'*
'The tooth? I have it'	*is*	*'Jino? Ninalo'*
'Teeth? I have them'	*is*	*'Meno? Ninayo'*
'The dog? I have it'	*is*	*'Mbwa? Ninaye'*
'The dogs? I have them'	*is*	*'Mbwa? Ninao'*

Summarising the last two sections, the insertion of 'o', (or yo, ye, zo, lo, o, cho, etc) adds the sense of which…, who…, that…. The very same short insert, (or in the case of 'o', just a single letter), placed at the end of the word amba, produces the same meaning.

Placed instead after 'na', it means 'with it/them'.
Placed after wana, it means 'We have it/some/them'.

The final grammatical point to make about the letter 'o' is that it is frequently the last letter of a noun, and indeed you can make some nouns by changing the last letter to 'o', e.g.:
Kusikia = to listen;   sikio = ear
Kucheza = to play mchezo = game
Kuisha = to finish   mwisho = end
Kufungua = to open   ufunguo = key

35.   Relatives of manner – jinsi; kama; kadiri

'They knew how to cook'	*is*	*'Walijua jinsi ya kupika'*
'I know the way to clean'	*is*	*'Ninajua jinsi ya kusafisha'*
'They do not know …'	*is*	*'Hawajui…*
'…how to cook…'	*is*	*'…jinsi ya kupika…'*
'…like they cooked…'	*is*	*'…kama walivyopika…'*
'…a long time ago'	*is*	*'…zamani'.*
'I am cooking like you cook'	*is*	*'Ninapika kama unavyopika'*
'I will help…'	*is*	*'Nitasaidia…'*
'…as much as I can'	*is*	*'…kadri ninaweza/niwezavyo'*
'As far as I have gone'	*is*	*'Kadri nimekwenda/nilivyokwenda'*

Grammatical notes:

Sometimes the second part of a sentence is related to the first in that it explains more about the manner of the first – egh the way in which things are done. The connection between the two will be either a word such as 'how...', or a short phrase such as 'as much as...' Technically, such a link is known as a 'relative of manner'. Typical examples are: 'how...', ('Jinsi'); or 'as far as...', ('kadri'); or as/like, ('kama'). These never change their form to agree with another word.

(In some Swahili-speaking cultures, kama is also used to translate the word 'if' – eg 'If I go' = 'Kama (ni)nakwenda'.)

The manner in which things are done can also be described by adverbs – words which in English end in '-ly' such as 'badly'. As already mentioned, these also do not change their form in the various settings. When you think about it, that is not surprising, as words relating to the manner in which something was done are relating to a verb, and in a verb, there is nothing to dictate any agreements.

Adverbs typically begin with 'vi' or 'ki', eg vizuri, (well); kifupi, (briefly). (In practice, these ki and vi beginnings sometimes seems to be interchangeable – you might well hear 'kizuri' instead of 'vizuri').

The 'vi' beginning can also be used with the 'relative' ending 'o', to produce the insert 'vyo'. This would therefore mean a description of the manner, and would be used where we would use a relative word, such as 'how' or 'as':

'They knew how to cook'	is	*'Walijua jinsi ya kupika'*
'They knew how I will cook'	is	*'Walijua nitakavyopika'*
'They cook how I cook' (or 'as I am cooking')		
	is	*'Wanapika ninavyopika'*
'... as/like they cooked...'	is	*'... kama walivyopika...', or*
'... as/like they cooked...'	is	*'... tulivyopika...'*

Note: 'Jinsi ya' way of saying 'how' was used with the infinitive, (how **to** cook), whereas the vyo form was used with the conjugated verb, (eg how I, or you, or we cook). If you want to emphasise, you can even use both, (but using just 'jinsi', not 'jinsi ya'):

'They knew how I will cook'	is	*'Walijua nitakavyopika' or*
'They knew <u>how</u> I will cook!'	is	*'Walijua jinsi nitakavyopika'*
'As far as I have gone'	is	*'Kadri nimekwenda', or*
'<u>As far as</u> I have gone!'	is	*'Kadri nilivyokwenda'*

This 'vyo' form can be used in many common situations, when you want to convey the way in which something was done, or even sometimes it can refer to what was said or done:

'I can't cook like I used to (be able to)'
                                        is   *'Siwezi kupika kama nilivyozoea'*
'I will cook as much as I can'
                                        is   *'Nitapika (kwa) kadri niwezavyo'*
'Have you understood what we said?'
                                        is   *'Umeelewa tulivyosema?'*

'-vyo' therefore means 'in that way'. It can be used in the form 'hivyo', precisely to mean 'in that way'. The related word, 'hivi', means 'thus'. (Again, with the 'vi' ending meaning relative), e.g.:

'I can't cook in that way'   *is*   *'Siwezi kupika hivyo'*
'Do it in this way / Do it thus'   *is*   *Ufanye hivi'*

The 'o' ending is also related to the words normally used for yes and no. The part preceding is 'ndi-', which is an emphatic form of 'ni', (it is). 'Ndi' can be added to pronouns for instance to produce an emphatic one, eg 'ndimi' = 'I really am'. When added to the relative ending we get:

'It really is thus'   *is*   *'Ndiyo/sawa'*
'It is not thus'   *is*   *'Siyo/sivyo'*

('Ndi-' meaning 'indeed' – which it sounds very much like! – can be used in other settings of emphasis, e.g.

'This is indeed the person'   *is*   *'Huyu ndiye (mtu)'*
'This is indeed the book'   *is*   *'Hiki ndicho kitabu'*
'This is indeed the shop'   *is*   *'Hili ndilo duka hasa'*
'This is the very dog'   *is*   *'Huyu ndiyo/ndiye mbwa'*

36.   N class words

'Journey' or 'Journeys'   *is*   *'Safari'*
'House' or 'Houses'   *is*   *'Nyumba'*
'Good father or fathers'   *is*   *'Baba mzuri'*
'Good car or cars'   *is*   *'Motokaa nzuri'*
'Bad car or cars'   *is*   *'Motokaa mbaya'*
'Black car or cars'   *is*   *'Motokaa nyeusi'*
'Long car'   *is*   *'Motokaa ndefu'*
'Good news'   *is*   *'Habari njema'*
'The rain has arrived'   *is*   *'Mvua imefika'*
'The flight has arrived'   *is*   *'Ndege imefika'*

'The flights have arrived'	is	'Ndege zimefika'
'The flight has not arrived'	is	'Ndege haijafika'
'The flights have not arrived'	is	'Ndege hazijafika'
'This flight has arrived'	is	'Ndege hii imefika'
'These flights have arrived'	is	'Ndege hizi zimefika'
'That flight has arrived'	is	'Ndege ile imefika'
'Those flights have arrived'	is	'Ndege zile zimefika'
'Where is the flight?'	is	'Ndege iko wapi?'
'Where are the flights?'	is	'Ndege ziko wapi?'
'My flight'	is	'Ndege yangu'
'My flights' (or 'My birds')	is	'Ndege zangu'
'Two flights' (or 'Two birds')	is	'Ndege mbili/wawili'
'My grandfathers have arrived'	is	'Babu zangu wamefika'
'My grandmother has arrived'	is	'Bibi yangu amefika'
'My daughter'	is	'Binti yangu'
'My sons'	is	'Mwanangu (wa kiume)'
'That friend has arrived'	is	'Rafiki yule amefika'
'Those neighbours have arrived'	is	'Jirani wale wamefika'

Grammatical notes:

Whereas M-Mi words begin with M or Mi, and Ki-Vi words begain with Ki or Vi, N-class nouns begin with a great variety of letters. They are called N-class, because the adjectives often have a front-end change to n- ... but by no means always, (see below).

A further confusion is that with N-class nouns, in some cases there is no natural plural – e.g. 'mvua' = 'rain'. In other cases, there is no natural singular – e.g. 'maji' = 'water'. Even when there <u>are</u> singulars and plurals, (e.g. 'paka' = 'cat'), the word itself does not change from singular to plural. Even the adjective does not change its agreement from single to plural, such that the phrase 'nice dog' is translated precisely the same as 'nice dogs', ('mbwa nzuri').

The way that you know whether you are talking of one dog or more than one is by looking at the change the noun produces either at the front of the verb, or in the demonstrative 'this' or 'that'.

In general, the agreement of adjectives with N-class words is 'n-' e.g. 'nzuri'. However, if the adjective begins with B, V and sometimes P, the agreement is 'm-', (e.g. '-baya' = 'bad'). If the adjective begins with a vowel, (e.g. '-eusi' = 'black'), then the agreement is 'ny-'. There are exceptions, eg 'good news', (the agreement is 'nj-'), and 'long', in which '-refu' becomes 'ndefu'.
Besides '-zuri', another word for 'good' is '-ema'. With an N-class noun, this becomes 'njema'.

The agreements for N-class words use 'i-' (or 'y') for singular, and 'z-' or 'zi-' for plurals. The possessive words of mine, yours, his, etc, begin with a 'y' for the singular, and a 'z' for the plural.

The words for 'this' and 'these'are 'hii', and 'hizi'. 'That' and 'those' are 'ile', and 'zile'.

When counting N-class things, there are no agreeing letters at the start of the number, even for those numbers that normally have them.

37. Ji-Ma Class of words

'New eye'	is	'Jicho jipya'
'New eyes'	is	'Macho mapya
'Big eye'	is	'Jicho kubwa'
'Big eyes'	is	'Macho makubwa'
'This eye'	is	'Jicho hili'
'These eyes'	is	'Macho haya'
'That eye'	is	'Jicho lile'
'Those eyes'	is	'Macho yale'
'My eye'	is	'Jicho langu'
'My eyes'	is	'Macho yangu'.
'Their eye'	is	'Jicho lao'
'Their eyes'	is	'Macho yao'.
'One shop'	is	'Duka moja'
'Two shops'	is	'Maduka mawili'
'Black tooth'	is	'Jino jeusi'
'Black teeth'	is	'Meno meusi'
'Big tooth'	is	'Jino kubwa'
'Big teeth'	is	'Meno makubwa'
'Dirty milk'	is	'Maziwa machafu'
'Dirty water'	is	'Maji machafu'.
'It is burning'	is	'Linawaka'
'They are burning'	is	'Yanawaka'
'It is not burning'	is	'Haliwaki'
'They are not burning'	is	'Hayawaki'
'The egg? I am burning _it_'	is	'Yai? Nina_li_unguza'
'The eggs? I am burning t_hem_'	is	'Mayai? Nina_ya_unguza'
'Where is the answer'	is	'Jibu liko wapi?'
'The tooth is in the bag'	is	'Jino limo/liko mfukoni'
'The teeth are in the bag'	is	'Meno yamo/yako mfukoni'
'The tooth is in the kitchen'	is	'Jino lipo/liko jikoni
'The teeth are in the kitchen'	is	'Meno yako/yapo jikoni'

Grammatical notes:

The Ji-Ma group of words especialy includes plants and plant produce – but it also includes some conceptual words, such as many of the well-recognised professions. To form the plural, you normally drop the 'ji-', and add 'ma-', (or sometimes 'me-'). Sometimes this does not happen.

Unlike the N-class nouns, which mainly do not begin with the letter N, Ji-Ma class noun frequently are recognisable by the 'ji-' or 'ma-' beginning. However, for many of the Ji-Ma words, the singular does not have the 'ji-' as the starting letters, though it will take 'ma-' in the plural.

The agreements at the front end of any adjective are: 'j-' or ji-' for the singular; 'm-' or 'ma-' for the plural. The word for black, ('-eusi'), because it starts with a vowel, has the agreements 'j-' and 'm-' (not 'ji' and 'ma').

With adjectives of more than one syllable, beginning with a consonant, note the absence of 'ji-' on the adjective in the singular, but the presence of 'ma-' in the plural. With actions involving Ji-Ma words, the agreements are 'li-' and 'ya-'. 'Mine'/'yours', and PKM plocation words also use 'li-' & 'ya-'.

38.   U class words

'This nice love has arrived'	*is*	*'Upendo huu mzuri umefika'*
'That bad love has arrived'	*is*	*'Upendo ule mbaya umefika'*
'My love has arrived'	*is*	*'Upendo/Mpenzi wangu umefika'*
'Their love has arrived'	*is*	*'Upendo wao umefika'*
'Their love? It has arrived'	*is*	*'Upendo wao? Umefika'*
'That love? He has destroyed it!'	*is*	*'Upendo ule? Ameuharibu'*
'A black wind has arrived'	*is*	*'Upepo mweusi umefika'*
'Black winds have arrived'	*is*	*'Pepo nyeusi zimefika'*
'Those two dirty black faces'	*is*	*'Nyuso zile mbili chafu nyeusi'*
'This big, long face'	*is*	*'Uso huu mkubwa, mrefu'*
'Those boards are burning'	*is*	*'Mbao zile zinawaka/zinaungua'*
'Their boards are burning'	*is*	*'Mbao zao zinawaka/zinaungua'*
'My boards? They are burning'	*is*	*'Mbao zangu? Zinawaka'*
'My boards? He is burning them'	*is*	*'Mbao zangu? Anaziunguza'*
'Some diseases are coming'	*is*	*'Magonjwa baadhi yanakuja'*
'Those diseases are coming'	*is*	*'Magonjwa yale yanakuja'*
'These diseases are coming'	*is*	*'Magonjwa haya yanakuja'*
'These diseases are not coming'	*is*	*'Magonjwa haya hayaji'*
'Dirty diseases are coming'	*is*	*'Magonjwa machafu yanakuja'*
'Big diseases are coming yanakuja'	*is*	*'Magonjwa makubwa/hatari*
'Black diseases are coming'	*is*	*'Magonjwa meusi yanakuja'*
'Their diseases are coming'	*is*	*'Magonjwa yao yanakuja'*

Grammatical notes:

When you want to turn an adjective, (eg good, bad), into an actual topic or subject or thing, (eg goodness or badness), you add 'u-' (or 'w') to the beginning. By definition, there is no plural form for such words. The agreement is normally 'u', as in 'umefika', ('it has arrived'). 'This' is 'huu', and 'that' is 'ule'.

To say 'mine' should be 'u-angu', but of course this gets changed to 'w' for all the possesives: wangu; wako; wake; watu; wenu; wao.

The main irregularity with U Class words is that the agreement for adjectives is not 'u', but is instead the same as for M-MI words – ie 'm-', (or 'mw-' before a vowel), eg 'beautiful love' = 'upenda mzuri'.

Unfortunately, the U-class is not purely of things which are singular, and does contain some words which have a plural version. In each case, the singular word starts with a 'u', but start of the plural has a number of options – e.g. no letter; 'ny-'; 'nd-'; or even occasionally 'm-'. Not only do the pluralslooks like N-class words, but their agreements are also for N-class. For adjectives, this varies according to the first letter of the rest of the adjective. The agreeing letter is typically 'n', but can be 'ny-', '-m-', or even 'nd'.

The other agreements for plural U-class words are based on the letter 'z':
'zi-' for 'they' or 'them'; 'hizi' for 'these'; 'zile' for 'those'; and 'zangu', 'zako', etc for 'mine', yours', etc:

With the words for 'quarrel' and 'disease': in the singular, they are normal U-class words. However, in the plural, the beginning of the word becomes 'ma-'. The 'ma-' beginning can be used in any situation where you want to really emphasise the bigness or seriousness, and, conventionally, you always do this with the plural of these words. This means also that these words, in the plural, function like Ma-class words, and their agreements are based on 'ma-' and 'ya-'.

In the English phrase 'those two black faces', the parts of speech are: demonstrative + quantity + adjective + noun. In Swahili, they are put precisely in the reverse order.

39.   Pa Class, plus more on location

'A good place with trees'   is   *'Mahali pazuri penye miti'*
'Some bad places are smelling bad'   is   *'Baadhi ya Mahali pabaya*
                              pananuka' (baadhi ya sehemu mbaya zinanuka)
'My place? I like it!'   is   *'Mahali pangu? Ninapapenda'*
'My place is in the village'
          is   *'Mahali pangu papo/pako kijijini' (kwangu ni kijijini)*
'This place is in the village'   is   *'Mahali hapa pako kijijini'*
'That place is in the village'   is   *'Mahali pale pako kijijini'*
'Their place is in the village'   is   *'Mahali pao pako kijijini'*
'That (ill-defined) large place has trees'
                              is *'Mahali pale pakubwa kuna miti'*
'My (ill-defined) place has trees'   is   *'... kwangu kuna miti'*
'His (ill-defined) place is burning'   is   *'...kwake kunawaka/kunaungua'*

'The nice rice inside is burning'
          is   *'... mchele mzuri ndani unawaka/unaungua'*
'That good area is burning'
          is   *'...mahala pale pazuri panawaka'*
'Inside my (village) there is a tree'
          is   *'... kijijini kwangu/mwangu mna / kuna mti*
'Inside my village there is a tree'
          is   *'Kijijini mwangu/kwangu kuna / mna mti'*
'Inside this village there is a tree' is   *'Kijijini humu mna/kuna mti'*
'Inside (this) good (village) it smells'
          is   *'... mzuri mnanuka' (katika kijiji hiki kizuri kunuka)*
'Inside this good village it smells'
          is   *'Katika kijiji hiki kizuri mnanuka /kunanuka'*

Grammatical notes:

The Pa class of words only has one word in it!: Mahali. 'Pa-' also means 'it' when referring to 'mahali':

When referring to an indefinite place, ('that place vaguely over there', 'that general area'), then you do not use 'mahali'. You simply drop the word for the place altogether, and just use the adjective and rest of the sentence

The '-ni' at the end of 'kijiji' implies that the sentence is about location, and tells you to look out for a P, K or M agreement.

However, when you use 'katika' as a way of saying 'inside', you do not use 'M' agreements – you use whatever other agreements are in the sentence. Also, you do not add the '-ni' to the end of the word for the place you are talking about.

40. Passive – insertion of '-w-'

'I will answer'	*is*	*'Nitajibu'*
'I will be answered'	*is*	*'Nitajibiwa'*
'I will eat'	*is*	*'Nitakula'*
'I will be eaten'	*is*	*'Nitaliwa'*
'The tree used the water'	*is*	*'Mti ulitumia maji'*
'The tree was used by the man'	*is*	*'Mti ulitumiwa na mwanaume'*
'The tree was used by the dog'	*is*	*'Mti ulitumiwa na mbwa'*
'The tree was cut by the man'	*is*	*'Mti ulikatwa na mwanaume'*
'The tree was cut by (or with) the knife'	*is*	*'Mti ulikatwa kwa kisu'*

Grammatical notes:

Where the action is being done to the subject, the letter 'w' is inserted just before the end of the verb. (Or sometimes '-liw-'; '-lew-'; or'-iw-').

If the verb ends in an 'i' or an 'u', then '-wa' or 'liwa' is added to the end.

When the action is being done by a human, the connecting word is 'na'.
When it is being done by a thing or things, the connecting word is 'na/kwa':

41. The stative – insertion of '-k-'

'I have been seen. I was seen by the child'
>   *is*   *'Nimeonwa/nimeonekana. Nilionwa na mtoto'*

'I am cut. I was cut by the child
>   *is*   *'Nimekatwa. Nilikatwa na mtoto'*

'The tree is burnt. It was burnt by the child'
>   *is*   *'Mti umeunguzwa/umechomwa.*
>   *(or 'Umeunguzwa/umechomwa na mtoto')*

'I can be seen by the child'	*is*	*'Naweza kuonwa na mtoto'*
'The book? It is open'	*is*	*'Kitabu? Kimefunguka/kimefunuliwa'*
'The bag? It is put out'	*is*	*'Mfuko? Umewekwa nje'*
'The tree? It can be burnt'	*is*	*'Mti? Unaweza kuunguzwa'*
'The tree? It can be used'	*is*	*'Mti? Unaweza kutumiwa/kutumika'*
'The bag? It smells bad'	*is*	*'Mfuko? Hunuka vibaya'*
'I am mistaken	*is*	*'Nimekosea'*
'We were very tired'	*is*	*'Tulikuwa tumechoka sana'*
'They will be very angry'	*is*	*'Watakasirika sana'*
'You have been lost'	*is*	*'Mmepotea/umepotea'*

Grammatical notes:

If you want to describe the <u>state</u> something is in, without specifying who made it into that state, then instead of an insertion based on the letter 'w', you use one based on the letter 'k'. When forming sentences using these words describing the state of something, you use it with the '-me-' tense, (the past perfect).

These sentences, denoting the state something is in, might also imply that the state is a possibility.

In the stative in English, we use two verbs – e.g. 'I am cut': 'am' is an auxiliary verb. There is no need to translate this is Swahili. The 'k' insertion conveys the sense of 'am' or 'have become'.

42.   Causing things to happen – '-isha'; '-esha'; '-ka' and '-za'

'We will make ready to journey'   is   'Tutajitayarisha kusafari'
'They have put right those poor people'
             is   'Wamewaweka sawa wale watu maskini'
'They will explain to these poor people'
             is 'Wataeleza kwa watu maskini hawa'
             (or Watawaelezea/watawafafanulia watu hawa masikini)
'I am going to listen to this person'
             is   'Nitamsikiliza mtu huyu'
'We are getting dressed now'
             is   'Tunavaa sasa hivi/tunajiandaa sasa'
'The people reached the town at 8pm'
             is   'Watu walifika mjini saa mbili usiku'

'We will feed the people at 8am'
             is   'Tutawalisha watu saa mbili asubuhi'
'The people will be fed by 8am'
             is   'Watu watalishwa saa mbili asubuhi'
'I have lost the child'   is   'Nimepoteza mtoto'
'I am going to fill the bag'   is   'Nitajaza mfuko'
'I am going to insert the things into the bag'
             Is   'Nitaingiza vitu ndani ya mfuko'
             (or nitajaza / nitaweka / nitapakia)
'We can drive to town'   is   'Tunaweza kuendesha kuelekea mjini'
'You will tire and will be lost'
             is   'Utachoka na utapotea' (Mtachoka na mtapotea)

Grammatical notes:
Swapping the last letter of a word for '-esha' or '-isha' typically implies that you are now talking about a cause – e.g. the change from 'kuoza' to 'kuozesha' changes the meaning from 'to rot' into 'to cause to rot'. The change is '-isha', typically when the word in question does not contain an 'o' or an 'e', otherwise it is '-esha'. Sometimes the ending used is '-za' or '-eza' or '-iza'. Sometimes an extra letter such as an 'l' is inserted

Swapping the last letter of a word for '-esha' or '-isha' therefore deals with actions that produce a result. It is not only verbs which can be dealt with in this way, but also adjectives.

Note that the word for 'poor' ('maskini'), being an adjective of Arabic orgin, does not take any front-end agreements.

Up to this point, the paragraph numbering in the second section has reflected that of the first. However, there are a few other issues of grammar which are explained for the first time here, as their explanation needs particular grammatical reference.

43.   The present indefinite tense: -a-

There are in fact more than one present tenses in Swahili. Much the most common is the 'na' tense – e.g. 'I am cooking' = '(ni)napika'. However, sometimes you may wish to convey that something happens from time to time – e.g. 'Do you cook?' (i.e. 'Do you cook sometimes?') If you translate this as 'unapika?' it would mean 'are you currently cooking?'

The correct way to express this phrase, then, is to omit the 'n' from 'na', and just insert 'a': 'Uapika?' Not surprisingly, this does not look right, and so the 'u' is changed to 'w': 'Wapika?

"Do you cook?'   is   *'Wapika/unapika?"*

The full list of pronouns, combined with the '-a-' tense marker is:
M-Wa class   I = na;   You = wa   s/he = a   We = twa   You (pl) = mwa   They = wa

M-MI class:	it = wa	they = ya
Ki-Vi class:	it = cha	they = vya
Ji-Ma class:	it = la	they = ya
N class:	it = ya	they = za
U class:	it = wa	they = za

E.g.:
'I read Swahili (sometimes)'   is   *'Nasoma Kiswahili'*
(note that this produces the same result as the common dropping of 'ni' at the start of the present continuous tense – eg 'Ninasoma' (I am reading) will often be said as '…nasoma'.)
'We try (sometimes)   is   *'Twajaribu'*
'We are trying (now)'   is   *'Tunajaribu'*

A peculiarity of this tense is that the 'ku' is dropped from monosyllabic verbs. This normally only happens with the indefinite tenses, (negative, imperative and subjunctive). However, the reason for dropping the 'ku-' is that this tense is actually itself indefinite – it does not say at all when you action is done, how often, etc.

Therefore:
'I eat (sometimes)'   is   *'Nala'*
'We come (sometimes)'   is   *'Twaja'*

44.   The 'Hu-' tense – 'usually'

The 'Hu' tense is, to an extent, not past present or future, because it deals with habitual actions – those things you usually did before, usually do now, and probably in the future will still usually do. It does not take any subject prefix, (ni, tu, wa, i, u, zi, etc). If you want to say who or what is usually doing the thing, you have to specify:

'I usually drink water'	*is*	*'(Mimi) hunywa maji'*
'The dog usually drinks water'	*is*	*'Mbwa hunywa maji'*
'The dogs usually drink water'	*is*	*'Mbwa hunywa maji' (same)*
'Water? The dog usually drinks it'	*is*	*'Maji? Mbwa huyanywa'*
'They usually like water'	*is*	*'(Wao) hupenda maji'*

Like the 'a' tense, monosyllabic verbs drop the 'ku':

'I usually eat food'	*is*	*'(Mimi) hula chakula'*
'The dog usually eats food'	*is*	*'Mbwa hula chakula'*
'The dogs usually eats food'	*is*	*'Mbwa hula chakula' (same)*
'Food? We usually try to eat it'	*is*	*'Chakula? Hujaribu kukila'*
'They usually go to town'	*is*	*'(Wao) huenda mjini'*
'You usually come to town'	*is*	*'Huja mjini'*

You may remember that the word for 'you', when talking in the negative in the present tense, is also 'hu'. The negative also drops the 'ku'. However, when dealing with present tense negative, the final 'a' of the vowel is changed to 'i'. With verbs of Arabic origin, this does not happen, so only context can tell you which tense is implied – even though meanings can be nearly opposite!:

'You usually come to town'	*is*	*'Huja mjini'*
'You do not come to town'	*is*	*'Huji mjini'*
You usually try'	*is*	*'Hujaribu'*
'You do not try'	*is*	*'Hujaribu' (Same!)*

45. The '-ka-' narrative tense: 'and so I...'; 'he went and...'; 'go and...', etc

In English, when telling a story, we often use different forms of verbs than when simply stating the bare English. So, for instance, the bare English might be 'He sold the book'; or 'Might I sell the book'. However, in a story, we might say, 'He went and sold the book'; or 'let me go and sell the book'. It is in such narrative circumstances that the 'ka' tense is used. It only is allowed, however, when you have already set the scene, and it is clear that you are telling a story.

So, for instance:

'He went into town that day...   is   *'Alienda mjini siku ile...'*
'... and he went and sold the book!'
                      is   *'...alienda na akauza kitabu!...'*
' ... and I said to him ...'   is   *'... nikamwambia ...'*
'... let me go and sell it!'   is   *'... ngoja niende nikakiuze!'*

Note that the story has to be introduced by a statement typically using the 'li' tense, that sets the scene that something happened in the past, and I am going to narrate something further. Thereafter, there are two ways in which the 'ka' tense has been used above: one in the 'indicative' – i.e. what happened – and one in the 'subjunctive' – what might be.

In relation to the indicative, the 'ka' tense can be translated as '...and so...'. There is no further definition as to when you are talking about, as you have already specified it at the beginning of the story. (This is a recognised story-telling technique: "I went to town. I open the car door, and there's a guy standing there. He asks me for a fag. I say I haven't got any..." etc.)

'... and so, he went and sold the book!'
          is   *'...hivyo, alienda akauza kitabu!...'*
'... and so, I brought the money...'   is   *'...hivyo, nikaleta pesa...'*

In the case of the subjunctive, it is used in slightly less of a story-telling mode, and can be translated as adding the sense of '...go and..':

'I sell it' (a book)   is   *'Ninakiuza'*
'Might I sell it?'   is   *'Naweza kukiuza?'*
'I hope that I might sell it'
          is   *'(Ni)natumaini/nadhani naweza kukiuza'*
'... let me go and sell it!'
          is   *'... Ngoja niende nikakiuze!' (Ngoja kikakiuze)*
'I eat'   is   *'Nala'*
'Might I eat?'   is   *'Naweza kula?'*
'Let me go and eat'   is   *'Ngoja niende nikale'*

'Let's go and drink'   is   'Tukanywe' or
'Let's go and drink' (i.e. 'we might go & we might drink')
                                        is   'Twende tukanywe'

46.   The infinitive, the gerund, and the uses of 'ku'

In English, I can say, '**Going** to work is good', or, with exactly the same meaning, '**To go** to work is good'. In the first example, the use of the '-ing' ending to make a sort of noun is called a gerund. In the second example, 'to go' is the infinitive, recognisably in Swahili by the 'ku-' prefix.

In Swahili, you use exactly the same word for both the gerund and the infinitive. The use of the infinitive as a gerund is an integral part of the language, and is an easy and correct way to translate sentences such as:

'I like reading'   is   '(Ni)napenda kusoma'
'To go to work is good'   is   'Kwenda kazini ni vizuri'
'Working is good'
         is   'Kufanyakazi/kujishughulisha ni vizuri/kuzuri'
'For children, playing is important'
         is   'Kwa watoto, kucheza ni muhimu'

When you look out for it, you will notice that there are many constructions where the gerund would be useful in Swahili, and it is translated using the 'ku-' form, exactly as for the infinitive. In effect, then, this makes the gerund a noun class in Swahili. The possessives, (mine /yours etc); the demonstratives, (this /that); the subject prefix, (it); and the 'of' & 'for' words are all based on 'ku' (or 'kw'):

'My reading is helping me'   is   'Kusoma kwangu kunanisaidia'
'Reading? It is helping me'   is   'Kusoma? Kunanisaidia'.
'This thinking is helping me a lot'
                    is   'Kufikiri huku kunanisaidia sana'
'That thinking is helping them a lot'
                    is   'Kufikiri kule kunawasaidia sana'
'Thinking of food helps me'
                    is   'Kufikiria chakula kunanisaidia'
'Thinking is suitable for pupils'
                    is   'Kufikiri kunafaa kwa wanafunzi'

The negative of the gerund is formed by putting the insert '-to'- after 'ku':

'Not reading is helping me'   is   'Kutosoma kunanisaidia'
'Not to be able to think is bad' is   'Kutoweza kufikiri ni vibaya'
'Not to eat was dangerous'   is   'Kutokula kulikuwa hatari'

'Not coming is not an option'   *is*   **'Kutokuja si hiari'**

The uses of 'ku' in Swahili, then, are multiple, and include:
- The infinitive   e.g. **ku**piga – to hit
- The gerund   e.g. **ku**piga – hitting
- Subject pronoun of the gerund eg kupiga **ku**nasaidia – hitting helps
- The demonstrative   e.g. hu**ku** – this
- Location   e.g. hu**ku** - hereabouts
- Combination eg **ku**piga hu**ku kuna**saida – this hitting helps
- Combination eg **ku**piga hu**ku kuna**saida – hitting hereabouts helps
- 'You' as an object   e.g. nina**ku**piga – I hit you
- The negative of 'li' in the past   eg hatu**ku**piga – we did not not hit
- Combination   e.g. hatu**kuku**piga – we did not hit you
- Combination   e.g. hatu**kuku**piga hu**ku** – we did not hit you hereabouts

Before leaving the gerund, it needs to be noted that sometimes, the gerund needs first to be put in the prepositional form. When preceded by a preposition, the sense is eg 'for cooking'. In this case, the word 'for' is translated as '-a', and is then followed by the prepositional form of the gerund:

'This knife is for cooking'   *is*   **'Kisu hiki ni cha kupikia'**
'This ball is for playing'   *is*   **'Mpira huu ni wa kuchezea'**

47.   Swahili translation of the word 'it' and 'they / them' – summary

In English, we use the words 'it' and 'they' or 'them' in a number of different ways, sometimes as an object and sometimes as a subject. A typical example of the use as an object would be: 'The book? I have it?' Use as a subject would be, e.g.: 'The book? It is here'. As we have seen, in Swahili, these pronouns are translated as an insert based on an agreement with whatever the object being referred to.

The words for 'it' and 'they' as a subject are identical to the words for 'it' and 'them' as an object. The only exception to this rule about subject pronouns being the same as object ones, is in the M-Wa class, which of course deals with people, so does not use 'it' and 'them'.

	Subject sing	Subject pl	Object sing	Object Pl
M-MI class:	it = u	they = I	it = u	them = i
Ki-Vi class:	it = ki	they = vi	it = ki	them = vi
Ji-Ma class:	it = li	they = ya	it = li	them = ya

N class:	it = i	they = zi	it = i	them = zi
U class:	it = u	they = zi	it = u	them = zi
Ku class	it = ku		it = ku	

However, we have just dealt with the 'a' tense, in which the object pronouns were for some reason different:

M-MI class:	it = wa	they = ya
Ki-Vi class:	it = cha	they = vya
Ji-Ma class:	it = la	they = ya
N class:	it = ya	they = za
U class:	it = wa	they = za

When dealing with location, (eg 'it is there') the normal inserts are added to the ending '-po':

M-Mi words:	It is:	Upo;	They are: Ipo
Ki-Vi words:	It is:	Kipo;	They are: Vipo, etc.

Sometimes, there is a need to use the word 'it' when there is no obvious noun to refer to, eg 'it is important'. In such cases, the simple word 'ni' is used in the present tense:

'It is good'   *is*   *'Ni nzuri/ni vizuri'*

In the past and future tenses, however, the N-class 'i' is used:

'It was good' ('It became good')   *is*   *'Ilikuwa nzuri/ilikuwa vizuri'*
'It will be good' ('It will become good')   *is*   *'Itakuwa nzuri/itakuwa vizuri'*

The N-class 'i' is used whenever you need to say 'it' without referring to anything in particular:

'It is raining'   *is*   *'Inanyesha'*

Finally, there is a shorthand for combining 'with' + 'it' or 'them':

M-MI class:	with it = nao/nayo	with them = nayo/nao
Ki-Vi class:	with it = nacho	with them = navyo
Ji-Ma class:	with it = nalo	with them = nayo
N class:	with it = nayo	with them = nazo
U class:	with it = nao	with them = nazo

48.   Summary of verb modifications to produce related meanings

Swahili very neatly allows you to create meaning in a predictable way, by using certain inserts into verbs. These inserts are mainly just before, (or replacing), the last letter:

The insertion of 'l' is the prepositional form. The insertion of 'w' or 'lew' describes the action in the passive, (e.g. to **be** cut; to **be** hit). Tha addition of 'na' makes it reciprocal:

'To cut'	is	*'Kukata'*
'To be cut for/to/on etc'	is	*'Kukatia/kukatiwa'*

(i = prepositional form)

'To be cut' (action of being cut) is *'Kukatwa' (w = to be...)*
'To be cut for' (combining the two above) is *'Kukatiwa' (i + w)*

'To guide'	is	*'Kuongoza'*
'To be guided'	is	*'Kuongozwa' (sometimes -lew-)*
'To be cut' (state of being cut)		is *'Kukatika'*

(k = describes a state)

'To cut one another'   is   *'Kukatana' (+na for reciprocal)*

The insertion of 'iz' or 'ish' (or similar), makes the verb describe an action leading to the state that something is in. To describe the actual state, the insertion is 'k'. in some cases, the change of meaning is subtle and /or metaphorical:

'To love'	is	*'Kupenda'*
'To cause to love'	is	*'Kupendeza' (z = causing)*
'To arrive'	is	*'Kufika'*
'To cause to arrive – ie to reach'	is	*'Kufikisha' (isha = also causing)*
'To wear/to cause to wear'	is	*'Kuvaa/ kuvalisha'*
'To dress/to cause to dress'	is	*'Kuvaa/ Kuvalisha'*
'To be tired'	is	*'Kuchoka'*
'To tire'	is	*'Kuchokesha'*

Even non-verbs can be treated this way:

'Must'	is	*'Lazima'*
'To matter'	is	*'Kujali/Kulazimisha'*
'Ready'	is	*'Tayari'*
'To make ready'	is	*'Kutayarisha'*
'Certainty'	is	*'Hakika'*
'To make certain'	is	*'Kuhakikisha'*
'To talk'	is	*'Kuongea'*
'To increase'	is	*'Kuongeza/kuongezeka'*
'To be increased'	is	*'Kuongezwa'*

'To guide'	*is*	*'Kuongoza'*
'To be guided'	*is*	*'Kuongozwa'*
'To be converted'	*is*	*'Kuongoka/kubadilishwa'*
'To direct'	*is*	*'Kuongoza/kuelekeza'*
'To be intelligible'	*is*	*'Kuelewa/kufahamu'*
'To follow a pattern'	*is*	*'kufuata mtiririko'*
'To explain'	*is*	*'Kueleza'*
'Explanation'	*is*	*'Maelezo/Elezo'*
'To go'	*is*	*'Kwenda/Kuenda'*
'To drive'	*is*	*'Kuendesha'*
'To be passable'	*is*	*'Kuendeka/kupitika'*
'To continue, to progress'	*is*	*'Kuendelea/kusonga (mbele)'*
'To adapt'	*is*	*'Kuzoea/Kuiga /kubadilika'*

For convenience of self-testing, the exercises of Section 2 are now presented again without explanation. Use this part to test yourself when you are fairly happy you have understood Section 2. If you are getting anything wrong, go back and find out why. The vocabulary has been kept very limited so that the main point of the test is understanding the grammar.

Once you are mainly getting the answers right, then record the sentences, and listen often and repeatedly – when you are walking, driving, doing the gardening, doing the cooking, etc. The grammar and this limited vocabulary will then painlessly sink in.

1. '-na-' Present continuous. M-Wa nouns

'The child is currently visiting the town' is *'Mtoto anazuru mji'*
'The children are visiting the town' is *'Watoto wanazuru mji'*
'The children are visiting the towns' is *'Watoto wanazuru miji'*
'The teacher is cooking bread' is *'Mwalimu anaoka mkate'*
'The teachers are cooking bread' is *'Walimu wanaoka mikate'*
'The pupil is hiding the bag' is *'Mwanafunzi anaficha mfuko'*
'The pupils are hiding the bag' is *'Wanafunzi wanaficha mfuko'*
'The pupils are hiding the bags' is *'Wanafunzi wanaficha mifuko'*
'The man is arriving' is *'Mwanaume anafika'*
'The women are arriving'' is *'Wanawake wanafika'*
'I am currently coming' is *'(Ni)nakuja'*
(When the meaning is obvious, the 'ni' part if often omitted in the spoken language)
'You are currently coming' (one person) is *'Unakuja'*
'S/he is currently coming' is *'Anakuja'*
'We are currently coming' is *'Tunakuja'*
'You are currently coming' (>1 person) is *'Mnakuja'*
'They are currently coming' is *'Wanakuja'*

2. M-Mi nouns

'The bread is burning' (i.e. aflame) is *'Mkate unawaka/unaungua'*
'The bag is sufficient' is *'Mfoko unatosha'*
'The smoke is smelling' is *'Moshi unanuka'*
'The body is smelling' is *'Mwilii unanuka'*
'The bodies are smelling' is *'Miili inanuka'*
'The hands are touching' is *'Mikono inagusa'*
'The plants are arriving' is *'Mimea yanafika'*
'The trees are burning' is *'Miti inawaka'*

'The mango trees are burning'	is	*'Miembe inawaka'*
'The tree? It is burning'	is	*'Mti? Unawaka'*
'The trees? They are burning'	is	*'Miti? Inawaka'*

3. Ki-Vi and Ch-Vy words

'The things are touching'	is	*'Vitu vinagusa'*
'The food is growing	is	*'Chakula kinaongeza'*
'The village is growing	is	*'Kijiji kinaongeza'*
'The man is bringing beds'	is	*'Mwanaume analeta vitanda'*
'The beds are arriving'	is	*'Vitanda vinafika'*
'The toilet is smelling'	is	*'Choo kinanuka'*
'The toilets are smelling'	is	*'Vyoo vinanuka'*
'The villages are burning'	is	*'Vijiji vinaungua'*

4. Na = To have

'Is-currently'	is	*'Na'*
'And'	is	*'Na'*
'With'	is	*'Na'*
'Have'	is	*'Na'*
'It has' (M-Mi class)	is	*'Una /ina'*
'They have' (M-Mi class)	is	*'Ina /wana'*
'It has' (Ki-Vi class)	is	*'Kina'*
'They have' (Ki-Vi class)	is	*'Vina'*
'I have a book'	is	*'Nina kitabu'*
'You have a book' (one)	is	*'Una kitabu'*
'S/he has a book'	is	*'Ana kitabu'*
'We have a book'	is	*'Tuna kitabu'*
'You (>1) have a book'	is	*'Mna kitabu'*
'They have a book'	is	*'Wana kitabu'*
'The villages have no food'	is	*'Vijiji havina chakula'*
'The village has no beds'	is	*'Kijiji hakina vitanda'*
'The village has beds'	is	*'Kijiji kina vitanda'*
'The child has a tree'	is	*'Mtoto ana mti'*
'The child has some trees'	is	*'Mtoto ana miti baadhi'*
'I have a bed and a book'	is	*'Nina kitanda na kitabu'*

'The villages have food'	is	*'Vijiji vina chakula'*
'The villages with food'	is	*'Vijiji vyenye chakula'*
'The villages without food'	is	*'Vijiji bila chakula'*
'The child has a bed and a book'	is	*'Mtoto ana kitanda na kitabu'*
'The child with a bed and a book'	is	*'Mtoto mwenye kitanda na kitabu'*
'The child without a bed and a book'	is	*'Mtoto bila kitanda na kitabu'*

'The village is increasing and has beds'
               is   'Kijiji kinaongezeka na kina vitanda'
'The books and the beds are burning'
               is   'Vitabu na vitanda vinawaka/vinaungua'
'I have food and books. They are sufficient'
               is   'Nina chakula na vitabu. Vinatosha'
'The child has no bed and no book'
               is   'Mtoto hana kitanda wala kitabu'

5. The verb 'To be'

'The man is good'	*is*	'Mwanaume ni mzuri'
'You are good'	*is*	'Wewe ni mzuri'
'You are not good'	*is*	'Wewe si mzuri'
'I am good'	*is*	'Mimi ni mzuri'
'I am not good'	*is*	'Mimi si mzuri'
'The tree is good'	*is*	'Mti ni mzuri'
'The book is good'	*is*	'Kitabu ni kizuri'
'The book is not good'	*is*	'Kitabu si kizuri'
'The food and the beds are good'	*is*	'Chakula na vitanda ni vizuri'
'The food and the beds are not good'	*is*	'Chakula na vitanda si vizuri'

6. 'He is not coming' - Expressing the negative of verbs

'I-not'	'You-not'	'S/he-not'	*is*	'Si-'	'Hu'	'Ha'
'We-not'	'You-not'	'They-not'	*is*	'Ha-tu'	'Ha-m'	'Ha-wa'
'It-not'	'They-not'	(M-Mi class)	*is*		'Ha-u'	'Ha-i'
'It-not'	'They-not'	(Ki-Vi class)	*is*		'Ha-ki'	'Ha-vi'

'The pupils do not come'	*is*	'Wanafunzi hawaji'
'He does not feed and does not wash'	*is*	'Halishi/hali na haoshi'
'<u>He</u> does not feed and does not wash'	*is*	'<u>Yeye</u> halishi na haoshi'
'The tree, it is not burning'	*is*	'Mti hauwaki'
'The plant does not feed'	*is*	'Mmea haulishi'
'The plants do not feed'	*is*	'Mimea hailishi'
'The toilet does not shut'	*is*	'Choo hakifungi'
'I do not have water'	*is*	'Sina maji'
'We do not have trees'	*is*	'Hatuna miti'

7. That is so! That is not so!

'That is so!'	*is*	'Ndiyo/ndivyo!'
'That is not so!'	*is*	'Siyo! (or sivyo)
'No'	*is*	'La' or can be 'Hapana'
'Are the bodies smelling?' – 'Yes!'	*is*	'Miili inanuka?' – 'Ndiyo!'
'Are the hands touching?' – 'Yes!'	*is*	'Mikono inagusa?' – 'Ndiyo!'

'Are the plants arriving?' – *'No!'*   is   *'Mimea yanafika?'* – *'Siyo!'* or *'La!'*
'Are the trees burning?' – *'They are!'*   is   *'Miti inawaka?'* – *'Ndiyo!'*
'The trees are not burning?' – *'They are!'*   is   *'Miti haiwaki?'* – *'Siyo!'*

8. Location – the PKM system

'The children are located hereabouts ...'	is	*'Watoto wako ...'*
'The children are located precisely...'	is	*'Watoto wapo ...'*
'The children are located within..'	is	*'Watoto wamo...'*
'The children are not located precisely...'	is	*'Watoto hawapo ...'*
'The book is located precisely .. .'	is	*'Kitabu kipo ...'*
'The books are located precisely ...'	is	*'Vitabu vipo ...'*
'The books are within ...'	is	*'Vitabu vimo ...'*
'Where?'	is	*'Wapi?'*
'Where are the children?'	is	*'Watoto wako wapi?'*
'Where are the books?'	is	*'Vitabu viko wapi?'*
'The books? They are not located ...'	is	*'Vitabu? Havipo ...*
'The books? They are not within ...'	is	*'Vitabu? Havimo ...*
'The children are not located within..'	is	*'Watoto hawamo...'*

9. Location – In; on; nearby = -ni.

'Where is the bread? It's on the table'
                          is   *'Mkate uko wapi? Upo mezani'*
'Where are the children? They're in the village'
                          is   *'Watoto wako wapi? Wapo/wako kijijini'*

'By the river'	is	*'Mtoni'*
'By the good river'	is	*'Katika mto mzuri'*
'By the rivers'	is	*'Mitoni'*
'By the good rivers'	is	*'Katika mito mizuri'*
'On the good bed'	is	*'Katika kitanda kizuri'*
'On the beds'	is	*'Katika vitanda/vitandani'*

10.   Location – Here = Hapa or Huku. There = Pale or Kule.

'The children are (located) right here'	is	*'Watoto wapo hapa'*
'The children are right there'	is	*'Watoto wapo pale'*
'The books are somewhere round here'	is	*'Vitabu viko huku'*
'The rivers are somewhere there'	is	*'Mito iko kule'*
'Where is the doctor?'	is	*'Mganga yuko wapi?'*
'The doctor is here somewhere'	is	*'Mganga yuko huku'*
'The doctor is not around here'	is	*'Mganga hayuko huku'*
'Is the doctor right here?'	is	*'Mganga yupo hapa?'*
'The doctor is not here.	Is	*'Mganga hayupo hapa...*
...He is in the village'	is	*Yuko kijijini'*
'The doctor is not there	is	*'Mganga hayupo pale...*

'...He is in the town somewhere'	is	'Yuko mjini'
'The books? They are not here'	is	'Vitabu? Havipo'
'The children? They are not here'	is	'Watoto? Hawapo hapa'
'Up there'	is	'Huko'

11. Location – (In that place) there is; there are: Pana, Kuna & Mna

'There are books right here'	is	'Pana vitabu hapa'
'There are books right there'	is	'Pana vitabu pale'
'There are some books hereabouts'	is	'Kuna vitabu baadhi huku'
'There are some books thereabouts'	is	'Kuna vitabu baadhi kule'

'There are books somewhere in the kitchen'

is   'Kuna vitabu mahali fulani jikoni'

'The books are somewhere in the kitchen'

is   'Vitabu viko mahali fulani jikoni'

'There are no books exactly here'	is	'Hakuna vitabu hapa'
'There are no books hereabouts	is	'Hakuna vitabu huku'
'There are books in the river'	is	'Mna vitabu mtoni'
'There are no books within the river'	is	'Hamna/hakuna vitabu mtoni'

12. Location – Nearby: this; these: H- Further away: that; those: -le

'This man'	is	'Mwanaume huyu'
'That man'	is	'Mwanaume yule'
'These men'	is	'Wanaume hawa'
'Those men'	is	'Wanaume wale'
'This tree'	is	'Mti huu'
'That tree'	is	'Mti ule'
'These trees'	is	'Miti hii'
'Those trees'	is	'Miti ile'
'This book'	is	'Kitabu hiki'
'That book'	is	'Kitabu kile'
'These books'	is	'Vitabu hivi'
'Those books'	is	'Vitabu vile'

'This nice book is burning'

is   'Kitabu hiki kizuri kinaungua'

'That nice book is burning'

is   'Kitabu kile kizuri kinaungua'.

13. Location – In front of, on top of, behind of, etc.

'Where is the book?'	is	'Kitabu kiko wapi?'
'The book is on top of the tree'	is	'Kitabu kipo juu ya mti'
'The book is in front of the tree'	is	'Kitabu kipo mbele ya mti'
'The book is among 'of' the trees'	is	'Kitabu kiko kati ya miti'
'The book is close to the tree'	is	'Kitabu kipo karibu na mti'
'The book is far from the tree'	is	'Kitabu kipo mbali na mti'
'Beside me'	is	'Kando yangu'
'Beside you' (One person)	is	'Kando yako'
'Beside him'	is	'Kando yake'
'Beside us'	is	'Kando yetu'
'Beside you' (>One person)	is	'Kando yenu'
'Beside them'	is	'Kando yao'

Location – Directions

'Towards'	is	'Kuelekea'
'To the right'	is	'Kulia' or 'Kwa kulia'
'He went to the right'	is	'Alikwenda kulia'
'Right hand'	is	'Mkono wa kulia'
'To the left'	is	'Kushoto'
'Near to'	is	'Karibu na'
'Before ...'	is	'Kabla ya'
'More than'	is	'Zaidi ya'
'In here'	is	'Humu'
'In there'	is	'Mle'
'Travel straight on...'	is	'Safiri kwa kunyoosha...'
'Travel straight on...'	is also	'Safiri moja kwa moja ...'
'... as far as the town'	is	'... mpaka mjini'
'Morogoro is far from Arusha'	is	'Morogoro ni mbali na Arusha'

14. Possession and the possessive

'Beside me'	is	'Kando yangu' (location)
'Beside you'	is	'Kando yako' (location)
'My pupil'	is	'Mwanafunzi wangu'
'Your pupil' (just one of you)	is	'Mwanafunzi wako'
'The pupil of the teacher'	is	'Mwanafunzi wa mwalimu'
'The pupil of the teachers'	is	'Mwanafunzi wa walimu'
'The pupils of the teacher'	is	'Wanafunzi wa mwalimu'
'The tree of the teacher'	is	'Mti wa mwalimu'
'The trees of the teacher'	is	'Miti ya mwalimu'
'The thing of the teacher'	is	'Kitu cha mwalimu'
'The things of the teacher'	is	'Vitu vya mwalimu'
'The things of the teachers'	is	'Vitu vya walimu'

'My pupils'	is	'Wanafunzi wangu'
'My tree'	is	'Mti wangu'
'My trees'	is	'Miti yangu'
'My book'	is	'Kitabu changu'
'My books'	is	'Vitabu vyangu'

'I am going to my house'
         is   '(Ni)nakwenda kwenye nyumba yangu'
'I am going to my house'
         Is also '(Ni)nakwenda nyumbani kwangu'

15. Adjectives

'A big man'	is	'Mwanaume mkubwa'
'Big child'	is	'Mtoto mkubwa'
'Big trees'	is	'Miti mikubwa'
'Big book'	is	'Kitabu kikubwa'
'Big books'	is	'Vitabu vikubwa'
'A good book'	is	'Kitabu kizuri'
'A very good book'	is	'Kitabu kizuri sana'
'An honest child'	is	'Mtoto mwaminifu' (m+a=mwa)
'Honest children'	is	'Watoto waaminifu' (wa+a=wa)
'A black child'	is	'Mtoto mweusi' (m+e=mwe)
'Part of the child'	is	'Mtoto mwingine' (m+i=mwi)
'Many children'	is	'Watoto wengi' (wa+i=we)
'Some black teachers'	is	'Walimu baadhi weusi' (wa+e=we)
'Some black trees'	is	'Miti baadhi myeusi' (mi+e=mye)
'Many trees'	is	'Miti mingi' (mi+i=mi)
'A black book'	is	'Kitabu cheusi' (ki+e=che)
'Black books'	is	'Vitabu vyeusi' (vi+e=vye)
'Dangerous men'	is	'Wanaume hatari'
'Dangerous food'	is	'Chakula hatari'
'Dangerous trees'	is	'Miti hatari'

'A bigger man'	is	'Mwanaume mkubwa kuliko'
'Bigger trees'	is	'Miti mikubwa kuliko''
'A better book'	is	'Kitabu kizuri kuliko''
'More dangerous men'	is	'Wanaume hatari kuliko'

'More dangerous men' (comparison)
         is   'Wanaume hatari zaidi/kuliko'
'More dangerous men' (more of them)
         is   'Wanaume hatari zaidi'

'More big trees'	is	'Miti mikubwa zaidi'
'More of those better books'	is	'Zaidi ya vile Vitabu vizuri'
'More than those books'	is	'Zaidi ya vitabu vile'
'More than three books'	is	'Zaidi ya vitabu vitatu'

'This child is bigger'   is   *'Mtoto huyu ni mkubwa zaidi/kuliko...'*
'This child is bigger than that one' *('to pass that one')*
       is   *'Mtoto huyu ni mkubwa kupita yule/zaidi ya yule'*
'This book is better than that one' is   *'Kitabu hiki ni kizuri kupita kile'*

16.   Greetings

'Hi!'   is   *'Jambo!'*
     Response: 'Jambo!'
'(polite greeting from child)   is Shikamoo!'*
     Response: 'Marahaba!'
'How's it going?' (to 1 person)   is   *'Hujambo?'*
     Response: 'Sijambo!'; or 'Safi!' (Pure!); or 'Poa!', (Cool!)
'How's it going?' (to 2+)   is   *'Hamjambo?'*
     Response: 'Hatujambo!'

'How are you?' 'Complete!'   is   *'U hali gani?' 'Mzima!'*
'What news?' 'Fine!'   is   *'Habari gani?'*   *:'Nzuri!' or 'Njema!'*
'How's things?'   is   *'Mambo vipi/Habari?' (i.e. News?')*
'Fine. How's things with you?' is   *'Poa/Nzuri. Habari yako' (Your news?)*

'Good morning, friend'   is   *'Habari za asubuhi, Bwana?'*
(i.e. 'What news of the morning?')
'Good!'   *(i.e. good news! – i.e. all OK)* is   *'Nzuri' or 'Njema!'*
'What news of the daylight?'   is   *'Habari ya mchana?'*
'Good day, ladies and gentlemen!'   is
            'Siku njema mabibi na mabwana!'
'God be with you until we meet again!'   is
            'Mungu awe nanyi mpaka tutakapoonana tena!'
'It's very good to be here!'   is
            'Ni vizuri sana kuwa hapa!'
'Goodbye!' (end of day)   is   *'Kwaheri!': 'Kwaheri!'*
'Goodbye!' (to 2+)   is   *'Kwaherini!'*
            (to 2+): 'Kwaherini!'
'May I come in? '   is   *'Hodi'*
'Yes, come in!'   is   *'Karibu!'*
            (or Karibuni if >1)

17. The past – to have done something = '-me-'; did something = '-li-'

'We have gone'	is	'Tumekwenda'
'We went'	is	'Tulikwenda'
'We have spoken'	is	'Tumesema /Tumeongea'
'We spoke'	is	'Tulisema /Tuliongea'
'The teachers have started'	is	'Walimu wameanza'
'The teachers started'	is	'Walimu walianza'
'I gave you'	is	'Nilikupa / nilikupatia'
'I have given you'	is	'Nimekupa'
'They are walking'	is	'Wanatembea'
'They have walked'	is	'Wametembea'
'They walked'	is	'Walitembea'
'They were walking'	is	'Walikuwa wakitembea'

('They became (that) they were walking')

'They had walked'	is	'Walikuwa wametembea'

('They became (that) they have walked')

18. Negative of the past – '-ja-', '-kwe-', '-ae-', '-hu-', '-ha-' and '-ku-'

'I have not gone'	is	'Sijakwenda'
'I did not go'	is	'Sikukwenda'
'You have not gone'	is	'Hujakwenda'
'You did go' (ie you went)	is	'Hulikwenda'
'You did not go'	is	'Hukukwenda'
'We have not gone'	is	'Hatujakwenda'
'We did not go'	is	'Hatukukwenda'
'S/he did not go'	is	'Hakukwenda'
'You did not go' (plural)	is	'Hamkukwenda'
'They did not go'	is	'Hawakukwenda'
'The doors have not shut'	is	'Milango haijafunga'
'The doors did not shut'	is	'Milango haikufunga'

19. The future – '-ta-'

'I will go'	is	'Nitakwenda'
'I will not go'	is	'Sitakwenda'
'We will speak'	is	'Tutasema'
'We will not speak'	is	'Hatutasema'
'The bag will open'	is	'Mfuko utafunguka'
'The bag will not open'	is	'Mfuko hautafunguka'
'The doors will shut'	is	'Milango itafunga'
'The doors will not shut'	is	'Milango haitafunga'

'They are wanting/going to go'	is	'Wanataka kwenda'
'It is wanting/going to rain'	is	'Inataka kunyesha mvua'
'I am going to fall'	is	Nitaanguka / nitadondoka'

20. The imperative and the subjunctive: Giving orders and making requests

'To cook'	is	'Kupika'
'Cook! (to one person)	is	'Pika...'
'Cook! (to 2+ people)	is	'Pikeni...'
'Would you cook...? (to one person)	is	'Upike...?'
'Would you cook...? (to 2+ people)	is	'Mpike...?'
'Would you not cook...? (to one person)	is	'Usipike...?'
'Would you not cook...? (to 2+ people)	is	'Msipike...?'
'Please'	is	'Tafadhali'
'Please would you cook ...?' (Already polite)	is	'Upike...?'
'<u>Please</u> would you cook ...?' (extra polite!)	is	'Tafadhali upike'
'Would you cook...? (to one person)	is	'Upike...?'
'I want you to cook' ('I want that you might cook')	is	

'Ninataka upike'

'It's best that you cook now'	is	'Bora upike sasa'
'I am cooking in order that you might eat'	is	'Ninapika ili ule'
'I am cooking in order that he might eat'	is	'Ninapika ili ale'
'Let him cook' (i.e. 'might he cook?')	is	'acha apike'
'Let's cook' (ie 'might we cook?')	is	'Ngoja/acha tupike'
'Let's not cook' (ie 'might we not cook?')	is	'Ngoja tusipike'
'I might cook'	is	'Nipike/naweza kupika'
'I might not cook'	is	'Nisipike/naweza nisipike'
'Am I not to cook?'	is	'Nisipike?' (same)
'Let me not cook'	is	'Nisipike' (same)
'Let them not cook'	is	'Wasipike'
'They might not cook'	is	'Wasipike' (same)
'Are they not going to cook?'	is	'Hawatapika?' (but with '?')
'We refused to let them cook'	is	'Tuliwakataza wasipike'

21. The conditional: If: '-ki-'. If not: 'kama' or 'sipo'

'If I cook...'	is	'Nikipika'
'If you cook'	is	'Ukipika'
'If I don't cook' (= if I might not cook)	is	'Kama nikipika
'If I <u>do not</u> cook'	is	'Ni<u>sipo</u>pika'
'Unless I cook'	is	'Nisipopika'
'We saw them cook<u>ing</u>'	is	'Tuliwaona wa<u>ki</u>pika'
'If I come'	is	'Nikija'

'If I come'	is	'Kama nikija'
'If I (will) come'	is	'Kama nitakuja'
'If I came'	is	'Kama nilikuja'
'If I do not come'	is	'Nisipokuja'
'If I will not come'	is	'Kama nisipokuja'
'Unless I come'	is	'Nisipokuja'
'We saw them cooking'	is	'Tuliwaona wakipika'
'The trees? We saw them burning'	is	'Miti? Tuliiona ikiwaka'
'The books? They saw them burning'	is	'Vitabu? Tuliviona vikiwaka'

'If I cook...'	is	'Nikipika'
'If you cook'	is	'Ukipika'
'If I come'	is	'Nikija'
'If you come'	is	'Ukija'
'If you come to Dar, you will see the sea'	is	
		'Kama ukija Dar, utaona bahari'

'If I come, I will bring some food'	is	
		'Kama nikija, nitaleta chakula'
'I would bring some food'	is	'Ningeleta chakula'
'I would like...'	is	'Ningependa...'
'I would do'	is	'Ningefanya'
'I would not like...'	is	'Nisingependa...'
'I would not do'	is	'Nisingefanya'

'I would be doing (if)...'	is	'Ningekuwa nikifanya / ninafanya...'
'They would be coming (if)...'	is	'Wangekuwa wakija / wanakuja ...'
'I would have liked / if I were to have liked...'	is	'Ningalipenda...'

'We would have been cooking (if)'	is	'Tungalikuwa tukipika'
'I would not have liked'	is	'Nisingalipenda...'
'We would not have been cooking (if)'	is	'Tusingalikuwa tukipika'
'I was cooking'	is	'Nilikuwa nikipika'
'I saw him cooking'	is	'Nilimwona akipika'

22. Object pronouns: Me, you, him/her, us, them

'They are giving me the tree'	is	'Wa-na-ni-pa mti'
(wa = they; na = currently; ni = to me; pa = give; mti = the tree)		
'They are giving you the tree' (to 1 person)	is	'Wana-ku-pa mti'
'They are giving him/her the tree'	is	'Wana-m-pa mti'
'They are giving us the tree'	is	'Wana-tu-pa mti'
'They are giving you the tree' (>1 person)	is	'Wana-wa-pa mti'
'They are giving them the tree'	is	'Wana-wa-pa mti'
'The book? It hit me'	is	'Kitabu? Kilinipiga'
'The book? It hit you' (hitting one person)	is	'Kitabu? Kilikupiga'

'The book? It hit us'		is	'Kitabu? Kilitupiga'
'The book? It hit you' (>one)		is	'Kitabu? Kiliwapiga'
'The book? It hit them' (people)		is	'Kitabu? Kiliwapiga'
'The book? It hit it' (hit a tree)		is	'Kitabu? Kiliupiga'
'The book? It hit them' (hit trees)		is	'Kitabu? Kiliipiga'
'The book? It hit it' (hit another book)		is	'Kitabu? Kilikipiga'
'The book? It hit them' (hit other books)		is	'Kitabu? Kilivipiga'

23. Adverbs: Descriptions of actions

'Nice'	is	'-zuri'
'Nicely' or 'well'	is	'Vizuri'
'Bad'	is	'-baya'
'Badly'	is	'Vibaya'
'Brief'	is	'-fupi'
'Briefly'	is	'Kifupi'
'Briefly'	is also	'Kwa kifupi'
'More than...'	is	'Zaidi ya...'
'Furthermore...'	is	'Zaidi ya....'
'Instead of...'	is	'Badala ya...'
'After that time...'	is	'Baada ya muda/wakati huo...'
'Before that time...'	is	'Kabla ya muda...'

'Truthfully'	is	'Kwa kweli/kiukweli'
'Usually'	is	'Kwa kawaida'
'Luckily	is	'Kwa bahati'
'Therefore'	is	'Kwa hiyo'
'Because...'	is	'Kwa sababu'
'Because of / On account of...'	is	'Kwa ajili ya' ('kwasababu')
'For the reason that...'	is	'Kwa maana ya' ('kwasababu')
'Together with...	is	'Pamoja na...'
'Far from...'	is	'Mbali na...'
'Close to...'	is	'Karibu na...'

'Afterwards'	is	'Kisha'
'In order that...'	is	'Ili...'
'Gently'	is	'Polepole'
'Equally'	is	'Sawasawa'
'Early' or 'Soon'	is	'Mapema'
'Especially'	is	'Hasa'
'So then ...'	is	'Hivyo basi'

24. Expressions of relationships in time

| 'Still', 'Not yet' | is | 'Bado' |
| 'Quite' | is | 'Kidogo' |

'Not quite yet'	is	'Bado kidogo'
'Later'	is	'Baadaye'
'Early'	is	'Mapema'
'Now'	is	'Sasa'
'Afterwards'	is	'Halafu'
'Before'	is	'Kabla ya'
'Always'	is	'Siku zote'
'Always'	is also	'Mara zote' or 'Mara kwa mara'
'Suddenly'	is	'Ghafula'
'Day'	is	'Siku'
'Today'	is	'Leo'
'Tomorrow'	is	'Kesho'
'Yesterday'	is	'Jana'
'This morning'	is	'Asubuhi ya leo'
'Tonight'	is	'Usiku wa leo'
'Last night'	is	Jana usiku'
'Next week'	is	'Wiki ijayo'
'Long ago'	is	'Zamani'
'The third' (of the month)	is	'Tarehe tatu'
'Period of time'	is	'Wakati' or 'Muda'
'After that time...'	is	'Baada ya muda'
'Before that time...'	is	'Kabla ya muda'
'At that time'	is	'Wakati huo'
'I do not know when they are coming'	is	'Sijui wanakuja muda wakati gani'
'When we are ready...	is	'Wakati tukiwa tayari...
...we can begin'	is	... tunaweza kuanza'
'I will do it...'	is	'Nitafanya/nitaifanya...
...when I have time'	is	'...wakati nikiwa na muda'

25.   Numbers and telling the time

'One tree'	is	'Mti mmoja'
'Two trees'	is	'Miti miwili'
'Two tables'	is	'Meza mbili'
'Eleven trees'	is	'Miti kumi na mmoja' (ten + one)
'One book'	is	'Kitabu kimoja'
'Two books'	is	'Vitabu viwili'
'Eleven books' (ten plus one)	is	'Vitabu kumi na kimoja'
'Eleven men'	is	'Wanaume kumi na mmoja'
'Twenty-two men'	is	'Wanaume ishirini na wawili'
'322 men'	is	'Wanaume mia tatu ishirini na wawili'

'What is the time now?'	is	'Saa ngapi sasa / Ni saa ngapi?'
'First hour am' (7 o'clock am)	is	'Saa moja asubuhi'
'First hour pm' (7 o'clock pm)	is	'Saa moja usiku'

'9.15pm' (i.e. third hour + quarter)	is	'Saa tatu na robo usiku'
'It's about nine o'clock'	is	'Ni kama saa tatu kamili' (about
the 3rd hour)		
'First'	is	'-a kwanza'
'First man'	is	'Mwanaume wa kwanza'
'First tree'	is	'Mti wa kwanza'
'First book'	is	'Kitabu cha kwanza'
'First answer'	is	'Jibu la kwanza'
'First house	is	'Nyumba ya kwanza'
'Third man'	is	'Mwanaume wa tatu'
'Third tree'	is	'Mti wa tatu'
'Third book'	is	'Kitabu cha tatu'
'Four hundred and twenty three'	is	'Mia nne ishirini na tatu'
'Seven hundred and four'	is	'Mia saba na nne'
'Seven thousand'	is	'Elfu saba'
'Seven thousand and four'	is	'Elfu saba na nne'
'14,403'	is	'Kumi na nne elfu, mia nne na tatu'
'First month' (January)	is	'Mwezi wa kwanza'
'Third month' (March)	is	'Mwezi wa tatu'
'The 1st day of the month'	is	'Tarehe moja'
'The 3rd day of the month'	is	'Tarehe tatu'

26.   Quantity

'How many trees?'	is	'Miti mingapi?'
'How many men?'	is	'Wanaume wangapi?'
'A few trees'	is	'Miti michache'
'A few men'	is	'Wanauma wachache'
'Many trees'	is	'Miti mingi'
'Many men'	is	'Wanaume wengi'
'Much bread'	is	'Mkate mingi'
'Many books'	is	'Vitabu vingi'
'Plenty of books'	is	'Vitabu vingi'
'Plenty of men'	is	'Wanaume wengi'
'Some bread'	is	'Mkate kiasi'
'Another tree'	is	'Mti mwingine'
'A whole (loaf of) bread'	is	'Mkate mzima'
'A whole book'	is	'Kitabu kizima'
'Each book'	is	'Kila kitabu'
'Each tree'	is	'Kila mti'
'Each person'	is	'Kila mtu'
'Every person'	is	'Kila mtu'
'Everybody'	is	'Kila mtu'

27. All and any: '-ote' and '-o -ote'

'All of us'	*is*	*'Sisi sote'*
'All of you'	*is*	*'Ninyi nyote'*
'All of them' (M-Wa class)	*is*	*'Wao wote'*
'All the trees' (M-Mi class)	*is*	*'Miti yote'*
'All the books' (Ki-Vi class)	*is*	*'Vitabu vyote'*
'They all went'	*is*	*'Wote walikwenda'*
'They all went' (M-Mi class)	*is*	*'Yote Ilikwenda'*
'They all went' (Ki-Vi class)	*is*	*'Vyote vilikwenda'*
'The whole (loaf of) bread is mine'	*is*	*'Mkate wote ni wangu'*
'All the loaves are mine'	*is*	*'Mikate yote ni yangu'*
'Any of them' (M-Wa class)	*is*	*'Yeyote yule' (plural)*
'Any of the trees' (M-Mi class)	*is*	*'Miti yoyote' (plural)*
'Any of the books' (Ki-Vi class)	*is*	*'Vitabu vyovyote' (plural)*
'Anyone' (M-Wa class)	*is*	*'(Mtu) yeyote' (singular)*
'Any of the bread' (M-Mi class)	*is*	*'Mkate wowote' (singular)*
'Any of the book' (Ki-Vi class)	*is*	*'Kitabu chochote' (singular)*
'Any of the good book'	*is*	*'Kitabu kizuri chochote'*

28. Indirect object pronouns: Actions to, at, or for someone or something

'They are going to town to bring books'
is   *'Wanakwenda mjini kuleta vitabu'*
'They are going to town to bring me a book'
is   *'Wanakwenda mjini kuniletea kitabu'*
'They are coming to town to answer'
is   *'Wanafika mjini kujibu'*
'They are coming to town to answer me'
is   *'Wanakuja mjini kunijibu'*
'They are returning to town tomorrow'
is   *'Wanarudi mjini kesho'*
'They are returning to town tomorrow for bread'
is   *'Wanarudia mkate mjini kesho'*

29. Making an action reciprocal – another use of '-na'

'They are washing'	*is*	*'Wanaosha'*
'They are washing one another'	*is*	*'Wanaoshana'*
'They will see'	*is*	*'Wataona'*
'They will see one another'	*is*	*'Wataonana'*
'We are answering'	*is*	*'Tunajibu'*
'They are coming to town to answer me' is		

'Wanakuja mjini kunijibu'

'They are coming to town to answer one another'   is
                              'Wanakuja mjini kujibiana'
'We are answering one another'   is   'Tunajibiana'

30.   Doing things to oneself – '-ji-' u

'To teach'	is	'Kufunza/kufundisha'
'To learn' (i.e. teach <u>onesself</u>)	is	'Kujifunza/kujifundisha'
'To see'	is	'Kuona'
'To see oneself'	is	'Kujiona'
'To beat'	is	'Kupiga'
'To beat onesself'	is	'Kujipiga'
'He taught himself'	is	'Alijifundisha'
'They beat themselves'	is	'Walijipiga'
'We have seen ourselves'	is	'Tumejiona'
'I myself have helped'	is	'Mimi mwenyewe nimesaidia'
'The tree itself has helped'	is	'Mti wenyewe umesaidia'
'The book itself has helped'	is	'Kitabu chenyewe kimesaidia'

31.   Conjunctions and adverbial connecting words

'Therefore, he came...'	is	'Kwa hiyo alikuja...'
'... instead of me'	is	'... badala ya mimi'
'His book is the same as theirs'	is	'Kitabu chake ni sawa na chao'
'I will go after eating'	is	'Nitakwenda baada ya kula'
'I am telling him about the town'	is	'Ninamweleza habari ya mji'
'I am telling him about the town'	is	'Ninamwambia kuhusi mji'
'Perhaps he might want to go'	is	'Labda atahitaji kwenda'
'Equally, he might want to go'	is	'Sawasawa atahitaji kwenda'

('Equally' can also be: 'vilevile' or 'pia')

'Thus, he will want to go'	is	'Hivyo atahitaji kwenda'
'We will also go together'	is	'Vilevile tutakwenda pamoja'

32.   Questions

'Where will he come?'	is	'Atakuja wapi?'
'Who will come?'	is	'Nani atakuja?'
'Why will he come?'	is	'Kwa nini atakuja?'
'When will she come/arrive?'	is	'Lini atafika/atawasili?'
'Which man will arrive?'	is	'Mwanaume gani atafika?'
'How many men will arrive?'	is	'Wanaume wangapi watafika?'
'What did you cook?'	is	'Ulipika nini?'
'In which way will you cook?'	is	'Utapika vipi?' or 'Utapikaje?'
'How did you cook?' 'Well!'	is	'Ulipikaje?' 'Vizuri!'

33.   Relatives: Who, which and whom – 'amba'

'The man whom I hit'   is   'Mwanaume ambaye nilimpiga'
'The man who is smelling bad'   is   'Mwanaume ambaye ananuka'
'The men who are smelling bad'   is   'Wanaume ambao wananuka'
'The tree which is smelling bad'   is   'Mti ambao unanuka'
'The trees which are smelling bad' is   'Miti ambayo inanuka'
'The things which I burned'   is   'Vitu ambavyo niliunguza'
 'The thing which is smelling bad'   is   'Kitu ambacho kinanuka'
'The things which are smelling bad'is   'Vitu ambavyo vinanuka'
'The things which are bad'   is   'Vitu ambavyo ni vibaya'
'The things which were bad'   is   'Vitu ambavyo vilikuwa vibaya'
'The things which had badness'   is   'Vitu ambavyo vilikuwa na
                                                                          ubaya'

'The person whose things were bad'
                              is   'Mtu ambaye vitu vyake vilikuwa vibaya'
 'The people who must work now
                              is   'Watu ambao lazima wafanye kazi sasa'
'The trees which must be seen'
                              Is   'Miti ambayo lazima ionwe/ionekane'
'The books which must be read'
                              Is   'Vitabu ambavyo lazima visomwe'

'The people who come'   is   'Watu ambao huja'
'The people who came'   is   'Watu ambao walikuja'
'The people who might come'   is   'Watu ambao wanaweza kuja'
'The people who must come'   is   'Watu ambao lazima waje'
'The man whom I hit'   is   'Mwanaume ambaye nilimpiga'
'The man whom I hit'   is   'Mwanaume niliyempiga'
'The tree which is smelling bad'   is   'Mti ambao unanuka'
'The tree which is smelling bad'   is   'Mti unaonuka'
'The things which I burned'   is   'Vitu ambavyo niliunguza'
'The things which I burned'   is   'Vitu nilivyounguza'

'<u>These</u> children are really good'   is   'Watoto hawa ni wazuri sana'
'<u>These</u> children are really good'   is   'Hawa watoto ni wazuri sana'
'<u>These</u> shops are really good'   is   'Maduka haya ni mazuri sana'
'A child? I have one'   is   'Mtoto? Ninaye mmoja'
'Children? I have them'   is   'Watoto? Ninao'
'Books? I have them'   is   'Vitabu? Ninavyo' etc.
'A child? I have come with one'   is   'Mtoto? Nimekuja naye'
'Children? I have come with them' is   'Watoto? Nimekuja nao'
'Books? I have come with them'   is   'Vitabu? Nimekuja navyo'

'The year which passed' (i.e. last year)   is   'Mwaka uliopita'

'The man whom I hit'	is	'Mwanaume ambaye nilimpiga'
'The man whom I will hit'	is	'Mwanaume nitakayempiga'
'The tree which is smelling bad'	is	'Mti ambao unanuka'
'The tree which will smell bad'	is	'Mti utakaonuka'
'The things which I burned'	is	'Vitu ambavyo niliunguza'
'The things which I will burn'	is	'Vitu nitakavyounguza'
'The man whom I will hit'	is	'Mwanaume nitakayempiga'
'The man whom I will not hit'	is	'Mwanaume ambaya sitampiga'
'The tree which will smell bad'	is	'Mti utakaonuka'
'The tree which will not smell bad'	is	'Mti ambao hautanuka'
'The things which I will burn'	is	'Vitu nitakavyounguza'
'The things which I will not burn'	is	'Vitu ambavyo sitaunguza'
'The things which I am not burning'	is	'Vitu nisivyounguza'
'The things which I did not burn'	is	'Vitu ambavyo sitaunguza'
'The man whom I will hit'	is	'Mwanaume nitakayempiga'
'When I will hit the man...'	is	'Nitakapompiga mwanaume'
'When I hit the man...'	is	'Nilipompiga mwanaume'

34. Preposition + object: 'With it' – Na +it

'The tree? I am cooking with it'	is	'Mti? Ninaopikia'
'The trees? I am cooking with them'	is	'Miti? Ninayopikia'
'The book? I am cooking with it'	is	'Kitabu? Ninachopika nacho'
'The books? I am cooking with them'	is	'Vitabu? Ninavyopika navyo'
'The tooth? I am cooking with it'	is	'Jino? Ninalopika nalo'
'The water? I am cooking with it'	is	'Maji? Ninayopikia'
'The egg? I am cooking with it'	is	'Yai? Ninalopikia'
'The eggs? I am cooking with them'	is	'Mayai? Ninayopikia'
'The tree? I have it'	is	'Mti? Ninao'
'Trees? I have some'	is	'Miti? Ninayo'
'The book? I have it'	is	'Kitabu? Ninacho'
'Books? I have some'	is	'Vitabu? Ninavyo'
'The tooth? I have it'	is	'Jino? Ninalo'
'Teeth? I have them'	is	'Meno? Ninayo'
'The dog? I have it'	is	'Mbwa? Ninaye'
'The dogs? I have them'	is	'Mbwa? Ninao'

35. Relatives of manner – jinsi; kama; kadiri

'They knew how to cook'	is	'Walijua jinsi ya kupika'
'I know the way to clean'	is	'Ninajua jinsi ya kusafisha'
'They do not know ...'	is	'Hawajui...'
'...how to cook...'	is	'...jinsi ya kupika...'
'...like they cooked...'	is	'...kama walivyopika...'
'...a long time ago'	is	'...zamani'.
'I am cooking like you cook'	is	'Ninapika kama unavyopika'

'I will help...'	is	'Nitasaidia...'
'...as much as I can'	is	'...kadri ninaweza/niwezavyo'
'As far as I have gone'	is	'Kadri nimekwenda'
'They knew how to cook'	is	'Walijua jinsi ya kupika'
'They knew how I will cook'	is	'Walijua nitakavyopika'
'They cook how I cook'	is	'Wanapika ninavyopika'
'... as/like they cooked...'	is	'... kama walivyopika...', or
'... as/like they cooked...'	is	'... tulivyopika...'
'They knew how I will cook'	is	'Walijua nitakavyopika' or
'They knew how I will cook!'	is	'Walijua jinsi nitakavyopika'
'As far as I have gone'	is	'Kadri nilivyokwenda'

'I can't cook like I used to (be able to)'
                                          is   'Siwezi kupika kama nilivyozoea'
'I will cook as much as I can'
                                          is   'Nitapika (kwa) kadri niwezavyo'
'Have you understood what we said?'
                                          is   'Umeelewa tulivyosema?'

'I can't cook in that way'	is	'Siwezi kupika hivyo'
'Do it in this way / Do it thus'	is	Ufanye hivi
'It really is thus'	is	'Ndiyo'
'It is not thus'	is	'Siyo'
'This is indeed the person'	is	'Huyu ndiye (mtu)'
'This is indeed the book'	is	'Hiki ndicho kitabu'
'This is indeed the shop'	is	'Hili ndilo duka hasa'
'This is the very dog'	is	'Huyu ndiyo mbwa'

36.   N class words

'Journey' or 'Journeys'	is	'Safari'
'House' or 'Houses'	is	'Nyumba'
'Good father or fathers'	is	'Baba mzuri'
'Good car or cars'	is	'Motokaa nzuri'
'Bad car or cars'	is	'Motokaa mbaya'
'Black car or cars'	is	'Motokaa nyeusi'
'Long car'	is	'Motokaa ndefu'
'Good news'	is	'Habari njema'
'The rain has arrived'	is	'Mvua imefika'
'The flight has arrived'	is	'Ndege imefika'
'The flights have arrived'	is	'Ndege zimefika'
'The flight has not arrived'	is	'Ndege haijafika'
'The flights have not arrived'	is	'Ndege hazijafika'
'This flight has arrived'	is	'Ndege hii imefika'
'These flights have arrived'	is	'Ndege hizi zimefika'
'That flight has arrived'	is	'Ndege ile imefika'

English		Swahili
'Those flights have arrived'	is	'Ndege zile zimefika'
'Where is the flight?'	is	'Ndege iko wapi?'
'Where are the flights?'	is	'Ndege ziko wapi?'
'My flight'	is	'Ndege yangu'
'My flights' (or 'My birds')	is	'Ndege zangu'
'Two flights' (or 'Two birds')	is	'Ndege mbili'
'My grandfathers have arrived'	is	'Babu zangu wamefika'
'My grandmother has arrived'	is	'Bibi yangu amefika'
'My daughter'	is	'Binti yangu'
'My sons'	is	'Mwanangu (wa kiume)'
'That friend has arrived'	is	'Rafiki yule amefika'
'Those neighbours have arrived'	is	'Jirani wale wamefika'

37.   Ji-Ma Class of words

English		Swahili
'New eye'	is	'Jicho jipya'
'New eyes'	is	'Macho mapya'
'Big eye'	is	'Jicho kubwa'
'Big eyes'	is	'Macho makubwa'
'This eye'	is	'Jicho hili'
'These eyes'	is	'Macho haya'
'That eye'	is	'Jicho lile'
'Those eyes'	is	'Macho yale'
'My eye'	is	'Jicho langu'
'My eyes'	is	'Macho yangu'.
'Their eye'	is	'Jicho lao'
'Their eyes'	is	'Macho yao'.
'One shop'	is	'Duka moja'
'Two shops'	is	'Maduka mawili'
'Black tooth'	is	'Jino jeusi'
'Black teeth'	is	'Meno meusi'
'Big tooth'	is	'Jino kubwa'
'Big teeth'	is	'Meno makubwa'
'Dirty milk'	is	'Maziwa machafu'
'Dirty water'	is	'Maji machafu'.
'It is burning'	is	'Linawaka'
'They are burning'	is	'Yanawaka'
'It is not burning'	is	'Haliwaki'
'They are not burning'	is	'Hayawaki'
'The egg? I am burning <u>it</u>'	is	'Yai? Nina<u>li</u>unguza'
'The eggs? I am burning <u>them</u>'	is	'Mayai? Nina<u>ya</u>unguza'
'Where is the answer'	is	'Jibu liko wapi?'
'The tooth is in the bag'	is	'Jino liko mfukoni'
'The teeth are in the bag'	is	'Meno yako mfukoni'
'The tooth is in the kitchen'	is	'Jino liko jikoni'
'The teeth are in the kitchen'	is	'Meno yako jikoni'

38.   U class words

'This nice love has arrived'	is	'Upendo mzuri huu umefika'
'That bad love has arrived'	is	'Upendo mbaya ule umefika'
'My love has arrived'	is	'Upendo wangu umefika'
'Their love has arrived'	is	'Upendo wao umefika'
'Their love? It has arrived'	is	'Upendo wao? Umefika'
'That love? He has destroyed it!'	is	'Upendo ule? Ameuharibu'
'A black wind has arrived'	is	'Upepo mweusi umefika'
'Black winds have arrived'	is	'Pepo nyeusi zimefika'
'Those two dirty black faces'	is	'Nyuso zile mbili chafu nyeusi'
'This big, long face'	is	'Uso huu mkubwa, na mrefu'
'Those boards are burning'	is	'Mbao zile zinaungua'
'Their boards are burning'	is	'Mbao zao zinaungua'
'My boards? They are burning'	is	'Mbao zangu? Zinawaka'
'My boards? He is burning them'	is	'Mbao zangu? Anaziunguza'
'Some diseases are coming'	is	'Magonjwa baadhi yanakuja'
'Those diseases are coming'	is	'Magonjwa yale yanakuja'
'These diseases are coming'	is	'Magonjwa haya yanakuja'
'These diseases are not coming'	is	'Magonjwa haya hayatakuja'
'Dirty diseases are coming'	is	'Magonjwa machafu yanakuja'
'Big diseases are coming'	is	'Magonjwa makubwa yanakuja'
'Black diseases are coming'	is	'Magonjwa meusi yanakuja'
'Their diseases are coming'	is	'Magonjwa yao yanakuja'

39.   Pa Class, plus more on location

'A good place with trees'	is	'Mahali pazuri penye miti'
'Some bad places are smelling bad'		
	is	'Baadhi ya mahali pabaya pananuka'
'My place? I like it!'	is	'Mahali pangu? Ninapapenda'
'My place is in the village'	is	'Mahali pangu pako kijijini'
'This place is in the village'	is	'Mahali hapa pako kijijini'
'That place is in the village'	is	'Mahali pale pako kijijini'
'Their place is in the village'	is	'Mahali pao pako kijijini'
'That large place has trees'	is	'Mahali pale pakubwa kuna miti'
'My (ill-defined) place has trees'	is	'... kwangu kuna miti'
'That (ill-defined) place is burning'	is	'...kwake kunawaka/kunaungua'
'The nice rice inside is burning'	is	'Mchele mzuri ndani unaungua'
'That good area is burning'	is	'Mahala pale pazuri panawaka'
'Inside my (village) there is a tree'	is	'... kijijini kwangu mna mti'
'Inside my village there is a tree'	is	'Kijijini mwangu kuna mti'
'Inside this village there is a tree'	is	'Kijijini humu kuna mti'
'Inside (this) good (village) it smells'	is	'katika kijiji hiki kizuri kunuka

40. Passive – insertion of '-w-'

'I will answer'	*is*	*'Nitajibu'*
'I will be answered'	*is*	*'Nitajibiwa'*
'I will eat'	*is*	*'Nitakula'*
'I will be eaten'	*is*	*'Nitaliwa'*
'The tree used the water'	*is*	*'Mti ulitumia maji'*
'The tree was used by the man'	*is*	*'Mti ulitumiwa na mwanaume'*
'The tree was used by the dog'	*is*	*'Mti ulitumiwa na mbwa'*
'The tree was cut by the man'	*is*	*'Mti ulikatwa na mwanaume'*
'The tree was cut by (or with) the knife'	*is*	*'Mti ulikatwa kwa kisu'*

41. The stative – insertion of '-k-'

'I have been seen. I was seen by the child'
        is   'Nimeonwa. Nilionwa na mtoto'
'I am cut. I was cut by the child
        is   'Nimekatwa. Nilikatwa na mtoto'
'The tree is burnt. It was burnt by the child'
        is   'Mti umeunguzwa. 'Umeunguzwa na mtoto'

'I can be seen by the child'	*is*	*'Naweza kuonwa na mtoto'*
'The book? It is open'	*is*	*'Kitabu? Kimefunguka'*
'The bag? It is put out'	*is*	*'Mfuko? Umewekwa nje'*
'The tree? It can be burnt'	*is*	*'Mti? Unaweza kuunguzwa'*
'The tree? It can be used'	*is*	*'Mti? Unaweza kutumiwa'*
'The bag? It smells bad'	*is*	*'Mfuko? Hunuka vibaya'*
'I am mistaken	*is*	*'Nimekosea'*
'We were very tired'	*is*	*'Tulikuwa tumechoka sana'*
'They will be very angry'	*is*	*'Watakasirika sana'*
'You have been lost'	*is*	*'Mmepotea'*

42. Causing things to happen – '-isha'; '-esha'; and '-za'

'We will make ready to journey'   is   'Tutajitayarisha kusafari'
'They have put right those poor people'
        is   'Wamewaweka sawa wale watu maskini'
'They will explain to these poor people'
        is 'Wataeleza kwa watu hawa masikini'
'I am going to listen to this person'
        is   'Nitamsikiliza mtu huyu'
'We are getting dressed now'
        is   'Tunavaa sasa hivi/tunajiandaa sasa'
'The people reached the town at 8pm'
        is   'Watu walifika mjini saa mbili usiku'
'We will feed the people at 8am'
        is   'Tutawalisha watu saa mbili asubuhi'

'The people will be fed by 8am'

                 is   'Watu watalishwa saa mbili asubuhi'

'I have lost the child'   *is*   'Nimepoteza mtoto'

'I am going to fill the bag'   *is*   'Nitajaza mfuko'

'I am going to insert the things into the bag'

                 is   'Nitaingiza vitu ndani ya mfuko'

'We can drive to town'   *is*   'Tunaweza kuendesha kuelekea mjini'

'You will tire and will be lost'   *is*   'Utachoka na utapotea'

43.   The present indefinite

''Do you cook?'	*is*	'Wapika/unapika?''
'I read Swahili (sometimes)'	*is*	'Nasoma Kiswahili'
'We try (sometimes)	*is*	'Twajaribu'
'We are trying (now)'	*is*	'Tunajaribu'
'I eat (sometimes)'	*is*	'Nala'
'We come (sometimes)'	*is*	'Twaja'

44.   The 'hu' tense – usually

'I usually drink water'	*is*	'Mimi hunywa maji'
'The dog usually drinks water'	*is*	'Mbwa hunywa maji'
'The dogs usually drink water'	*is*	'Mbwa hunywa maji'
'Water? The dog usually drinks it'	*is*	'Maji? Mbwa huyanywa'
'They usually like water'	*is*	'Wao hupenda maji'
'I usually eat food'	*is*	'Mimi hula chakula'
'The dog usually eats food'	*is*	'Mbwa hula chakula'
'The dogs usually eats food'	*is*	'Mbwa hula chakula'
'Food? We usually try to eat it'	*is*	'Chakula? Hujaribu kukila'
'They usually go to town'	*is*	'Wao huenda mjini'
'You usually come to town'	*is*	'Huja mjini'
'You usually come to town'	*is*	'Huja mjini'
'You do not come to town'	*is*	'Huji mjini'
You usually try'	*is*	'Hujaribu'
'You do not try'	*is*	'Haujaribu'

45.   The '-ka-' narrative tense: 'and so I...'; 'he went and...'; 'go and...', etc

'He went into town that day...	*is*	'Alienda mjini siku ile...'
'... and he went and sold the book!'		
	is	'...alienda na akauza kitabu!...'
' ... and I said to him ...'	*is*	'... nikamwambia ...'

'... let me go and sell it!'	is	'... ngoja niende nikakiuze!'
'... and so, he went and sold the book!'		
	is	'...hivyo, alienda akauza kitabu!...'
'... and so, I brought the money'	is	'...hivyo, nikaleta pesa...'

'I sell it' (a book)	is	'Ninakiuza'
'Might I sell it?'	is	'Naweza kukiuza?'
'I hope that I might sell it'	is	'(Ni)natumaini naweza kukiuza'
'... let me go and sell it!'	is	'... Ngoja niende nikakiuze!'
'I eat'	is	'Nala'
'Might I eat?'	is	'Naweza kula?'
'Let me go and eat'	is	'Ngoja niende nikale'
'Let's go and drink'	is	'Tukanywe'

46.   Gerunds, and the uses of Ku.

'I like reading'	is	'Ninapenda kusoma'
'To go to work is good'	is	'Kwenda kazini ni vizuri'
'Working is good'	is	'Kufanyakazi ni vizuri'
'For children, playing is important'		
	is	'Kwa watoto, kucheza ni muhimu'
'My reading is helping me'	is	'Kusoma kwangu kunanisaidia'
'Reading? It is helping me'	is	'Kusoma? Kunanisaidia'.
'This thinking is helping me a lot'		
	is	'Kufikiri huku kunanisaidia sana'
'That thinking is helping them a lot'		
	is	'Kufikiri kule kunawasaidia sana'
'Thinking of food helps me'		
	is	'Kufikiria chakula kunanisaidia'
'Thinking is suitable for pupils'		
	is	'Kufikiri kunafaa kwa wanafunzi'

'Not reading is helping me'	is	'Kutosoma kunanisaidia'
'Not to be able to think is bad'	is	'Kutoweza kufikiri ni vibaya'
'Not to eat was dangerous'	is	'Kutokula kulikuwa hatari'
'Not coming is not an option'	is	'Kutokuja si hiari'
'This knife is for cooking'	is	'Kisu hiki ni cha kupikia'
'This ball is for playing'	is	'Mpira huu ni wa kuchezea'

Annexe 1: Vocabulary Summary

Verbs			
Arrive	-fika	Lend	-kopesha
Answer	-jibu	Listen	-sikiliza
Be /Become	-wa	Lose	-poteza
Be angry	-kasirika	Love	-penda
Be born	-zalika	Make ready	-tayarisha
Be lost	-potea	Open	-fungua
Be mistaken	-kosa/kosea	Please	-pendeza/tafadhali
Be sufficient	-tosha	Put out	-toka/zima/toa
Be tired	-choka	Put right	-sawazisha/rekebisha
Beat	-piga	Rain	-nyesha mvua
Bring	-leta	Reach	-fikisha/fika
Burn	-waka	Return	rudi
Carry	-chukua/beba	See	-ona
Come	-ja	Shut	-funga
Cook	-pika	Smell bad	-nuka
Cut	-kata	Speak	-sema/zungumza
Destroy	-haribu	Start	-anza
Drive	-endesha	Succeed/pass	-fanikiwa/faulu
Eat	-la	Talk	-ongea
Explain	-eleza	Teach	-fundisha
Fall	-anguka	Tell	-ambia/sema
Feed	-lisha	Tire	-chokesha
Feed	-kulisha	To be able	-weza
Fill	-jaza	Touch	-gusa
Forget	-sahau	Travel	-safiri
Get dressed	-valisha/vaa	Use	-tumia
Give	-pa/toa	Visit	-zuru/tembelea
Give to	-patia	Walk	-tembea
Go	(Kw)enda	Want	-taka
Grow	-otesha	Wash	-osha
Hand out to	-tolea	Find	-tafuta/pata
Help	-saida	Do	-fanya
Hide	-ficha	Search	-tafuta
Increase	-ongeza	Look at	-tazama
Insert	-ingiza	Smell good	-nukia
Know	-jua	Put or place	-weka

Nouns	
Child/ren	Mtoto /Watoto
Answer/s	Jibu /Majibu
Bag/s	Mfuko /Mifuko
Bed/s	Kitanda /Vitanda
Beer	Bia (N class)
Board/s	Ubao/Mbao
Book/s	Kitabu /Vitabu
Crop/s	Zao/mazao
Daughter	Binti
Disease	Ugonjwa
Doctor	Mganga
Dog/s	Mbwa (N class)
Egg/s	Yai /Mayai
Eye/s	Jicho /Macho
Face/s	Uso /Nyuso
Fire/s	Moto /Mioto
Food	Chakula (Ki-Vi plural)
Friend/s	Rafiki/marafiki
Goodness	Uzuri
Grandfather	Babu
Grandmother	Bibi /Nyanya
Hand/s	Mkono /Mikono
House/s	Nyumba (N class)
Journey	Safari
Kitchen/ fireplace	Jiko /Meko (Ji-Ma)
Knife/s	Kisu /Visu
Loaf of Bread /Breads	Mkate /Mikate
Love	Upendo/penda/mpenzi
Maize porridge	Uji wa mahindi/gali
Man/Men	Mwanaume /Wanaume
Mango tree/s	Mwembe /Miembe
Neighbour/s	Jirani
News	Habari
Person /People	Mtu /Watu
Place	Mahali
Pupil/s	Mwanafunzi /Wanafunzi
Quarrel/s	Ugomvi/Magomvi
Rain	Mvua
River/s	Mto /Mito
Shop/s	Duka /Maduka
Smoke	Moshi/vuta sigara
Son	Mwana/kijana
Stone/s	Jiwe /Mawe

Sun	Jua
Table/s	Meza (N class)
Teacher/s	Mwalimu /Walimu
Thing/s	Kitu /Vitu
Toilet/s	Choo /Vyoo
Tooth /Teeth	Jino / Meno
Town/s	Mji /Miji
Tree/s	Mti /Miti
Village/s	Kijiji /Vijiji
Water	Maji (Ji-Ma plural)
Wind/s	Upepo /Pepo
Woman	Mwanamke

Adjectives

Good	-zuri; -ema;
Bad	-baya
Best	Bora
Big	-kubwa
Black	-eusi
Clean	Safi
Cold	-a baridi
Dangerous	-a hatari
Dirty	-chafu
Good (N class)	njema
Honest	-aminifu
Hot	-a moto
Little	-dogo
Long (N class)	ndefu
New	-pya
Old	-kuukuu
Poor	maskini

Common Adverbs	
..so that...	..ili...
...it's best that...	...bora...
About, regarding	Juu ya/husiana na
After	Baada ya
Also	Vilevile/pia
Always	Sikuzote/mara kwa mara
As much /far as	Kadri
As, like	Kama
Badly	Vibaya
Briefly	Kwa kifupi
But	Lakini
Bible	Biblia
Equally	Sawasawa
Especially	Hasa
Gently	Pole pole
Good	Vizuri
How to	Jinsi ya
Instead	Badala ya
Luckily	Kwa bahati
More than	Zaidi ya
Nearly	Karibu na
No	La! Hapana!
Now	Sasa
On purpose	Kwa kusudi
Please!	Tafadhali!
Plenty /Many	...ingi
Possibly /Perhaps	Labda
Quickly	Kwa haraka
Quite	Kidogo
Ready	Tayari
Same as	Sawa na
Slowly	Polepole/taratibu
Some /Part /Another	...ingine
Soon	Mapema
Suddenly	Ghafula
That is not so!	Siyo hivyo!
That is so!	Ndiyo/ndivyo!
Therefore	Kwa hiyo
Thus	Kwa hiyo /hivyo
Together	Pamoja
Truthfully	Kwa kweli
Usually, normally	Kwa kawaida
Very	Sana

Whole	...zima
Whom, which	Amba-
Within /in	Ndani ya / Katika

Kiswahili Adverbs, Prepositions & Conjunctions	
Aidha	Moreover
Akali/chache	A few
Ama	Either / or
-amba	That
Au	Or
Baada ya...	After that time.../after
Baadaye	Afterwards
Badala ya...	Instead of...
Bado	Not yet / Still
Baina ya / Katikati ya ...	Between / Among
Chini ya...	Under / Below
Chache / Haba	Few / Very little
Hapa	Here
Hapo	There /Then
Hasa	Especially
Hata/hadi	Until / up to
Hata kidogo	Not at all
Hatimaye/mwishowe	Finally
Hivi / Hivyo	Thus
Hivyo / Hivi	Thus / In that way
Huenda / Labda	Perhaps
Ikiwa / Kama / Iwapo	If
Ila	Except
Ili	In order that
-inge	Many / much
-ingine	Some / Other /Another
Isipokuwa	Unless
Japo	Although
Jinsi ya	How / in what manner
Juu	Up / Above
Juu ya	Over / Down / From
Juujuu	Superficially
Kabla ya	Before that time...
Juu ya	About
Kadha	Various / Such-and-such
Kadha wa kadha/na kadhalika	Etcetera
Kama	As / Like / If /Whether
Kamwe	Never / Not at all

Kana kwamba	As if
Kando	Aside
Kando ya	Beside
Kidogo	Less by
Katikati ya../kati ya...	Between / Among
Katika / -ni	In
Katika hali hiyo	In such a case
Kidogo	A little
Kidogo zaidi/kiduchu	Much less / Much more
Kifupi	Briefly
Kila	Every
Kile	That
Kingi	Much
Kisha	Just then
Kokote	Anywhere / Whereever
-kubwa	Big / Large
Kuliko	Than
Kubwa / -ingi	A lot
Kuhusiana na	Concerning…
Kuhusu / juu ya	Concerning…
Kwa	For / Of / By / To
Kwa ...	In the manner of ...
Kwa ajili ya X	'For X's sake
Kwa bahati	Luckily
Kwa hiyo	Therefore
Kwa kawaida	Usually
Kwa kifupi	Briefly
Kwa kweli	Truthfully
Kwa sababu / kwa kuwa	Because
Kwa tayari	Readily
Kwanza / Mwanzoni	At first / First
Labda	Perhaps
Lazima iwe vile	It must be that…
Licha ya..	Not only
Maadamu	While / As
Hivi karibuni	Recently
Mapema	Early' or 'Soon
Mara moja	At once
Mbali	Far
Mbele ya...	In front of
Minajili/kwa ajili ya…	Because of
Pasipo/kasoro	Without / Except
Mintarafu	Concerning

Miongoni mwa	Among
Mithili ya...	Like / As if
Mnamo	About
Mno	Exceedingly
Mmoja mmoja	One by one
Moja kwa moja	Straight ahead
Mojawapo	One of
Mpaka/hadi	Until / As far as / Up to
Ipi inaenea/inafaa	What is fitting
Mwingine	Someone else / Another
Ndani	Inside
Nje	Outside
Nyote / Wote / Ninyi nyote	You all / All of you
Pale pale	Just there / Just then
Pamoja	Together
Pamoja na	Together with
Papo hapo	Just right here / then
Pasipo	Without
Peke yangu	By myself
Pole pole/taratibu	Gently
Sana	Very much
Sasa	Now
Sawa	Equal / Alike
Sawasawa/pia	Equally
Sio –a kawaida/ Si kawaidi	Unusual
Sivyo	Not so / Not thus
Tangu	While / Since
Tangu leo	From today
Tena	Again
Tu	Only
Upesi	Quickly
Vibaya	Badly
Vilevile	Just the same
Vingi	Many
Vingine	Some /Others
Vivyo hivyo/vilevile	Likewise
Vizuri	Nicely
Wala	Neither ... nor
Yaani	That is to say
Zaidi na / kadhalika	Furthermore / And so on
Zaidi	More

Numbers & Quantities	
1	-moja
2	-wili (mbili)
3	-tatu
4	-nne
5	-tano
6	Sita
7	Saba
8	-nane
9	Tisa
10	Kumi
11	Kumi na mmoja/moja
20	Ishirini
30	Thelathini
40	Arobaini
50	Hamsini
60	Sitini
70	Sabini
80	Themanini
90	Tisini
100	Mia
1000	Elfu
100000	Laki
1000000	Milioni
And	Na
Half	Nusu
Third	Theluthi
Quarter	Robo
Point	Pointi/hoja
%	Kwa mia/asilimia
7th	-a saba
8th	-a nane
Few	-chache
Many, plenty	-ingi
Each	Kila
All	-ote
Any	-o -ote

Questions	
When?	Lini?
What?	Nini?
Why?	Kwa nini? (for what?)
How many?	...ngapi?
Where?	Wapi?
Which?	Gani? Ipi?
Who?	Nani?
How?	-aje?

Location & Direction	
Under	Chini ya
Among	Kati ya
As far as	Mpaka
Behind	Nyuma ya
Beside	Kando ya
Far from	Mbali na
In front of	Mbele ya
In here	Humu
In there	Mle
Near	Karibu na
Straight on	Nyoosha/moja kwa moja
To the left	Kushoto
To the right	Kulia
Towards	Kuelekea

Time	
Where?	Wapi?
Then	Kisha
Already	Kwisha/tayari
Before	Kabla ya
Not quite yet	Bado
Now	Sasa
Early /soon	Mapema
After	Baada ya
Afterwards	Halafu
Later	Baadaye
Since	Tangu
Until	Mpaka
Long ago	Zamani
Recently	Hivi karibuni

Yesterday	Jana
Last night	Jana usiku
Morning	Asubuhi
Afternoon	Alasiri
Day	Siku
Today	Leo
Night	Usiku
Tonight	Usiku wa leo
Tomorrow	Kesho
7am (1st hr of morning)	Saa moja asubuhi
7pm (1st hr of night)	Saa moja usiku
1pm	Saa saba mchana
1am	Saa saba usiku
3rd of the month	Tarehe tatu
What's the time?	Saa ngapi sasa?

Annexe 2: (Ki)Swahili Metaphorical Expressions

Kiswahili Metaphorical Expressions	
Gari langu halitumii mafuta (MIGUU)	*My car doesn't need fuel/gas (LEGS)*
Huku mlima na kule mlima, katikati bonde (MATAKO)	*a mountain on either sides and a valley in the middle (BUTTOCKS).*
Huwawa na uzazi wake (KINYONGA)	*Dies giving birth (CHAMELEON)*
Kila mtu humwabudu apitapo (MLANGO)	*Everyone worship it when passing (DOOR)*
Kuku wangu katagia miibani (NANASI)	*My hen has laid an egg on the thorns (PINEAPPLE)*
Mashetani yangu yakikugusa huponi (UKIMWI)	*Once my demons touch you, you won't survive (HIV/AIDS)*
Mzungu kajishika kiunoni (KIKOMBE)	*A Whiteman with his hand on his waist (CUP)*
Namsikia saa zote lakini simwoni (UPEPO)	*I hear him/her/it all the time but I don't see him/her/ it (WIND)*
Ninapompiga mwanangu, watu hucheza (NGOMA)	*Whenever I hit my child, people start dancing (DRUM)*
Nyumba yangu haina mlango wala madirisha (YAI)	*My house has neither door nor windows (EGG)*
Nyumba yangu haina taa (KABURI)	*My house has no lights (GRAVE)*
Nyumba yangu ina mlango juu (CHUPA)	*My house has a door on the top/roof (BOTTLE)*
Nyumba yangu ina nguzo moja (UYOGA)	*My house has a single pillar (MUSHROOM)*
Nzi hatui juu ya damu ya simba (MOTO)	*The fly cannot settle on the lion's blood (FIRE)*
Parraa! Hata/mpaka Maka (UTELEZI)	*Parrr! Straight to Mecca (SLIPPERINESS)*
Popoo mbili zavuka mto (MACHO)	*Two areca nuts crossing the river (EYES)*
Popote ninapoenda ananifuata (KIVULI)	*It is with me wherever I go (SHADOW)*
Taa yangu inaangazia dunia nzima (JUA)	*My lamp illuminates the entire world (SUN)*

Uji wa mwana mtamu (USINGIZI)	A child's porridge is delicious (SLEEP)
Watoto wa binadamu wakiondoka hawarudi (MAJINI)	Once gone never come back/return (LEAVES)

Annexe 3: (Ki)Swahili Proverbs

Kiswahili Proverbs	
Ahadi ni deni	A promise is a debt
Akiba haiozi	A reserve will not decay
Akili ni mali.	Intelligence is wealth/an asset
Akili ni nywele kila mtu ana zake	Brains are like hair, each person has his/her own
Akili nyingi huondoa maarifa	Too many ideas (wit) drive wisdoms away
Asiyefunzwa na mamaye hufunzwa na ulimwengu	A child who is not taught by its mother will be taught by the world.
Asiyekubali kushindwa si mshindani	He who does not admit/concede defeat is not a competitor
Asiyesikia la mkuu huvunjika guu	One who does not listen to the elders breaks his leg
Baada ya dhiki faraja	After hardship comes relief
Bendera hufuata upepo	A flag follows the direction of the wind
Chanda chema huvikwa pete	The best finger gets the ring
Chovya - chovya humaliza buyu la asali	A constant dipping empties a gourd of honey (dipping a finger to taste repeatedly depletes a jar full of honey)
Dalili ya mvua mawingu	Clouds are the sign of rain
Damu nzito kuliko maji.	Blood is thicker than water.
Dawa ya moto ni moto	The remedy for fire is fire (An eye for an eye)
Elimu haina Mwisho	No limit to education
Elimu ni bahari	Education is an ocean (it has no end)
Fuata nyuki ule asali	Follow the bees to eat honey (no easy way to success)
Haba na haba hujaza kibaba	Little by little fills up the container
Hakuna kama mama	No one like mom
Hakuna marefu yasiyokuwa na ncha/Chenye mwanzo kina	Everything that has a beginning must have

mwisho	an end
Hakuna siri ya watu wawili	There can never be a two-people's secret
Hakuna siri ya watu wawili.	There is no secret for two people
Haraka haraka haina baraka	Hurry, hurry, has no blessings
Hasira hasara	Anger brings damage/Anger is loss
Jogoo la shamba haliwiki mjini	The village cock does not crow in town
Kama elimu ni ghali, jaribu ujinga	If education is expensive, try ignorance
Kutoa ni moyo usambe ni utajiri (kutoa ni moyo si utajiri)	To give is something of the heart, not riches
Kuuliza si ujinga	Asking is not ignorance/stupidity
Kuvuja kwa pakacha nafuu kwa mchukuzi	Leakage of a bag brings relief to its carrier.
Macho hayana pazia	Eyes have no curtain
Macho hayana pazia	Eyes have no screens or shades
Maji hufuata mkondo	Water follows the current (like father like son)
Majuto ni mjukuu	Regrets are like grandchildren (they never end)
Maskini akipata matako hulia mbwata	When a poor man becomes rich his buttocks jiggle
Mbio za sakafuni huishia ukingoni	A race on the floor ends at the edge/wall.
Mficha maradhi kifo humuumbua	Who hides diseases, death will reveal him/her.
Mganga hajigangi	A doctor cannot cure himself/herself
Mgeni njoo, mwenyeji apone	Let the guest come so that the host or hostess may benefit/enjoy
Milima haikutani, binadamu hukutana	Mountains never meet, but people always meet
Mkulima ni mmoja walaji ni	The farmer is one but those who

wengi	enjoy the fruits of his labour are many
Mshika mbili moja humponyoka	One who grasps two things, must allow one to go
Mtaka cha uvunguni sharti ainame	He who wants to fetch something under the bed must bend over (no pain, no gain)
Mtegemea cha nduguye hufa maskini	He who relies on his brother's property dies poor
Mtoto akililia wembe, mpe.	If a child cries for a razor-blade, give it to her/him (burnt child dreads fire)
Mtoto kwa mzazi hakui	To a parent, a child is always a child
Mtoto umuleavyo ndivyo akuavyo	The way you bring up a child is how he/she ends up being.
Mtoto wa nyoka ni nyoka	The child of a snake is a snake (like father like son)
Mtu ni watu	A person is people (no man is an island)
Mungu si Athumani	God is not a human being/Mr. Athumani
Mungwana ni kitendo	A good person is judged by his actions
Mvumilivu hula mbivu	The patient person eats that which is ripe
Mwenye macho haambiwi tazama.	Who has eyes, do not need to be directed to see.
Mwenye nguvu mpishe	Make way for the strong one (survival of the fittest)
Mwenye nguvu mpishe	Make a way for a strong one.
Ndege mjanja hunaswa katika tundu bovu.	A clever bird gets caught in a defective hole/nest
Njia ya muongo ni fupi	A liar's path is short.
Nyota njema huonekana alfajiri/asubuhi	The lucky star is seen at dawn/morning (good luck begins in the morning)
Paka akiondoka, panya hujitawala	If the cat goes away, mice rule.

Penzi ni kikihozi, haliwezi kujificha	*Love is like a cough, [it] can never be hidden*
Pole pole ndio mwendo	*Slow, slow is the way to go (slow but sure)*
Samaki mkunje angali mbichi	*Bend a fish while it is still fresh (the earlier, the better)*
Samaki mmoja akioza, wote wameoza	*If one fish rots, they all rot (A rotten apple spoils the whole bushel)*
Shukrani ya punda ni mateke	*Gratitude of a donkey is kicks.*
Siku za mwizi ni arobaini	*A thief can stay at large for only 40 days*
Subira yavuta heri	*Patience begets blessedness*
Tabia ni ngozi	*Habit is a skin (people don't change easily)*
Uchungu wa mwana, aujuaye mzazi	*The labour of childbirth is known to the mother*
Ukila na kipofu usimushike mkono	*As you are eating with a blind don't touch his/her hand.*
Ukiona vyaelea, jua vimeundwa	*when you see the vessels afloat, know they have been made*
Ulimi hauna mfupa	*A tongue has no bone*
Ulimi hauna mfupa	*A tongue has no bone*
Usimwamshe aliyelala utalala wewe	*Do not wakeup who has fallen asleep, you will sleep yourself.*
Vyote ving'aavyo usifikiri ni dhahabu	*All that glitters are not gold*
Wengi wape	*Majority wins/prevails*

Street phrases & Slang	
Acha uboya	Stop nonsense
Acha usoro	Stop nonsense
Barida	Cool
Bi mkubwa/ Bi mdashi	Mother
Bigi	Fat man
Boda boda	bicycle & motorcycle taxis
Bomba	Cool/it's okay/ awesome/nice
Bondeni/kwa Madiba	South Africa
Bongo	Tanzania/Dar es Salaam
Bringi- bringi	To wear fashionable clothes
Broo	Brother
Buku moja	One thousand
Buzi	Sugar daddy
Changudoa/mama huruma/shangingi	Prostitute
Cheki	Have a look/see
Chukulia poa	Take it easy
Chuna	Extort money
Dada poa	Prostitute
Daladala/Kipanya/Matatu	Commuter bus/ minibuses
Demu	Girlfriend/ woman
Denti/wakusoma	Student/pupil
Dingi/ mshua	Father
Dogo	Young man
Dolo	Broke/penniless
Fala	Stupid/Idiot
Fataki	Sugar daddy
Fiti	Fit/strong
Freshi	Fresh/cool
Funga Kamba	Deceiving someone/telling lies
Ganja	Marijuana
Geti kali	Mansion/modern house usually with a fence
Hamna noma	It's okay
Hamna noma	No problem
Jelo	Five hundred Tanzanian Shillings

Jimama	*Sugar mammy*
Kaa chonjo	*Stay alert*
Kabumbu/Kandanda	*Football*
Kama kawa	*As usual*
Kausha	*Keep quiet/silent/don't report something*
Kauzibe	*Hindrance*
Kibosile	*A boss or manager*
Kichapo	*To be beaten*
Kicheche	*A person who has multiple lovers*
Kidume	*A boy/man*
Kiepe	*Chips*
Kijiweni/kijiwe (-jiwe)	*Office/workplace/A place where drug abusers meet /a place where people meet in the evening to drink coffee and exchange ideas about politics or gossips.*
Kilonga longa	*Mobile phone*
Kimeo	*Something bad/defective*
Kipute	*A football match*
Kitimoto	*Pork*
Kitu kidogo	*Bribe*
Konda	*Bus conductor*
Kuacha solemba (-acha solemba)	*End a relationship/avoiding someone*
Kufulia/kuwamba (-fulia/-wamba)	*Penniless/broke*
Kujikataa	*To leave/exit*
Kukata gogo (-kata gogo)	*Defecate*
Kula bata	*Let's have fun/enjoy life*
Kula kona	*Run away*
Kula pamba	*Dress up nicely*
Kula shaba	*To be shot/gunned down*
Kumbwaya	*Fear*
Kumchomolea (-chomolea)	*To deny him/her*
Kupiga sound/ verse	*To seduce someone/wooing*
Kusagana	*Relating to lesbianism*
Kutia timu (-tia timu)	*To arrive somewhere*
Kutimba (-timba)	*To arrive*

Kutumbua (-tumbua)	To fire someone (usually, corrupt public officials)
Kutusua	Be successful/Succeed
Kuuza sura	Showing off
Kuzingua (-zingua)	Refuse/cause trouble/failure to honour promise
Kwa Malkia/Kwa Mama	U.K.
Machinga	Street vendor/hawker or petty traders
Majuu	Abroad/ Europe
Mama-ntilie	Food vendor (usually, women)
Mambo vipi kaka/dada	How are doing brother/sister?
Mangi	Chaga people/Shopkeeper
Manzi	A girlfriend
Mapene/Mkwanja	Money
Maskani/Skani	Home
Mbulula	Foolish person
Mchizi	Friend
Mchongo	A deal
Mchovu (-chovu)	Lazy person
Mchuchu	Beautiful woman
Mchuma (-chuma)	A car
Mduwanzi	Ignorant/stupid person
Mguu wa kuku	Pistol
Michosho	Something boring
Mkenge	Misleading someone
Mkwanja /mpunga/mavumba	Money
Mnoko	Someone who is very strict (likely to report an incident to the relevant authority or to take action)
Mpiga debe (-piga debe)	A tout
Msela /masala	Street men/friend/gangster/bachelor/single
Msenge	Stupid person/gay
Mshikaji	Friend
Msimbazi	Ten thousand Tanzanian Shillings
Msosi	Meal/Lunch/Dinner
Mtanange	Competition/match (usually, a

	football match)
Mtoko	Going out (to a party, beach, date, etc).
Mtoni/mamtoni	Europe/America/Abroad
Mtoto wa kishua	Someone from a wealth family
Muhenga	Old person
Mwake	Exactly/great/okay
Mwanga	Witch/sorcerer
Mwela/afande	Policeman
Mzuka	Energetic/Excellent/fantastic/Be excited
Mzungu/mtasha	White people/European
Nakozi	To be beaten
Namzimia/Nakuzimia (-zimia)	To like/love someone
Ndinga	An expensive car
Ndomu/Buti	Condom
Ng'atuka	To retire
Ngeli/ Ung'eng'e	English language
Ngeta/roba	Robbery
Ngoma/miwaya	HIV/AIDS
Nguna/Sembe/Dona	Ugali/hard porridge
Niaje	How are you?
Nipe tano	Give me five
Niteme	Leave me alone
Noma	Danger
Noma	Problem/trouble
Nyodo	Arrogance/Be arrogant
Nyomi	High turnout
Pedeshee	A person with a lot of money and like showing off
Piga bonji	Sleep
Piga denda/Nyonya mate	Deep kiss
Piga fiksi	Tell lies
Piga kibesi	Threaten someone
Piga kimya	Be silent
Piga maji	Drink alcohol
Piga mzinga/bomu	To beg for money from someone
Piga puli	Masturbate

Pige telo	Search someone
Pimbi	A Short person
Pipa	A plane
Poa	Fine
Punga	A gay person
Serengeti boys	Young men dating old women
Shaa-shaa	Faster/make it in hurry
Sharobaro	A smart boy
Shega	Good/okay/fine
Shilawadu	Gossip/ showbiz news
Shoga	Friend/gay
Shosti	Close friend
Shwari	Cool/ smooth/even
St. kayumba	Public school
Tambaa	Go/leave
Teja	Drug user
Tigo	Homosexual/anus
Tira rira	Taking too much alcohol
Toka nduki	To run away (high speed)
Tuliza boli	Keep quiet/calm down
Tusepe	Let's go
Ubuyu	Gossips
Ukapa	Broke/penniless
Umetokelezea (-tokelezea)	You look good/sexy
Unga	Illegal drugs
Unga/ ngada	Drug abuse
Unyunyu	Body spray/perfume
Usipime	Incredible/immeasurable
Uswazi/uswahilini	Slum
Vigogo	Top government officials
Vunga	Stop doing something
Wa-bushi/ mlugaluga/ mporipori/ wa-kuja	Layman/villager/uncivilised
Wowowo/bambataa	Big buttocks (usually, women)
Zana/Soksi	Condom
Zinga la mnuso	Big party/delicious food
Zungu la unga	Drug dealer

Annexe 5: (Ki)Swahili Taboo Words

TABOO WORDS	English Version	ALTERNATIVE WORDS	ENGLISH TRANSLATION
Choo/Chooni	Toilet	Msalani/maliwato	Toilet/ WC/Bathroom
-kojoa	Urinate	Kujisaidia/haja ndogo	Short call
Kudindisha/-dindisha/nyege	Phallus/penis erect/ horny	Kusimamisha/-simamisha	Sexual excitement
Kufa	Die	-tangulia mbele ya haki/-tutoka	Pass away
Kuma	Vagina	Uke/Sehemu ya siri	private part/sexual organ
Kunya	passing faeces	Kujisaidia/haja kubwa	Long call
Matako	Buttocks	Makalio/kiuno	Buttocks
Mavi/Mkojo	Faeces/urine	Kinyesi/haja ndogo	Stool/urine
Mboo/-uboo	Penis	Uume/Sehemu ya siri	private part/sexual organ
Tomba/Kutomba/ Kutombana	Sexual intercourse	Kujamiiana/Kufanya tendo la ndoa/ Kufanya mapenzi	To make love

Annexe 6: (Ki)Swahili links

Swahili use in Regional Forums

The Swahili language has increasingly been used in regional forums in Africa as an official language. Some of the International Forums, Summit, Exhibitions and festivals which have adopted Swahili as one of the official languages include:

- African Union
- East African Community
- First African Ladies' Summit
- International Conference on the Great Lakes Region
- Southern Africa Development Community
- Swahili International Tourism Expo.
- Zanzibar International Film Festival

International Swahili Broadcast

Listening skills is one of the most important component in learning any language. As such, the following international radios and TVs' Swahili broadcast might be of interest to you in developing you're listening and speaking skills:

BBC Swahili (Idhaa ya Kiswahili BBC/Dira ya Dunia) – Radio, Television & Social media.

Website: www.bbcswahili.com

Channel Africa/SABC (Sura ya Afrika/Kiswahili News - Channel Africa) – Radio & Social media.

Website: http://www.channelafrica.co.za/sabc/home/channelafrica/programmes

CRI Swahili/ China Radio International (Idhaa ya Kiswahili ya China) – Radio & Social media.

Website: http://swahili.cri.cn/

DW Swahili/ Deutsche Welle (Idhaa ya Kiswahili Ujerumani) – Radio & Social media.

Website: www.dwswahili.com

IRIB Swahili/Parstoday – Iran (Idhaa ya Kiswahili ya Radio Tehran) - Radio & Social media.

Website: http://Parstoday.com/sw

NHK World – Swahili (Idhaa Ya Swahili Radio Japani) – Radio & Social media.

Website: https://www3.nhk.or.jp/nhkworld/sw/

RFI Swahili/ Radio France International (Idhaa ya Kiswahili ya Ufaransa) - Radio & Social media.

Website: www.rfikiswahili.com

UN Radio Swahili (Radio ya Umoja wa Mataifa/ Idhaa ya Redio ya UM) - Radio & Social media.

Website: www.unmultimedia.org/radio/kiswahili

Vatican Radio Swahili (Idhaa ya Kiswahili Vatican) - Radio & Social media.

Website: www.vaticanradio.net

VoA Swahili/Voice of America (Idhaa ya Kiswahili ya Sauti ya Amerika) - Radio & Social media.

Website: www.voaswahili.com

Note: The above media houses also have special weekly programmes on Swahili learning.

Annexe 7: (Ki)Swahili-speaking countries

It is believed that there are more than 100 million Swahili speakers in Africa. Thus, making it the most spoken language in Africa, with over 45 million speakers in Tanzania alone.

Regionally, Kiswahili language is a *lingua franca* of Eastern, Central and South-Eastern Africa. It is also a national or official language of the African Great Lakes Region *i.e.* Tanzania, Uganda, Burundi, Rwanda, Kenya and Congo DRC.

Outside of Africa, there is a remarkable number of Swahili speakers in Yemen, Oman and Saudi Arabia. This is due to the historical ties (i.e. trade, migration, intermarriage, religion and settlement) between the Middle-East on the one hand, and the East African coast on the other since 800 A.D. to date.

Map of Kiswahili-speaking countries

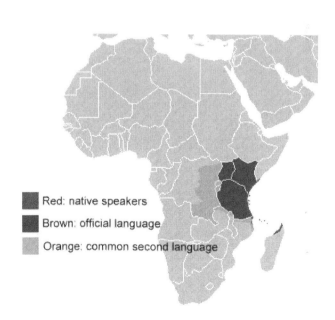

Red: native speakers

Brown: official language

Orange: common second language

Countries where (Ki)Swahili is spoken		
Country	Region	Continent
1. Tanzania	Great Lakes/East Africa	Africa
2. Kenya	Great Lakes/East Africa	Africa
3. Uganda	Great Lakes/East Africa	Africa
4. Rwanda	Great Lakes/East Africa	Africa
5. Burundi	Great Lakes/East Africa	Africa
6. South Sudan	East Africa	Africa
7. D.R.C	Central Africa	Africa
8. Mozambique	Southern Africa	Africa
9. Somalia	Central Africa	Africa
10. Malawi	Southern Africa	Africa
11. Ethiopia	Central Africa	Africa
12. Madagascar	Southern Africa	Africa
13. Comoros Islands	Southern Africa	Africa
14. Zambia	Southern Africa	Africa
15. Yemen	Middle-East	Asia
16. Oman	Middle-East	Asia
17. Saudi Arabia	Middle-East	Asia

Learn Swahili quickly and easily –
Final thought

Don't give up!!

Just about every child – even those much less clever than you – ends up speaking the language fluently. The reason that they manage it is that they keep listening until the unfamiliar becomes familiar.

Then, and only then, with the grammar and vocabulary stick in the 'deep learning' part of your head. Your ears are the main route to your brain's language centre, not your eyes or your intellect!

The building of vocabulary and ease in talking comes either by immersion in a Swahili-speaking culture, or by listening to Swahili as spoken in real life. Or both! This is the easy final part of your being fairly fluent in Swahili. If you had just had immersion and listening alone, it would have taken you to a good level, but would have taken a long time to get a mastery.

In this book, however, your work on Sections 1 & 2 has short-circuited this time, and has made it possible to arrive quickly at the point where listening leads to deep learning.

Listen. Relax. Check anything you did not understand. Why was it expressed that way?

Then listen again.

Safari njema!

About the authors

Laurence Wood was previously Lead Obstetrician at University Hospitals Coventry. He left that role to set up and run a charitable project in rural Tanzania - 'Tushikamane' - setting up women's groups in rural hamlets, to help tackle high maternal and child death rates.

He worked at national level as an expert in education. As an educationist, he relished the opportunity to make the learning of Swahili digestible and accessible.

Jaba Tumaini Shadrack is a Tanzanian and native Swahili Speaker. He majored in Swahili and English studies in High School, the subjects which he later taught at Kibara Secondary School in 2004 and early 2005. His main area of interest relates to literature and grammar.

He runs a Swahili blog known as "Mashairi ya Jaba" (http://tanzaniapoetry.blogspot.co.uk/). He is also an established lawyer, and law teacher at the University of Dar es Salaam (Tanzania). Jaba is currently at the University of Warwick (U.K.) as a Commonwealth Scholar and PhD student.

Made in the USA
San Bernardino, CA
05 February 2020

64015630R00158